Promoting Student Development Through Intentionally Structured Groups

Roger B. Winston, Jr.
Warren C. Bonney
Theodore K. Miller
John C. Dagley

ююююююююююю

Promoting
Student Development
Through Intentionally
Structured Groups

Principles, Techniques,
and Applications

 Jossey-Bass Publishers

San Francisco • London • 1988

PROMOTING STUDENT DEVELOPMENT
THROUGH INTENTIONALLY STRUCTURED GROUPS
Principles, Techniques, and Applications
  by Roger B. Winston, Jr., Warren C. Bonney, Theodore K. Miller, and
  John C. Dagley

Library of Congress Cataloging-in-Publication Data

Promoting student development through intentionally
  structured groups.

  Bibliography: p.
  Includes index.
  1. College student development programs.   2. Personnel
service in higher education.   3. Group guidance in
education.   I. Winston, Roger B.
LB2343.4.P76   1988   378'.194   88-42803
ISBN 1-55542-113-X

JACKET DESIGN BY WILLI BAUM

FIRST EDITION

Code 8845

ιοιοιοιοιοιοιοιοι

The Jossey-Bass
Higher Education Series

Contents

ΙΟΙΟΙΟΙΟΙΟΙΟΙΟΙΟΙΟΙΟΙ

Preface

Hundreds of books have been written about groups, group leadership, group dynamics, group counseling and psychotherapy, and small-group exercises. Most of these books have focused on (1) the study of behavior and the evolution of leadership in naturally occurring groups, (2) using an understanding of human behavior in small groups to increase the effectiveness of organizations, (3) understanding the process of group development and how it affects psychotherapeutic interventions, or (4) teaching participants about principles of group process through the use of planned exercises and "games." There is a distinct void, however, in the area of the application of structured or planned groups in college settings. Specifically, there is little that describes working with groups of students in the higher education environment or that makes a direct connection between theories of college-student development and the use of groups to facilitate and encourage that development. Student affairs professionals and others in higher education interested in using group techniques to reach large portions of their student populations and to enhance students' education and lives have had little to assist and guide them.

This book grew out of the frustration we experienced when attempting (without a concise, comprehensive guide) to teach graduate students how to plan and lead what we have come to call intentionally structured groups. Also, as we watched professionals on college campuses in a variety of settings, we found that they viewed group interventions as counseling or therapy or as a class or as "fun and games." All these approaches have limited potential for promoting the development of college students. Most college students do not need therapy and respond negatively to groups whose structures are similar to psychotherapy groups. However, when staff members in counseling centers endeavor to meet the legitimate and often overwhelming career-development needs of students in groups that are little different from the academic classes in which students are already enrolled, they often do little to help students make satisfying career decisions because insufficient attention is paid to developing and utilizing the group *qua* group. Or when young professionals resort to fun-and-games exercises to fill training sessions for student paraprofessionals, they do not prepare these students to do their jobs and they do not significantly affect their personal development or interpersonal effectiveness, even though students often respond positively to such experiences because they are entertaining. In addition to these professionals, who use groups in a well-intentioned but often inappropriate way, we have also observed many seasoned student affairs professionals who have come to view all group interventions as "touchy-feely" stuff that has no legitimate place in higher education. This book is dedicated to all these colleagues in the hope that they will understand and appreciate the value of well-planned and well-implemented intentionally structured groups for encouraging the personal development of students.

In this book we advocate the use of intentionally structured groups (ISGs) to promote the personal development of college students and as an effective vehicle for training staff members. Although ISGs are basically psychological in nature, they are different from therapy groups or unstructured growth groups in two important ways: First, their goals are educational rather than therapeutic. That is, ISGs are composed of individuals who are basically normal, with healthy personalities, faced with predictable life events and experiences, rather than being composed of maladjusted or mentally ill persons. Second, the leaders envision specific outcomes as a result of participation, and those outcomes are communicated to prospective participants before the group begins. ISGs are more than a series of loosely connected group exercises and activities. Group exercises are often utilized in ISGs, but they must have a specific, well-thought-out purpose based on a sound understanding of both student development and group dynamics.

The planning model, theory of group development, and leadership model proposed in this book are appropriate for use with diverse populations in many settings. We, however, have chosen to focus this book on one setting, higher education, and one population, college students, because ISGs must be grounded in a solid theoretical foundation that explains the developmental tasks of the target population and must be set in a specific social context. Many of the principles and techniques presented here can be applied elsewhere, provided the user has a detailed knowledge of the developmental tasks the target population faces and understands the participants' milieu.

In writing this book we have crystallized for ourselves a set of values of which the reader should be aware:

- It is the responsibility of colleges and universities to be concerned about and to purposefully address the psychological, social, career, esthetic, intellectual, ethical, and physical development of their students, not just their academic development.
- Small groups, when carefully planned and adroitly led, can have great power for contributing to the growth of participants.
- Interventions that promote the interpersonal interaction of group members and allow the natural dynamics inherent in most groups to function have the greatest likelihood of success.
- Leaders have responsibility for providing structure or helping the group develop it. Structure does not necessarily inhibit personal freedom but may, in many instances, liberate individuals to explore new ideas or to experiment with new behavior patterns and ways of viewing themselves or responding to others.
- We are committed to democratic processes and the worth and dignity of the individual. In working with small groups, these values are paramount.
- ISGs are one way to help college students understand them-

selves and the society in which they live and to develop their ability to assume responsibility for their own educations and take command of their lives now and in the future. To paraphrase Socrates, the unexamined life is not worth living, or, as he said in the *Crito* (48b), "the really important thing is not to live but to live well."

This book was constructed with six goals in mind. First, it is intended to provide practical guidance for planning, evaluating, and leading group experiences in a collegiate environment. Second, drawing on two relatively distinct bodies of knowledge — group dynamics and student-development theory — the book proposes to increase practitioners' understanding of effective group interventions with college students. Third, it points out, and we hope will help correct, some of the abuses and inappropriate uses of group techniques (especially structured exercises). Fourth, this book is intended to increase practitioners' appreciation of the potential of group experiences that fall between the extremes of fun-and-games activities on the one hand and in-depth psychotherapy on the other. Fifth, it proposes to present theory, amply illustrated with examples and applications, and detailed suggestions and guidelines for effectively implementing group experiences without becoming a "cookbook." Emphasis is on understanding principles and the "why" of techniques, with less attention to step-by-step directions or how-to-do-it recipes. Finally, many of the ethical, professional, and political issues that practitioners should consider when planning and leading groups on college campuses are identified, and suggestions are offered for dealing with them.

Who Should Read This Book?

This book is intended for all in higher education who are concerned about the personal development of college students, especially outside the formal classroom. We hold that ISGs have many applications on a college campus — for example, (1) in helping students deal with their college experience and personal development in a variety of settings such as counseling centers, residence halls, academic advising centers, international student programs, academic assistance programs, student centers, career planning and placement centers, and developmental studies programs; (2) in professional staff development; (3) in training peer helpers such as resident assistants, peer academic advisors, orientation leaders, peer tutors, peer counselors, and peer educators in areas such as AIDS education or health and wellness promotion; (4) in the development of student leaders; and (5) as part of a regular academic class.

This book is intended to help practitioners become skilled at selecting appropriate interventions. We assume that readers have a minimal knowledge of group dynamics and a modest understanding of student development theories. For those with limited experience, this book provides a conceptual foundation and pragmatic suggestions for implementing group interventions. For experienced practitioners, we offer some new ideas, raise some questions about planning ISGs, and challenge them to reexamine and systematically improve the quality or quantity of their offerings. A special effort has been made to avoid the seductive trap of offering ISGs as a panacea for addressing all the developmental needs of students. Rather, in the absence of a definitive cause-and-effect relationship between group process and outcomes, this approach is offered as a direct intervention strategy that has utility for meeting some of the specific needs of students.

Overview of the Contents

The book is divided into three parts. Part One provides a definition of ISGs, presents a broad overview of important group-dynamics principles, and provides brief summaries of student-development theory in eight broad categories. Part Two is concerned with the planning, evaluating, leading, implementing, and closing of ISGs. The Sample ISG Manual at the end of the book is included to illustrate the concepts and suggestions provided in the main body of the book.

The reader will note that many topics (such as leadership skills, stages of group development, and basic group dynamics such as cohesiveness, norms, and pressures to conform) are covered in several sections of the book. Although there may be a certain amount of repetition, these important topics are addressed several times from different perspectives because successful use of ISGs requires a thorough understanding of these concepts and techniques. Repetition is also necessary because of the basic nature of groups: Groups must be understood as wholes; once divided they no longer exist. This is what makes them so fascinating to study and so difficult to understand.

University of Georgia   Roger B. Winston, Jr.
Athens, Georgia   Warren C. Bonney
July 1988   Theodore K. Miller
                                                     John C. Dagley

ЮЮЮЮЮЮЮЮЮЮЮ

The Authors

Roger B. Winston, Jr., is professor in the Student Personnel in Higher Education Program and graduate coordinator in the Department of Counseling and Human Development Services, College of Education, University of Georgia. He received his A.B. degree (1965) from Auburn University in history and philosophy, his M.A. degree (1970) from the University of Georgia in philosophy, and his Ph.D. degree (1973) from the University of Georgia in counseling and student personnel services.

Winston's primary research activities have been directed at measuring the psychosocial development of traditional-aged college students, studying academic advising as a developmental intervention, and investigating the utilization and training of student paraprofessionals in student affairs. In 1984 he received an award for outstanding research from the National Academic Advising Association, and in 1987 he was honored with the senior professional Annuit Coeptis Award from the American College Personnel Association.

He has served as a member of the American College Personnel Association's executive council and on the boards of directors of the National Academic Advising Association and the Council for the Advancement of Standards for Student Services/Development Programs (CAS). He currently serves on the editorial board of the *Journal of College Student Development* and has served as associate editor of the *College Student Affairs Journal* and on the editorial board of the *Journal of College Student Personnel*. He was the founding editor of *ACPA Developments*.

Winston's books include *Developmental Approaches to Academic Advising* (1982, with S. C. Ender and T. K. Miller), *Administration and Leadership in Student Affairs: Actualizing Student Develop-*

ment in Higher Education (1983, with T. K. Miller and W. R. Mendenhall), *Students as Paraprofessional Staff* (1984, with S. C. Ender), *Developmental Academic Advising: Addressing Students' Educational, Career, and Personal Needs* (1984, with T. K. Miller, S. C. Ender, and T. J. Grites), and *Fraternities and Sororities on the Contemporary College Campus* (1987, with W. R. Nettles and J. H. Opper). His test publications include the Student Developmental Task Inventory (1974, 1979, with T. K. Miller and J. S. Prince), the Student Developmental Task and Lifestyle Inventory (1987, with T. K. Miller and J. S. Prince), and the Academic Advising Inventory (1984, with J. A. Sandor).

Before joining the faculty of the University of Georgia in 1978, he served as dean of men and associate dean of students at Georgia Southwestern College. During the past ten years he has taught peer-helping skills to resident assistants using an ISG format and has coled numerous workshops on training student paraprofessionals and on developmental academic advising in the United States and Canada.

Warren C. Bonney is professor of education emeritus in the Counseling Psychology Program in the Department of Counseling and Human Development Services, College of Education, University of Georgia. He received his B.A. degree (1948) from Ohio State University in psychology, his M.A. degree (1950) from North Texas State University in psychology, and his Ph.D. degree (1958) from the University of Texas in counseling psychology.

Bonney's research activities have included the study of personality development and group dynamics, with particular focus on group counseling and psychotherapy. He has served as a consultant on group process to industry, educational institutions, government agencies, state departments of education (Texas, Illinois, Indiana, and Georgia), and the United States Army. He has conducted individual and group counseling in private practice, clinics, and a college health service. He has written numerous articles on group process for a variety of professional journals and is a consulting editor for the *Journal of Group Psychotherapy, Psychodrama, and Sociometry*.

Before joining the faculty at the University of Georgia in

1965, Bonney served on the faculties of the University of Illinois, University of Texas, and Texas A&M University.

Theodore K. Miller is professor and coordinator of the Student Personnel in Higher Education Program and director of the Student Development Laboratory in the College of Education at the University of Georgia. He received B.S. (1954) and M.A. (1957) degrees from Ball State University and an Ed.D. degree (1962) from the University of Florida.

Miller has done research mainly on the normal developmental processes of young-adult college students as influenced by their higher education experiences. He was instrumental in the development of the Tomorrow's Higher Education Student Development Process Model and of the professional standards and guidelines for the Council for the Advancement of Standards.

Miller has authored, coauthored, and edited numerous professional books, chapters, and articles, and has served on the editorial board of three professional journals. He is currently coeditor of the *Georgia Journal of College Student Affairs*. His books include *The Future of Student Affairs* (1976, with J. S. Prince), *Students Helping Students* (1979, with S. C. Ender and S. S. McCaffrey), *Developmental Approaches to Academic Advising* (1982, with R. B. Winston and S. C. Ender), *Administration and Leadership in Student Affairs* (1983, with R. B. Winston and W. R. Mendenhall), *Developmental Academic Advising: Addressing Students' Educational, Career, and Personal Needs* (1984, with R. B. Winston, S. C. Ender, and T. J. Grites), and *CAS Standards and Guidelines for Student Services/Development Programs* (1986, with W. L. Thomas and S. C. Looney). His psychometric instruments include the Student Developmental Task Inventory (1974, 1979, with R. B. Winston and J. S. Prince), the Student Developmental Task and Lifestyle Inventory (1987, with R. B. Winston and J. S. Prince), and the Student Profile and Assessment Record (with R. B. Winston).

Miller has been professionally active over the years and is currently president of the Council for the Advancement of Standards for Student Services/Development Programs. He is past

president of the Georgia College Personnel Association (GCPA)
(1969–1970) and the American College Personnel Association
(1975–1976) and member of the board of directors of the American Personnel and Guidance Association (1978–1981) and the
Council for Accreditation of Counseling and Related Educational Programs (1980–1987). Miller's honors include receipt of
the Mel Hardee Professional Contribution Award (Southern
Association for College Student Affairs, 1976), Outstanding
Professional Award (GCPA) (1980), Professional Service Award of
the American College Personnel Association (ACPA) (1981), Annuit Coeptis Senior Professional Award (ACPA) (1986), and the
ACPA President's Award (1986).

Prior to joining the faculty of the University of Georgia in
1967, Miller was an assistant professor and counseling psychologist at the State University of New York, Buffalo, and head
resident counselor to men at the University of Florida.

John C. Dagley is associate professor of counseling psychology in the Department of Counseling and Human Development
Services, College of Education, University of Georgia. He received his B.A. degree in business administration (1964) from
Culver-Stockton College, his M.S.Ed. degree in student personnel in higher education (1965) from Indiana University, and his
Ph.D. degree in counseling psychology (1972) from the University of Missouri.

Dagley's primary research activities have been in the areas
of career development, career guidance and counseling, and
computer-assisted career-guidance programs. He has served as a
trustee and board member of the National Career Development
Association, a member of the Council for Accreditation of
Counseling and Related Educational Programs, a member of
the National Council for the Credentialing of Career Counselors, president of the Georgia Association for Counseling and
Development, and president of the Georgia Vocational Guidance Association. He has received distinguished-service recognition from the American Mental Health Counselors Association
(1982) and the National Career Development Association
(1980).

Dagley has maintained an active counseling caseload for two decades, leading numerous groups, particularly career-exploration groups and parenting groups, and has also received several grants for career-guidance research and program development. His publications include coauthorship of a series of ten monographs on career guidance, a series of assessment instruments on career guidance, *Career Guidance in Georgia* (1976, with D. Hartley), and *Parent-Assisted Career Education* (1977, with M. A. Neeley and P. L. Dagley).

Before joining the faculty of the University of Georgia in 1972, Dagley served as instructor of psychology at Culver-Stockton College and as assistant project director at the University of Missouri. Dagley has also served as a counseling psychologist in the Counseling and Personal Evaluation Center of the University of Georgia's College of Education since 1975.

Promoting
Student Development
Through Intentionally
Structured Groups

Principles and Purposes of Intentionally Structured Groups

The first part of this book provides a theoretical base in the principles of student development and group dynamics and identifies the premises used to conceptualize intentionally structured groups (ISGs). We maintain that all people carry within them the potential for self-actualization and self-direction through continuous development.

As Carl Rogers (1961) elucidated, individuals are most likely to realize their full potential in an empathic, accepting, and encouraging environment; but most students are not even aware of the possibilities for personal development within an accepting and democratic group context. The microculture of an ISG can ignite an awareness of this potential and can help students move toward self-responsible action. A group experience with these broad goals, however, does not come about accidentally or simply by good intentions. It can happen with any degree of regularity only through careful planning, theory-grounded design, and thoughtful and skillful leadership. The planning and design need to be based on a thorough knowledge and understanding of the theoretical principles and practical functioning of small interactive groups, the environment in which they occur, and the developmental stages and dynamics of the participants. Part One provides a theoretical foundation for understanding ISGs and for conceptualizing effective ISGs with college students.

Chapter One examines the use of the peer group to enhance the personal development of college students. ISGs are defined, a model is presented for conceptualizing and planning them, and basic guidelines for conducting ISGs are given.

Chapter Two explores the basic principles of small-group dynamics, with emphasis on cohesiveness, group norms, conformity pressures, and role behavior. The concept of stage development of groups is discussed, and a developmental-stage model specific to ISGs is presented.

Chapter Three summarizes major theories of college-student development and identifies the basic processes and principles inherent in them. The identified developmental tasks and processes (developmental domains) are related to the model for conceptualizing ISGs with specific examples.

What Is an Intentionally Structured Group and How Does It Work?

One of the distinguishing characteristics of American higher education has been the concern for and acceptance of responsibility for educating the "whole student," not only the student's intellect. Student affairs as a profession came into existence to fill the void created by the faculty's withdrawal of interest in students' out-of-class lives. The landmark position paper published in 1972 by the Council of Student Personnel Associations in Higher Education (COSPA) asserted that human beings seek to become free and self-directed through developmental processes and that it is the role of student affairs professionals to assist them in that process (Commission on Professional Development. . . , 1972/1983). That statement was a major impetus in focusing the student affairs field on student development as both a theoretical foundation for practice and a professional raison d'être.

The COSPA statement charged student affairs divisions with responsibility for assisting the development of all students, not just responding to students with problems. Such a mammoth undertaking requires strategies other than one-to-one interventions because otherwise there will never be sufficient staff to accomplish the profession's goals. One feasible, but not fully appreciated or utilized, approach is to use groups as the intervention medium.

Enhancing Student Development Through Group Interventions

Groups as a medium for enhancing student development have a number of advantages: (1) Groups are economical. Because no college has sufficient staff to attempt to influence the personal development of students solely one-to-one, group interventions can be an efficient use of personnel and limited resources. (2) Groups appear less threatening than individual counseling or therapy. Students are often less reluctant to address concerns that trouble them after they learn that others have similar difficulties. (3) Groups often have a synergetic effect—that is, the members of the group gain more from the experience than they would have through individual interventions. The opportunity to interact with other students and to observe and imitate behaviors of peers can also be an effective learning stimulus and source of support. (4) Groups often focus attention on developmental areas for which the stimulus for change is too diluted in the overall campus environment. For example, students who need to work on developing tolerance may not have readily accessible opportunities to learn directly about their prejudices and to experience their hurtful impacts because students (as with people in general) naturally tend to seek out others who share common backgrounds and *Weltanschauungen*. (5) Students generally give positive evaluations of and report enjoying well-designed and implemented group experiences. Groups and group leaders who acquire a reputation for being effective are attractive to students. (6) Group interventions are versatile; they can focus on a given population of students, an identified problem, or a developmental task. (7) Group settings can provide a "safe" place to try out new roles and to practice different ways of relating to others. (8) Well-designed and implemented groups make excellent use of the instructional strategies identified in several models of student-development interventions (Miller and Prince, 1976; Morrill, Hurst, and Associates, 1980; Barrow, 1986).

A final and important advantage of using groups to enhance development is that college students, especially young adults, generally exhibit strong needs to belong to an identity group. This connection with the peer group is an important aspect of personal development and is essential to healthy personality growth. The power of the peer group to enhance the development of individual students makes groups an excellent strategy to consider.

Feldman and Newcomb (1969a, 1969b) document many different functions and influences of the student peer group:

- Peer groups help individuals make the transition from the dependent role in the family to full membership in the postcollege adult world.
- Peer groups can either support or discourage acceptance of the academic goals of the college.
- Peer groups can provide students occasions for practice in getting along with people whose backgrounds, interests, and values are different from their own.
- Through value reinforcement, peer groups can provide support for the status quo, or they can "challenge old values, provide intellectual stimulation, and act as a sounding board for new points of view, present new information and new experiences to the student, help to clarify new self-definitions, suggest new career possibilities, and provide emotional support for students who are changing" (p. 237).

Peer groups thus have wide-ranging and significant influences on how students view themselves and approach higher education. Consequently, it would seem that one way to harness the potent force of the peer group is to provide opportunities for students to enhance and enrich their lives in planned group settings. In this book we propose that one way to affect the personal development of students is through the careful and considered use of intentionally structured groups.

Intentionally Structured Groups: A Definition

Within the universe of types of group work, there is a family of interventions that we call "intentionally structured groups" (ISGs). Several unique characteristics distinguish them both from traditional counseling or therapy groups and from naturally occurring social or task groups.

An *intentionally structured group* is an intervention de-signed to promote specific goals; it has a planned structure or framework and a specified duration—usually relatively short; generally from four to thirty hours total, lasting not more than fifteen weeks or one academic term. An ISG (1) occurs in a planned social environment, (2) has preestablished goals (which have sufficient latitude to allow for members' modifications), (3) is designed to affect one or more areas of human develop-ment, and (4) has specific ground rules designed to maintain the essential structure of the group (for example, time parameters, goal specification, level of self-disclosure promoted, and defini-tion of leader and member roles). Tasks and activities are de-signed to create opportunities through which members may:

• Examine attitudes and feelings
• Acquire new information
• Develop and practice skills
• Receive feedback in a supportive climate
• Integrate knowledge with affect to form personally mean-ingful and useful constructs

ISGs are planned and implemented in ways that utilize the dynamics of the group to promote the ISG's goals and individual behavior change. The overall intervention is grounded in an understanding of the developmental content and processes typical of the population for which the ISG is intended. In this book the focus is on a specific population—college students and the higher education environment—and therefore the theory base is student-development theory.

We have chosen to call these kinds of interventions inten-tionally structured groups for several reasons:

• ISGs are planned and implemented with specified goals in mind, which means that leaders have the responsibility of keeping the group focused on the stated purposes and of eliminating or minimizing influences and behaviors that detract from attaining goals.

- Activities and processes are planned that focus attention on the goals and that amplify learning (Drum and Knott, 1977).
- The leader assumes major responsibility for selecting the content addressed and the processes utilized.
- Behavior change and learning are stimulated and reinforced principally by the personal interactions among members and by the dynamic forces of the group as a group. ISGs are specifically planned and purposefully led to maximize the effects of these psychological forces.

Preestablished Goals. An ISG has specific purposes or goals that should be formulated prior to convening the group (see Chapter Four) and should be explained to potential members in order to allow them to make informed decisions about whether they wish to participate. Pfeiffer and Jones (1973, p. 178) speak of the leader and the members forming a "contract." They contend that an ISG-type experience has an increased chance of being effective if the participants come into it knowing what to expect, why they are there, and what they have contracted to do.

Social Structure. ISGs are artificial social systems that have rules or norms established or promoted to facilitate and enhance learning. As Middleman and Goldberg (1972, p. 203) note, "When one structures a learning situation, one imposes a certain frame of reference on it. This frame of reference emphasizes some aspects of the situation and screens out others. Thus, the social situation is delimited, and a particular focus emerges." ISGs are a closed social system deliberately constructed to promote learning related to the ISG's preestablished goals or purposes. The rules or norms of the system should be articulated to participants by the leader in sufficient detail to enable them to determine whether they wish to participate. Should the group begin to stray from its intended purpose, the leader has the responsibility to refocus the group on its purposes or to focus the group's attention on what is happening as a prelude to the group's making a deliberate decision about the direction it wishes to take.

Activities generally fall into two categories: relatively formally structured tasks or exercises and relatively nonstructured
(or informally structured) activities. Either of these may be
designed to address specific content or to focus on process or
both. Formally structured exercises have explicit rules or specified ways of interacting, as with "games" and simulations. The
content may be irrelevant (for example, to focus on cooperation,
participants may be required to complete a nonsense task that
can be accomplished only when members share information
known only to individuals) or may require extensive knowledge
(for example, participants may be asked to rank order a list of
personal values that can ultimately be related to a variety of
occupations).

Unstructured or informally structured activities generally
focus on sharing perceptions or reactions to a stimulus through
discussion. The content may or may not be germane to the
learning focus. For example, to develop awareness of the need
for active listening, group members might discuss their reactions to terrorism in the world and then summarize each others'
reactions. The specific content—reactions to terrorism—is not
crucial. However, having group members talk about their feelings the last time they were frightened or appalled may be quite
germane in an interpersonal-communications training group.
These activities are structured only to the extent that a topic for
discussion is identified. Both the manifest and the latent content
are important (Middleman and Goldberg, 1972).

Group Dynamics. An effective ISG makes use of the principles of group dynamics to accomplish goals. An ISG is not a
collection of people who simply experience the same stimuli. A
number of people in the same room do not necessarily constitute a group.

For a collection of people to be considered a group, (1) a
rudimentary level of trust must exist among them; (2) they must
identify themselves as group members; (3) an informal communication network and system of interpersonal relationships
must be established; and (4) some identifiable purpose or goal
for the group needs to be understood. An ISG is built on the

principle of utilizing the group as a means to support or accomplish goals. Members are likely to experience behavior or attitude change within a supportive environment when experimentation is accepted, even expected. When members feel that they have control or major influence over the group's functioning, they are likely to support others within the group and to invest the time and make the commitment required to bring about personally meaningful learning. (These issues are dealt with in detail in Chapter Two.)

Cartwright (1951, pp. 386–387) proposed a number of group-dynamics principles that must be recognized and may be utilized to promote or encourage behavior or attitude change (or both) among group members:

- "If the group is to be used effectively as a medium of change, those people who are to be changed and those who are to exert influence for change must have a strong sense of belonging to the same group."
- "The more attractive the group is to its members the greater is the influence that the group can exert on its members."
- "In attempts to change attitudes, values, or behavior, the more relevant they are to the basis of attraction to the group, the greater will be the influence that the group can exert upon them."
- "The greater the prestige of a group member in the eyes of other members, the greater the influence he[she] can exert."
- "Efforts to change individuals or subparts of a group which, if successful, would have the result of making them deviate from the norms of the group will encounter strong resistance."
- "Strong pressure for changes in the group can be established by creating a shared perception by members of the need for change, thus making the source of pressure for change lie within the group."
- "Information relating to the need for changes, plans for change, and consequences of change must be shared with all relevant people in the group [if change is to be realized]."
- "Changes in one part of a group produce strain in other

related parts which can be reduced only by eliminating the change or by bringing about readjustment in the related parts."

Essential Psychological Nature. ISGs are always psychological in emphasis and process. Regardless of the explicit goals of the ISG, the process must focus on the self-exploration of each individual in relation to the ISG goals and the management of the natural dynamics of the group. An ISG with career exploration as the goal, for example, generally has a dual process focus: (1) procedures for locating and examining career information and (2) the psychology of decision making—that is, each individual's attitudes toward and beliefs about careers and the significance of work, and how each individual associates different careers with particular life-styles. The interaction among group members facilitates their gaining a broad understanding of their personal values in a particular context. In an ISG, the intervention plan must include strategies for promoting significant psychological interactions.

A Model for Conceptualizing ISGs

To assist those who desire to use ISGs in their work with college students, we have developed a model inspired by and adapted from the Colorado State Cube Program Development Model (Morrill, Oetting, and Hurst, 1974; Oetting, Morrill, and Hurst, 1980; Hurst and Jacobson, 1985). As can be seen in Figure 1, this three-dimensional model covers the intervention focus, the process focus, and developmental domains.

Intervention Focus. The focus of an ISG-type intervention may be enhancement, prevention, or remediation. These categories are not mutually exclusive, but each has a distinct purpose. *Enhancement* activities help participants enrich their quality of life or functioning or realize their potentials. These activities primarily promote positive growth and deal with the "normal" concerns or issues associated with a particular stage or phase of life. An ISG for traditional-aged college students on

Figure 1. A Model for Conceptualizing ISGs.

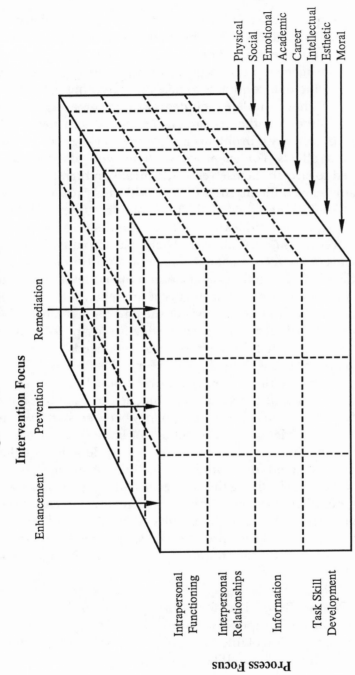

developing an understanding of intimacy and the skills and attitudes associated with establishing satisfying intimate relationships could be thought of as being enhancing. The development of intimacy is a task begun in earnest during the college years and one that continues to take on increasing importance for many as they complete their degree programs and move into young adulthood and early careers. *Prevention* activities are designed to anticipate problems and to prevent them or ameliorate their effects. For example, students who have not been required to stretch themselves academically in high school will probably have difficulty in a college with high academic standards. An ISG designed to help incoming students develop effective study techniques and skills can be viewed as preventive in nature. *Remediation* activities help participants deal with problems or correct or change behaviors or attitudes that prevent them from functioning at an acceptable level. There are three possible causes for problems: a discrepancy between the student's skills and the demands of the environment, behaviors of the student that are no longer effective (or possibly never were), or a mismatch between the student's needs and the environment (Oetting, Morrill, and Hurst, 1980). Examples of each of these problems are: (1) feelings of loneliness and isolation due to lack of the social skills needed to establish a new friendship group in college (discrepancy between skill level and environmental demands), (2) feelings of homesickness persisting after the first few weeks of college (overly dependent behavior), and (3) a minority student's feelings of alienation and isolation caused by living in a residence hall where there are few, if any, members of the same minority group (mismatch between the environment and the student's affiliation and support needs). As a general rule, problems college students experience that require remedial attention have antecedents in high school or earlier.

Process Focus. The focus of the process for effecting change can be intrapersonal functioning, interpersonal relationships, provision of information, or task skill development. It is not uncommon for an ISG to have all four foci. These categories are presented for heuristic purposes; in reality they seldom exist in a pure or distinct state. In any given ISG the process focus is a matter of emphasis. Different techniques or strategies are required, however, for each process focus; therefore, planners need to have a clear understanding of what they are attempting to accomplish.

Intrapersonal functioning covers individuals' perceptions of themselves and their relationship to the world around them, the meaning they make of their experiences, and the emotions that are associated with various behaviors and situations. Intrapersonal functioning deals with subjective, internal states that include self-concept, self-assessment, degrees of self-understanding, and ability to analyze accurately one's experiences and motives, as well as a suffusive collection of values and attitudes largely internalized from family and rarely verbalized. One cannot directly affect intrapersonal functioning without using interpersonal relationships and interactions.

Interpersonal relationships are interactions with others: forming and maintaining relationships, giving and receiving feedback (both positive and critical), understanding others' perspectives (developing and showing empathy), cooperating with others, and becoming a contributing member of a group. The quality and nature of the interpersonal interactions are crucial in all ISGs. It is primarily through the interaction among group members that individuals are challenged to evaluate critically their behavior, values, and attitudes, to explore themselves, and to begin to risk trying new behaviors. Because the intervention is based in the group, it makes interpersonal relationships apparent and immediate and encourages self-evaluation and change.

Information provision includes providing ideas, data, facts, and theories about a given subject matter. Because ISGs, unlike T-groups or some counseling groups, begin with a stated purpose, participants always need to acquire a certain amount of information. The quantity of information presented in ISGs may vary considerably, however, depending on the group's purpose. For example, an ISG on study skills would have a heavy emphasis on content (information) dissemination; an ISG on developing personal autonomy would have less of an emphasis on information about autonomy and a much greater emphasis on self-examination and personal decision-making processes and styles. Groups that have as their only purpose the dissemination of information should not be considered ISGs because they lack the essential aspect of purposively using group interaction and dynamics to further the learning goals.

Task skill development is learning to apply knowledge or to exercise manual dexterity or both. Generally, skill development in ISGs involves at least two of the other process foci. Skill development comes through practice of new behaviors either within the group through activities such as role playing or outside the group through homework assignments (participants may be requested to practice a skill or behavior taught in the group with non–group members between sessions and then to share their experiences with others in the group).

Developmental Domains. ISGs are grounded in student-development theory—that is, they are designed to deal with the "normal" growth and development of college students and the problems or crises that students typically encounter while pursuing higher education (see Chapter Three). For the purposes of this model, we have categorized eight broad areas of development: physical, social, emotional, academic, career, intellectual, esthetic, and moral.

Physical development involves maintaining good health (through diet, exercise, avoidance of harmful drugs for substance use or abuse, and hygiene) and developing physical skills (through recreation, playing sports, and exercise). Drum (1980) proposes three levels of physical health development: unintentional practices—the student adopts practices from others uncritically and unsystematically; selective management—the student has an "increased sense of internal management of healthful behaviors [that] leads to a period of experimental activity in which...[he or she] tries new behaviors...and loosens his or her reliance on habits incorporated from parents" (p. 32); personal responsibility—the student shows awareness and understanding of the consequences of physically abusive practices and is able to judge the short-term and long-term health effects of specific actions.

Social development involves establishing relationships with peers that are characterized by trust, independence, and individuality and that allow for acceptance of differences and periods of disagreement with friends without destroying the relationship. Social development also involves interdependence—that is, mature dependence. Students recognize that if they are to receive the benefits of society they must be willing to make contributions as well. Students are also able to accept persons from different cultures and social/racial backgrounds and to establish effective working and social relationships (Chickering, 1969; Winston, Miller, and Prince, 1979; Chickering and Havighurst, 1981).

Emotional development for young-adult college students includes (1) becoming aware of feelings and trusting them, recognizing that they provide relevant information for decision making; (2) controlling emotions so that they are expressed in socially acceptable, nondestructive ways; and (3) being free from the need for continuous reassurance and approval from others and reliance on others (especially parents) in making decisions (Chickering, 1969; Winston, Miller, and Prince, 1979). For older students emotional development includes reestablishing emotional autonomy, which may have been disrupted or challenged by life transitions (the departure of children from home, divorce, career changes, or, for some women, redefining autonomy itself)(Chickering and Havighurst, 1981; Straub, 1987).

Academic development involves acquiring the knowledge, skills, and habits necessary to satisfy academic demands and learning to manipulate the collegiate environment to meet individual needs. Academic development may include learning how to use the library, use laboratory equipment, or structure out-of-class time to allow for completion of assignments and class preparations. Academic development involves gaining experience with various disciplines in order to assess personal interests and abilities and to acquire the skills and background needed to make a satisfactory choice of academic major or concentration.

Career development for most college students involves both the identification of personal interests, values, and abilities or talents, and the acquisition of information about a variety of career or occupational areas—educational requirements for entry, personality characteristics of successful practitioners, and typical job demands. As Super (1983) describes the process, most individuals move through the cycle of (1) crystallization—formulation of ideas about one's self and the nature of work, and the differentiation of interests and values; (2) specification—a narrowing process, taking necessary steps to identify likes and dislikes, interests, abilities, and personal values; (3) implementation—completion of education and entry into the work force; (4) stabilization—settling down in a field of work; and (5) consolidation—establishing a secure and comfortable position in an occupational field. Most traditional-aged college students deal only with stages 1, 2, and the beginnings of 3.

Many older students return to college as part of their plans to change occupational fields or to enter the world of work-for-pay for the first time. "For these men and women, moving into occupations or developing new careers can be a high-risk, high-gain period. It can be full of excitement, self-validation, growing self-esteem, and sense of competence. . . . But this can also be a period of frustration, anxiety, trial, and self-doubt" (Chickering and Havighurst, 1981, p. 42).

Intellectual development has to do with how students go about making meaning of their experience or how they conceptualize the nature of knowledge and truth. For persons within the "normal" range, it has little, however, to do with native ability or intelligence as measured by IQ tests. Perry (1970) proposes the most complete theory of the intellectual development of college students. He postulates nine positions that may be summarized in four stages or steps: (1) dualism, which is characterized by dichotomous thinking (that is, the world falls into categories of right/wrong, good/bad, either/or); (2) multiplicity, in which the student comes to see knowledge or truth as being subject to a multitude of interpretations, all having approximately equal weight or validity; (3) relativism, in which students move from simply acknowledging different perspectives to seeing the various points of view as fitting into a larger whole—"the context within which points of view exist has been established" (King, 1978, pp. 38–39); and (4) commitment in relativism, in which students accept relativism but are able to make "an active affirmation of themselves and their responsibilities in a pluralistic world," establishing their identities in the process (King, 1978, p. 39). Research studies suggest that most traditional-aged college students do not progress beyond the multiplicity stage during their undergraduate years (Kitchener and King, 1981; Polkosnik and Winston, in press).

Esthetic development has been a traditional goal of higher education, especially of liberal arts education. Drum (1980) proposes three levels of esthetic development: instilled preference, in which the student's tastes and judgments are adopted or copied from others (parents and especially peers)—"I know what I like, but I can't tell you why"; broadened appreciation, in which "esthetic judgments and preferences are built less on imitation of others' tastes and more on the basis of personal experimentation" (p. 28) or on experiencing a wide range of "cultural stimuli"; and enhanced sensitivity, in which "development of a specific set of esthetic preferences is not viewed as being as important as building an appreciation for the intricacy and beauty present in a wide range of life events" (p. 29).

Moral development primarily concerns how students make judgments with a moral content but does not directly concern the specific content of the judgments. As Smith (1978) notes, theories of moral development cover the "'whys,' not the 'whats,' or the content of the judgment" (p. 54). Kohlberg (1971), the best-known theorist of moral development, proposes three levels (with six stages): (1) at the preconventional level, the person (child) learns the cultural rules and mores and determines "good" and "bad" according to physical or hedonistic consequences of action (punishment, reward, exchange of favors); (2) at the conventional level, the person makes judgments based on a desire to maintain the social order, with a lessened concern for immediate consequences—"the attitude is not only one of *conformity* to personal expectations and social order but of loyalty to it, of actively *maintaining*, supporting, and justifying the order, and of identifying with persons or groups involved in it" (Smith, 1978, p. 55); (3) at the principled level, the individual makes an effort to define moral values and principles that have validity and application across groups, cultures, and situations. Gilligan (1982) questions the application of this formalization to women. She asserts that women reason in "a different voice" — that is, they place less emphasis on laws and principles of justice in making moral judgments and place greater emphasis on the maintenance and enhancement of relationships and how actions affect others who are important to them.

Rest (1985) expands the concept of moral development by pointing out that there are interconnected cognitive, affective, and behavioral aspects. He maintains people must carry out four relatively distinct psychological processes in order to behave morally: (1) They must evaluate the situation objectively — that is, determine who is involved, what lines of actions are possible for those involved, and how each line of action would affect the other parties. (2) They must judge the alternative lines of action as to which will be most just or fair or morally correct. (3) They must also assess other interests in the situation — that is, they need to recognize their own desire for success, cultural values, institutional goals, or other interests that may conflict with moral goals. They then must choose among the competing interests and values. (4) Finally, they must act on a decision to pursue a moral course of action and persist until the moral goal is accomplished.

Uses of the Model. This model is presented to help ISG designers focus on both goals and process objectives. It is important that planners have a clear understanding of what they are attempting to do with an ISG before convening the first session. By carefully conceptualizing the ISG and then designing activities directly related to goals (see Chapter Four), designers increase the likelihood of success. Our experience in designing and leading ISGs over the years has clearly demonstrated that good intentions and a caring attitude are not sufficient to produce successful learning experiences for students consistently. Careful planning—based on accurate assessment data from the population to be addressed, a good working knowledge of group dynamics, and a clear understanding of developmental theory—is essential.

Types of Group Work: A Context for Understanding ISGs

In order to understand ISGs fully, the reader needs a broad conceptual framework within which to place them. As Conyne (1985b) correctly notes, no truly adequate model for conceptualizing all group work currently exists. Most of what has been written concerns traditional counseling groups, which were designed to assist participants to overcome emotional problems and concerns in their lives or to teach specific skills, such as interpersonal communications or assertiveness.

To assist the reader in appreciating the full range and richness of group approaches and to provide a context for understanding the place of ISGs within that universe, we have developed a model, although at the outset we readily acknowledge that it is far from perfect. Categories in the model reflect emphases; they are not pure classifications. In addition, categories often overlap within a given group depending on the leader's style and theoretical orientation and the composition of the group. The model has three major dimensions: degree of structure, purpose, and desired outcomes. (See Figure 2.)

Degree of Structure. Structure refers primarily to the amount of control or direction the leader exercises, the degree to which members perceive the group as having a purpose or goals, and the degree to which the assigned roles for members and the leader are understood and fulfilled. The more the roles of members and the leader are consistently maintained and accepted by the members, the higher the degree of structure. The greater the ambiguity about roles and goals, the less structured is the group. (A detailed treatment of structure in groups is provided in Chapter Two.)

Figure 2. A Model of Types of Groups.

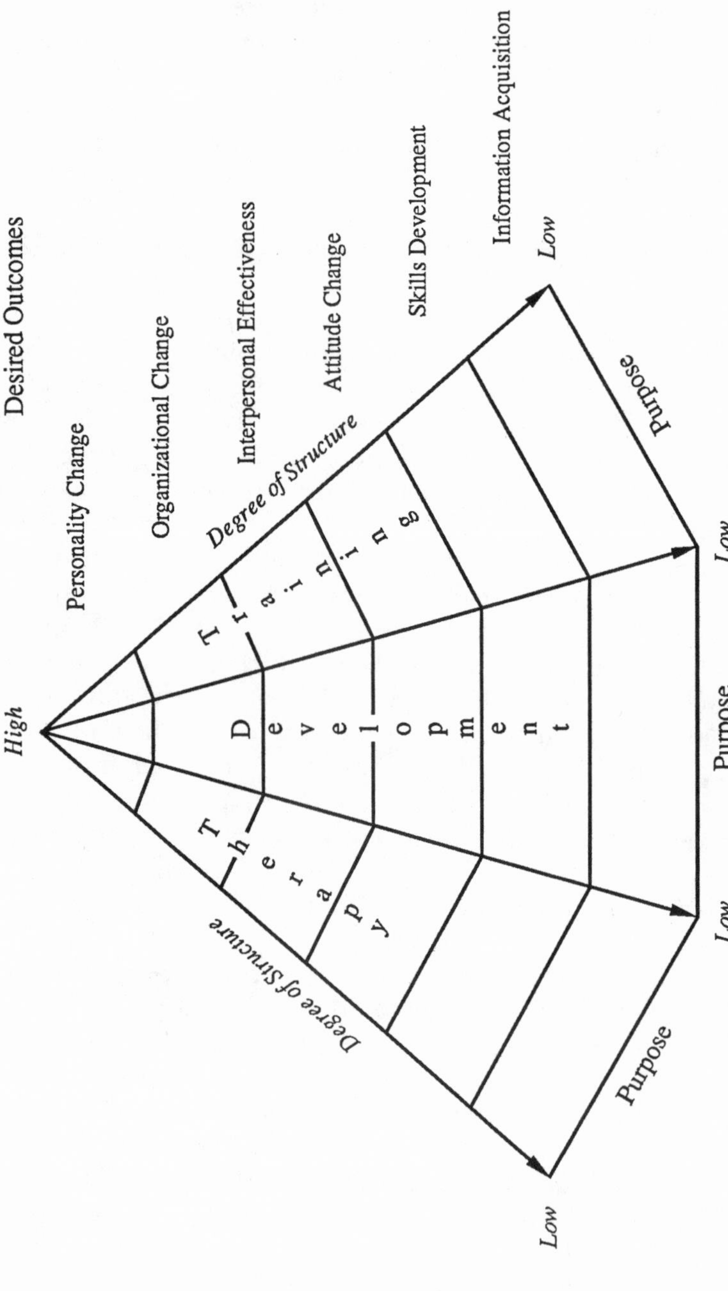

Desired Outcomes

Personality Change

Organizational Change

Interpersonal Effectiveness

Attitude Change

Skills Development

Information Acquisition

High

Low

Degree of Structure

Degree of Structure

Training

Development

Therapy

Purpose

Low

Low

Purpose

Low

Low

Purpose

There is no such thing, then, as an unstructured group. It is appropriate to speak only about the relative degree of structure evident or planned in a group. However, a relatively highly structured group may not use structured group exercises, which are often associated with structured groups. This dimension of the model may thus be conceived as a continuum ranging from low to high.

An example of a group low in structure is the T-group (training group). T-groups, which were "discovered" at the National Training Laboratory (NTL) in the late 1940s, are characterized by the leader's refusal to define content or tasks for the group or to interpret events that occur in the group. In other words, participants develop their own structure and define the content of the group's discussion and activity. Before a structure emerges, however, the group usually experiences a great deal of frustration, and some members may verbally attack the leader for insensitivity and dereliction of duty (Aronson, 1980; Clack, 1985). But the basic tenet of the T-group is that through the process of discovering or inventing a structure significant learning takes place. The discovery process is essential to the learning process.

At the other end of the structure continuum is the Systematic Group Discussion (Hill, 1985), which employs a series of predetermined steps or rules that are followed strictly. The content is sharply focused on the assigned reading materials. Typically used in a class setting, the steps are: "(1) definition of terms and concepts, (2) general statement of author's message, (3) identification of major themes or subtopics, (4) allocation of time, (5) discussion of major themes or subtopics, (6) integration of the material, (7) application of the material, (8) evaluation of author's presentation, and (9) evaluation of group and individual performance" (p. 158).

Purpose. The purpose of the group can be therapy, development, or training. As with the other categories in this model, they may overlap—that is, elements of two or more purposes may be present in any given group. One can, however, usually speak of the primary or principal purpose as falling into one of the three categories.

Therapy is intended to assist participants in dealing with or overcoming perceived problems. The therapeutic purpose is to "correct" or ameliorate whatever is "wrong." Problems may be severe, such as dealing with the effects of incest or chronic depression, or relatively minor in comparison, such as meeting members of the opposite sex. Therapy is needed when a person does not feel competent to deal with a problem alone or when past attempts at dealing with the situation have proven unsuccessful.

Another purpose for a group is *development;* the goal is not to correct a problem but to help participants with the tasks and concerns that are a "normal" part of life and the maturation process. For example, traditional-aged college students face predictable tasks, such as deciding on an academic major and a postcollege career, redefining the nature of their relationships with parents, and establishing personal identity (Chickering, 1969; see also Chapter Three). Development enhances or improves the quality of participants' lives and promotes members' growth and the realization of their potentials.

Training assists participants in acquiring the skills and knowledge needed to accomplish tasks or to deal effectively within an area of their life or interpersonal functioning. In other words, training is teaching participants how to do something. The subject matter may be physical operations, such as how to use a piece of computer software or how to operate a machine, or interpersonal functioning, such as how to improve active listening skills (attending and responding), or psychophysical functioning, such as how to do biofeedback or how to meditate in order to control physiological functions such as blood pressure or muscle tension.

Desired Outcomes. The last dimension of the model is the desired outcomes or how members are expected to be different or to have changed as a result of having participated in the group. As a general rule, most groups have multiple expected outcomes. Most effective group interventions are designed, how-

ever, with a limited number of outcomes in mind. These outcomes may be cateogorized as (1) information acquisition—
members will become knowledgeable about a given subject; (2)
personality change—members' typical or characteristic ways of
responding to people, ideas, or things will be altered in some
fundamental way (for most relatively short-term groups, this is
an unrealistic goal seldom attained because of the great difficulty associated with basic personality change); (3) skills development—participants will learn how to do something with
which they were previously unacquainted or they will increase
their skill level; (4) attitude change—participants will alter the
basic ways they view the world or some part of it (like personality
change, this is a difficult process unlikely to be accomplished in
short-term groups); (5) organizational change—organizations
will become able to deal with problems such as intergroup
communications or conflict or will increase productivity or
quality control, as with quality circles (Conyne, 1983, 1985a); (6)
interpersonal effectiveness—members will gain an increasingly
accurate perception or understanding of how and why others
respond to them as they do and will have the opportunity to
practice new ways of relating to others in a basically supportive
environment.

ISGs in the Universe of Group Interventions. If we use the
model presented in Figure 2, ISGs encompass the upper half of
the model—that is, the degree of structure is moderate to high.
The purposes of ISGs can be (1) therapy—advocated by Ivey and
Galvin (1982) as "microtraining" and by Drum and Knott (1977)
as "life theme and life transition groups"; or (2) development,
in what Drum and Knott (1977) and Gazda (1982) describe as
"life skills groups"; or (3) training, as exemplified by Lippitt's
(1985) "community futuring and planning groups" and by
communication-skills training (Ivey and Authier, 1978; Gazda
and others, 1984; Francis, McDaniel, and Doyle, 1987). Likewise,
an ISG can have any of the six desired outcomes, but as a rule
ISGs are most effective when they have information acquisition,
skills development, or interpersonal effectiveness as the goal.

Guidelines for Conducting ISGs

Planners and leaders of ISGs need to consider carefully a number of guidelines and rules relating to selection of participants and conduct of sessions. They are presented here to forewarn potential designers and leaders of crucial practical and ethical considerations that should always be kept in mind.

Screening and Selection. As a general rule it is desirable to screen prospective ISG members before the beginning of the group. Potential members can be requested to complete a short questionnaire and have an interview with one of the ISG leaders as part of the application process. During this interview the leader should explain the purposes of the ISG (should give the prospective member a short written summary of the goals and a brief description of the group activities and techniques that are planned) and give a general explanation of what is expected of participants, as well as gather information about why the student is interested in participating. The interview also gives students a chance to ask questions and have points clarified. Other variables about which the leader should seek information include capacity for insight, level of motivation to participate, level of maturity or readiness to address the ISG's topic, and evidence of severe mental disorders. Students who are currently receiving counseling or therapy of any kind should not be accepted into the group without first consulting with the professional already providing services. (As a general rule it is not desirable to include such persons in most ISGs.)

The screening interview also serves another purpose: It allows a leader and each participant to begin forming a relationship, which can help considerably in the early stages of the group because it helps members deal with the anxiety often associated with beginning the group (Hansen, Warner, and Smith, 1980).

Depending on the nature of the group, it may be desirable to ask potential participants to complete one or more questionnaires or psychological instruments, the results of which can (will) be used in the course of the ISG. For example, for a career-exploration group it may be desirable to have information about interests, which can be gained from the Strong Vocational Interest Blank (Strong, Hansen, and Campbell, 1985), or about level of career development and knowledge, which can be gained from the Career Development Inventory (Super and others, 1981) (which requires several weeks' lead time for computer scoring). The use of such instruments is also a way to begin building baseline data for summative evaluation (see Chapter Five). Asking students to complete inventories can also help a leader gauge their level of commitment and involvement.

Constraints of time and resources may prevent the acceptance of all qualified applicants and so decisions must be made about the composition of the group. For example, should the group be homogeneous or heterogeneous on variables such as class standing, gender, place of residence, age, or academic major? What is the maximum (and minimum) size of the ISG? Because leaders have professional and ethical responsibilities to assure that all qualified students receive assistance, a waiting list should be established of persons who will be given an opportunity within a reasonable time to participate in another ISG. (For students, "reasonable" probably means within the same academic term.) Or it may be possible to refer students to other services on campus where their concerns can be addressed more quickly—for example, individual counseling, an academic course, or self-paced instruction such as a computer program.

When planning on using an ISG with an intact group— for example, a staff—selection is not an issue. It is important, however, that members have a completely free choice about whether to participate and that they be given an opportunity to present their ideas about the content, processes, and duration of the ISG. If the staff members are not committed to accomplishing the ISG goals, little of consequence will generally result from the experience. Therefore, ISG leaders need to be sure that the content and process are perceived by participants as relevant and important to their job responsibilities.

As a general rule, self-selection is the most effective means for screening out potentially unsuitable ISG participants. If students have a clear picture of the ISG's goals, of the general nature of the processes and activities that are planned, and of expectations regarding their involvement and commitment, then they usually will not elect to participate in ISGs that are too threatening (developmentally inappropriate) or that require more than they are willing or able to give. We do not think it necessary, or even desirable, to require extensive testing or extended interviews as a prerequisite for participation. ISG leaders need to be concerned primarily with identifying students who are obviously unsuited for the planned activities or whose personalities or interpersonal communication styles appear to mediate against creating the kind of climate or process requisite for accomplishing the goals of the ISG. (For example, an ISG composed predominately of apprehensive or shy students is likely to be unsuccessful if high levels of interaction are required.) A high degree of homogeneity is not necessary and often is undesirable because homogeneous groups fail to provide sufficient stimulation or challenge to sustain participants' interest and promote growth. (This caution, however, applies more to group composition than to the determination of fitness of potential participants.)

Ground Rules and Ethics. All ISGs should have a concisely stated set of ground rules that are clearly communicated to participants. Leaders, at the beginning of a group, need to describe these rules as being essential to the functioning of the group and need to state that they will intervene if the rules are violated. Members should be given a copy of the ground rules during the first session and afforded opportunities for responding, questioning, and suggesting changes. Spending time on establishing the basic ground rules may well prevent many problems from occurring.

An important topic to cover in the ground rules is *confidentiality*. Trust is essential to the effective functioning of ISGs. In order for members to have trust they must feel that others respect them enough not to disclose what is said during an ISG to anyone outside the group or to discuss what transpired in the group outside the group — even with other group members.

Members should be assured that they will not be pressured into disclosing sensitive areas of their lives. They, however, should also be warned that no assurances can be given that everyone will abide by the rules of confidentiality proposed and that no legal sanctions can be imposed on those who break the rules. Participants should also be informed that the leader reserves the right to consult with other professionals about members of the group. If the leader determines that individuals are likely to harm themselves, another person, or others' property, then the leader is obligated to inform the potential victim(s) and the appropriate institutional and legal authorities (see Van Hoose and Kottler, 1977; American College Personnel Association, 1981; American Association for Counseling and Development, 1982; Association for Specialists in Group Work, 1982).

The ground rules should also emphasize *voluntary participation* in ISGs. An absolute rule in ISGs is that members may elect not to participate in any exercise or activity without being pressured by the leaders or other members. Members have the right to say simply "I pass" to any exercise or activity without being required to give an explanation and, likewise, to discontinue membership in the group at any time.

Substance use is another area that should be included in the ground rules. Members and leaders may not use alcohol or other drugs during group sessions and should not come to sessions under the influence of such substances.

Attendance and involvement requirements need to be listed. As a general rule, members are expected to attend all sessions and to be prompt because their absence or tardiness affects all group members. Leaders may wish to formulate a policy about notification of the leaders in advance in cases of emergency or illness. Expectations about attendance should be clearly specified during the screening interview and reviewed during the first session. The kinds of activities or work expected of members outside the group should be specified, and members should be informed that failure to complete assignments will adversely affect their learning and the learning of others in the group as well. Membership in the group signifies a commitment not only to devote the effort required to accomplish the group's goals but also to contribute to the learning and growth of other group members.

Members should avoid *sexual involvements* with others in the group for the duration of the ISG because the formation of these kinds of relationships almost always adversely affects the experience for other group members. Also, as stated by the Association for Specialists in Group Work (1982), "Group leaders shall abstain from inappropriate personal relationships with members throughout the duration of the group and any subsequent professional involvement" (p. 173). The American College Personnel Association (1981) is even more explicit: "Members [of the Association] are aware that sexual relationships hold great potential for exploitation. Consequently, members refrain from having sexual relationships with anyone for whom they act as counselors or therapists. Sexual relationships with staff members or students for whom one has supervisory or evaluative responsibilities have high potential for causing personal damage and for limiting the exercise of professional responsibilities and are therefore unprofessional and unethical" (p. 185).

Use or threats of physical *violence* are never permitted. Likewise, verbal abuse is not acceptable, and leaders have a responsibility to intervene should it occur. The Association for Specialists in Group Work states: "Group leaders shall protect member rights against physical threats, intimidation, coercion, and undue peer pressure insofar as is reasonably possible" (1982, p. 173).

Notifying Members of Potential Risks. Members should be informed of the potential risks of participating in the ISG, including possible life changes (Association for Specialists in Group Work, 1982). These risks should be raised first in the screening interview and again early in the life of the ISG. The greater the degree of risk, the greater the responsibility of leaders to communicate the risk factors, insofar as they can be anticipated, explicitly to members.

Notifying Members of Recording or Testing. Members should be informed if audio or video recording of sessions is to occur and what the disposition of those tapes will be—that is, who will have access to them and how long the tapes will be retained. Likewise, if members are to complete inventories, tests, or questionnaires during the course of the ISG, they should be informed in advance of their purpose (for example, for summative evaluation), their ultimate disposition, and the level of confidentiality to be afforded them.

Other Ethical Principles. The overarching ethical principle in leading groups is the avoidance of harm (Kitchener, 1985). Leaders have the responsibility to protect individuals from both physical and psychological damage. In order to avoid doing harm, leaders must carefully assess their abilities, skills, and levels of competence for leading an ISG. As a general rule leaders should not attempt an exercise that they have not taken part in as members or participants. If that is not feasible, then leaders should carefully explore the anticipated dynamics during an exercise and think through possible problems and responses. As Napier and Gershenfeld (1983, p. 40) caution leaders: "Going beyond your level of competence is dangerous. It is not taking a risk; it is inviting disaster." The welfare of participants takes precedence over all other considerations.

Leaders must be aware of the power they have over others in the group by virtue of holding the position. As models, they are watched carefully by members. When members detect a discrepancy between behavior and espoused principles or values, the incongruence detracts from the leaders' effectiveness and can undermine accomplishment of the ISG's goals.

Leaders have the responsibility to follow-up with members after any session in which they detect distress, discomfort, or unresolved issues or problems. Assistance may take the form of individual sessions with the leader or referral to others on the campus or in the community who possess the expertise and experience needed to provide appropriate help. Leaders also have the ethical responsibility to have identified, before beginning the ISG, backup professionals who are willing to provide consultation to the leaders should the need arise or to give assistance to members who require it.

Minimum Leader Knowledge, Skills, and Experience

It is difficult to specify a particular educational background or a list of essential skills that leaders should possess in order to lead ISGs successfully. Nevertheless, we can propose some broad categories of knowledge, skills, and experiences that are needed. These include knowledge of (1) theory, (2) group facilitation/process skills, (3) diagnostic skills, (4) content knowledge, (5) supervised practice, (6) experience as a participant, and (7) self-awareness.

Theory. ISG leaders need knowledge of human-development theory appropriate for the population for whom the ISG is intended, such as traditional-aged students, older returning students, or members of particular minority groups. Leaders need to know what to expect in both the content and process of human development. Leaders also need a good grounding in group-dynamics theory. They need to know how groups develop, to be able to identify cues that indicate various levels of development, to be able to identify obstacles to effective group functioning, and to understand the basic principles that explain the individual behavior of group members.

Group Facilitation/Process Skills. Leaders must be able to assist the group in developing trust, mutual caring, and cohesiveness, without which ISGs are seldom effective. The leader also needs to know how to help the group move from a superficial level of socializing and defensiveness at the beginning of the ISG and to assist the members in developing a commitment to the ISG's goals, to concerned mutual assistance, and to their own behavior or attitude change (Gazda, 1978). (Specific leadership skills are discussed in Chapter Six.)

Diagnostic Skills. To be effective, ISG leaders need well-developed diagnostic skills. They need to be able to identify the dynamics operating within the group, to detect when individuals are hurting in order to protect them, to identify members who are psychologically unsuited for membership in a given ISG, and to evaluate the effects of activities, exercises, and interactions.

Content Knowledge. ISG leaders need to have a firm grasp and understanding of the content at which the ISG is directed. For instance, in a career-exploration ISG, the leader needs a clear, in-depth understanding of the content and process of career development. There is no substitute for a thorough grounding in the theory and research related to the ISG's subject matter. Practical experience performing the role or tasks or dealing with persons who have experienced difficulty in the area adds to the leader's credibility in the eyes of members.

Supervised Practice. No matter how perceptive or bright, the leader needs the benefit of evaluations and critiques of performance from a knowledgeable and perceptive professional. Because of subjective biases it is impossible for group leaders to obtain a clear picture of their performance without objective feedback from someone experienced and knowledgeable about leading ISGs. All ISG leaders need this feedback, in conjunction with systematic feedback based on either audiotapes or videotapes, before assuming the role of principal group leader. Ideally, neophyte leaders should first colead groups with an experienced leader and then lead alone or as the senior leader.

Experience as a Participant. ISG leaders need extensive experience as participants in ISGs and in less-structured group experiences as well. There is no substitute for the experience gained as a group member. Without such experience, the leader will generally have difficulty developing an empathic understanding of group members. Whenever possible, ISG leaders should participate in activities and exercises before leading them.

Self-Awareness. ISG leaders need an understanding of themselves and their ways of relating to people, and they need to model effective behavior, particularly in the area that the ISG addresses. Persons who have not resolved developmental issues satisfactorily for themselves should not attempt to lead groups in those areas. For example, leaders who have difficulty expressing themselves in appropriate ways should not attempt to lead an ISG on assertiveness. Or someone going through a painful breakup of a relationship should not lead an ISG dealing with relationship enhancement because personal issues would likely interfere with effective leadership; the ISG might become a vehicle for dealing with the leader's problems rather than focusing on the members' needs. Only through self-awareness can such difficulties be avoided.

Efficacy of ISGs as Student-Development Interventions

Although nearly all students have a common set of developmental needs, these needs become manifest in different ways and at different times for different people. It is, therefore, impossible to predict precisely when a given student will begin to have a specific need or what form that need will take. (Age and class standing, for example, are not necessarily good predictors of individual students' needs or levels of development in many areas.) The ISG approach is grounded in student-development theory. Consequently, ISGs, if conceptualized and implemented as we advocate, can provide opportunities for students to experience conditions that promote growth and development—such as the stimulation of being exposed to a new idea, the challenge of finding a solution to a personal concern, and exposure to alternative ways of resolving problems and making decisions—when students are ready to deal with these issues.

In many ways the use of ISGs by student affairs professionals and others concerned with the development of students enhances and expands the students' general or liberal education and can promote the ideal of personal excellence as well. When the out-of-class activities of students complement the in-class academic programs by providing educational experiences that may not be available otherwise, the quality of the total educational experience is enhanced. The use of intentionally structured developmental groups is a good way to assure that students' educations will be comprehensive and meaningful. As Astin (1977, 1985) so strongly advocates, student involvement in the educational experience is a key factor in the value received and satisfaction derived from higher learning. One important way to enhance the total education of students and to increase their potential for becoming self-directed human beings and contributors in a democratic society is to expose them to numerous opportunities to increase their awareness, challenge their thinking, and expand their horizons. Well-conceived and skillfully implemented ISGs are viable vehicles for attaining these goals.

Group Dynamics
and Stages
of Group Development

Sam, the group leader, sweats and racks his brain about what to do next. He has just completed the first hour of a planned two-hour session on career exploration (which is part of a projected four-session workshop). He used the same icebreaker exercise he had used successfully several times before, but this time it did not produce the desired and expected effect. He then attempted another exercise he had copied from a collection of group exercises and games, and it produced equally disappointing results. The students refused to get involved, asked irrelevant questions, carried on side conversations, and appeared totally uninterested. Sam tried a couple of jokes, but no one laughed. He is confused, frustrated, and desperate because he cannot figure out what went wrong and, most important, what can be done to save this group.

Sam's situation is not an uncommon one for group leaders. The confusion does not have to persist, however, if the leader is adequately prepared, is knowledgeable about group dynamics, and understands how groups develop. The most important factor in the successful conduct of an ISG is the leader's knowledge and management of the natural dynamics of small groups. These dynamics are in force in any small group; they differ only in form and mode of expression according to the group's membership, purpose, and setting.

Group leaders who do not know about these forces may be at a total loss when events occur within the group that were not anticipated, and they may subsequently lose the group (that is, the members may desert) or lose control over its direction. This disastrous development is most likely to occur as a conse-

34

quence of one or more of these conditions: (1) The leader fails to understand, and thus violates, the expectations of the members. (2) The leader persistently follows a set procedure that worked previously with other groups but does not fit the present one. (3) The leader attempts to follow a published "canned" exercise without awareness of its pertinence to the group's task or its suitability given the developmental level of the members. Consistently successful leaders remain flexible and are sensitive to the feelings and desires of the participants. Flexibility is based in the leader's ability to identify and understand the dynamics of the group process. The capacity to shift direction or emphasis appropriately depends on the leader's comprehension of what is occurring dynamically within the group itself. Without this understanding any success the group achieves will be merely fortuitous.

This chapter about group dynamics and stages of group development establishes a firm foundation for understanding ISGs and a common frame of reference for the remainder of the book. It addresses three major areas. The first part of the chapter focuses on basic principles of group behavior that are typical and fairly constant across types of groups: characteristics and properties, formal and informal structure, norms, cohesiveness, group pressures, and the role behavior of individuals in groups. The second part of the chapter investigates the processes by which a group progresses toward effective, mature functioning, beginning with a historical overview of the concept of developmental stages applied to groups. Four representative models are presented. Finally, in the third part of the chapter, a developmental stage sequence model specifically relevant to ISGs is described.

Characteristics and Properties of Groups

The field of group dynamics is the study of those forces that produce a psychological entity referred to as a "group." Psychologically a group is different from a collection of people, an aggregate, a crowd, an audience, or other gatherings of individuals who do not depend on each other to achieve their separate goals. It may also be differentiated from an organization, in which identification is primarily with an impersonal system that specifies formal status relationships.

A group is an entity in which members

- Have similar goals
- Perceive benefits from membership
- Anticipate that the group will continue
- Share at least one common goal
- Show a willingness to cooperate in attaining goals
- Trust and accept other members within the group
- Share similar perceptions of the structure or order within the group
- Perceive the leadership function as being fulfilled
- Identify themselves as members
- Have a network of informal interpersonal relationships
- Experience standards of acceptable and unacceptable behavior

Some comparative examples may help clarify these characteristics. A collection of people waiting at a street corner for a traffic light to change or for a bus to arrive have a similar goal but do not need each other for the achievement of that goal; therefore, they are not a group. Membership in an audience of a stage production or concert is characterized by several of the attributes listed. Members have similar goals—to witness the performance; show a willingness to cooperate; and share a common perception of the order within the group—they behave themselves according to expectations for that kind of performance, which would differ markedly for a performance of a symphony orchestra and for a performance of a rock band. For the audience the other points are relevant only generally or not at all. Some of the characteristics listed hold true for a mob bent on the destruction of an individual or a place, but a group may be distinguished from a mob by the following traits: group members trust and accept one another, identify themselves as members, have an informal network of relationships, and anticipate that the group will continue. A delinquent youth gang meets all the criteria for a group, although its goals are anti-social. Most well-functioning ISGs can also be expected to exhibit all the characteristics listed.

Groups as Psychological Entities. In a psychological sense an organization and a group are not synonymous. The group may be an extension of an organization and may be essentially controlled by it, but groups have unique properties not shared with organizations. Within any organization there may be several groups that differ from each other in many significant ways. The degree to which the larger organization allows autonomy of purpose and action generally determines the vitality of the groups within it. A student government senate within a college is a prime example of this dynamic. When a student senate is allowed to assume or assumes a relative degree of autonomy from administrative controls and formulates its own direction and goals in response to expressed student needs, it can become a significant force in campus life (and on small campuses may exhibit many of the characteristics of groups). Fraternities and sororities are another example of organizations that often have groups (sometimes known as cliques) within them. Successful fraternity and sorority colonies when first organizing on a campus exhibit all the properties of a group; the larger and more institutionalized they become after gaining their charters, however, the less grouplike they remain. These organizations frequently develop subgroupings, and it is not uncommon to find individual members who are isolated or rejected by other members (in some large student organizations some members may be only marginally acquainted with each other). However, it is also not uncommon for the students in a residence hall to become a truly cohesive group and an identifiable psychological unit.

We may conclude, therefore, that a psychological group cannot be created by administrative fiat (but may become cohesive in reaction to administrative fiat) or by a designed structure alone because the factors that determine a cohesive and productive group must come from within the group itself. If we want to encourage the formation of groups, we must use strategies that allow students to create their own structure and purpose.

Attractiveness. The influence or impact a group has on its members, at least initially, is directly proportional to how attractive or desirable membership is perceived to be. (Often attractiveness is enhanced when there are high standards or selective membership criteria. For many students the most desirable group or organization is the one in which it is most difficult to gain membership.)

In a review of research studies on factors affecting group cohesion, Stockton and Hulse (1981) conclude that "attraction to the group can be enhanced by structure, composition, leader behavior, and a variety of other interventions such as self-disclosure and feedback" (p. 193). Nevertheless, attractiveness may be facilitated or hampered by forces outside the group. Some examples of external forces are the degree to which the group is perceived as satisfying the emotional needs of its members, the prestige of the group in relation to other groups, and the attractiveness of other members of the group to each individual. These and other forces may be managed intentionally to activate those dynamics inherent within groups that are most likely to create an efficacious group experience.

For the purposes of this book ISGs are an extension of the college, usually under the auspices of a student affairs unit. Thus, the character of the ISG will likely be influenced by the organizational structure of the larger system. The nature and extent of this influence should be considered carefully in the development of an ISG. A violation of the philosophy, regulations, and social norms of the college's leadership can destroy the entire enterprise. Such instances have occurred, and it has taken years to overcome their effects. Student affairs practitioners, however, can become overly concerned with conformity and administrative disapproval to the extent that they neglect students' needs and violate their personal and professional integrity.

Group Structure

Examples of spontaneous, informal groups are late-night bull sessions in residence halls or beer-drinking groups at college hangouts. There are no formal rules or expectations and no agendas in such groups, but over time certain topics of conversation tend to be predictable, and certain others are never broached. A particular tavern, cocktail lounge, or restaurant may attract a consistent type of clientele (philosophy majors, sports fans, graduate students in a given department, businessmen, or career women), some of whom become regulars. Informal leaders may emerge who determine the tone of the gatherings, but they would never attempt to impose any formal regulations on the proceedings. A lunch group from an organization may behave in a similar fashion. Formal decisions are rarely made, but plots for various activities may be hatched or incubated.

Functions of Structure. These informal groups are not far removed from the town meetings of early New England, through which every citizen had an equal voice in community governance; these meetings were an attempt at pure democracy. Perhaps present-day informal gatherings are a cultural precipitate or more likely meet an inherent need that is not satisfied by any other aspect of a highly structured and increasingly complex society. Because of population growth and other factors, cities and towns have been forced to abandon pure democracy in favor of representation, which in turn demands formal structures.

The word *formal* is important here because informal town meetings, bull sessions, and "lunch bunches" have structure, but are established out of individual needs and emerging group purposes that seldom need to be stated. The egalitarian quality of such gatherings, however, is not quite as pure as might appear from casual observation. For example, even though everyone had an equal voice in the town meetings, some voices had more power than others. This is part of what is meant by informal group structure (which is discussed in the section on group norms later in this chapter).

If a group does not have some structure, formal or informal, it is simply not a group. Formal structure is imposed in order to increase the efficiency of the operation. Structure often serves other purposes as well, often with questionable legitimacy. Parliamentary procedure may be used by group leaders to control or manipulate the direction and outcome of a discussion; minority opinions and creative ideas can be effectively stifled. The efficient use of time is another factor that necessitates some degree of formal structure. All student activities are, of necessity, time limited. An ISG program is an effort to strike a balance between the efficiency of formal structure and the freedom for individual growth provided by a spontaneous group experience.

Definition of Structure. The structure of a group or an organization may be defined as the degree to which positions and roles among members remain fixed. In a highly structured small group the relationship of the leader to the members remains the same from one day or one week to the next. In a large organization the formal relationships of the president to the vice-presidents and their relationships to the next level in the hierarchy seldom change. The degree to which this structure is maintained may be identified by the flow of power (who gives directions to whom) and the flow of information (who talks to whom about what). The flow of power is rarely violated, but the flow of information often is circumvented. Secretaries in different offices may discuss imminent policy changes, cutting across the lines of power, which can threaten the organizational structure. It is not uncommon in the military service for a sergeant to hear through the grapevine of a decision before the captain of the company receives the information through regular channels (Cartwright and Zander, 1968).

Caveats for ISGs. This military example may seem far afield, but similar processes occur within colleges and even within the limited domain of student affairs. An understanding of these factors becomes especially important in planning any new or potentially controversial student activity. Sensitive issues within the hierarchy must be given due consideration in the development of an ISG program because an unexpected defaulting of support can seriously jeopardize the entire venture. Authorization from the chief student affairs officer to conduct ISG interventions within the residence halls without the prior knowledge and support of the housing staff would be a grave error in most colleges. Launching such a program with only the knowledge and permission of the housing office could be equally problematical, especially on small campuses. In order to avoid trespassing on someone else's position or having information leak out when planning an ISG program, all concerned parties should be contacted within a relatively short time span. In summation, in the planning and development of an ISG program, student affairs practitioners must understand not only the dynamics of small groups but also the formal and informal structure of the organization within which it occurs.

Cohesiveness, Group Norms, and Pressures Toward Conformity

Three of the most important dynamic forces (actually they are conceptual representations of dynamic forces) affecting the formation and maintenance of a group are cohesiveness, group norms, and pressures toward conformity. Each is often talked about or written about independently of the other two for simplicity or a particular emphasis. In the functioning of a group, however, no one of these can be fully understood without reference to the others.

Cohesiveness. For the purposes for which ISGs are constructed, we may consider cohesiveness as the centerpoint around which all other dynamics converge. A formal definition of cohesiveness has been stated by Festinger, Schachter, and Bock (1950, p. 164) as "the total field of forces which act on members to remain in the group." This definition is certainly inclusive and therefore difficult to contest, although other researchers (Evans and Jarvis, 1980) have argued with it. The difficulty with the definition is in identifying the forces and the relative influence each exerts on the resultant cohesiveness. In research the problem remains unresolved, with many differences of opinion existing particularly in reference to emphasis and methods of measurement (Shaw, 1981).

The identification of the presence or absence of these forces becomes a primary concern of the group leader. Anticipation of the manner in which these forces may operate must also be of concern in the conceptualization and planning of any group experience. A cohesive group tends to be productive, with group members willing to be influenced by the leader and each other, and their experiences tend to be perceived as personally satisfying (Shaw, 1981). If a group is not cohesive, individuals tend to become defensive and rigid, cooperation among members falters, and the experience is regarded as unsatisfying or even unpleasant. If the group is overly cohesive, the experience may be regarded as emotionally satisfying, but nothing of substance or lasting value is likely to be accomplished. Evans and Jarvis (1980) also note the negative effects of too much cohesion when it is based primarily on attraction: "*Too cohesive* a group may cause members to be more concerned with the group itself than with the purpose for which the group exists. Members who are highly attracted to a group may have difficulty confronting negative aspects of the experience and may allow themselves to be unduly influenced by other members of the group" (p. 368).

The cohesiveness of a group is an elusive factor, difficult to validate, but is readily apparent by its presence or absence. One can sense the difference between involvement in a cohesive group and in one that is not. The presence or absence of cohesiveness is not absolute; the degree and quality of cohesiveness vary from one group to another and within the same group from one time period to another. The primary attribute of a cohesive group is the identification of its members with the group and their desire to maintain its unity. The basis for this identification will determine the consistency and durability of the cohesiveness and of the group itself. The most solid basis for a cohesive group is the development of respect among the members, particularly in relation to the purpose of the group (Bonney, 1974). The cohesiveness of a group typically starts with some other base — for example, social attraction, common interests, common problems, common identity with a larger social entity, a shared disaster, and even fear of a common enemy or an anticipated fate. Unless the group can move beyond the original basis for mutuality and toward interpersonal respect, group cohesiveness will remain limited and somewhat fragile. The use of techniques and procedures by which this movement may be facilitated is integral to an ISG.

Group Norms and Conformity Pressures. Group norms and conformity pressures are essential factors in the development of cohesiveness in ISGs. The norms of a group do not refer to the normal distribution curve of what is average or usual. They are the expectations and hopes of the group and a recognition of the group's limitations. They are the rules and standards by which the group operates and that control the behavior of its members. A formal definition of group norms is "the limits of allowable behaviors of individual members of the group, which also includes variable rewards and punishments when the behavior exceeds the allowable limits. Put in simpler terms, the group norm defines what one can get away with... and still remain an acceptable member of the group" (Bonney, 1974, p. 449).

Rules and standards of behavior may be imposed on the group from external sources (the group leader or the larger organization), but the most powerful source is the membership of the group itself. If the externally imposed rules do not meet the psychological needs of members or violate the accepted social conventions of the group members or seem irrelevant to the members, they will be ignored or circumvented, and group cohesiveness will not develop. Alternatively, a group may become cohesive by presenting a solid front in opposition to the external rules. Such informal group norms are never written and are rarely stated openly; they are simply understood. Although group leaders cannot dictate the nature of the informal group norms, they can actively participate in the formation of these norms. By doing so, they become members of the group but without abdicating the leadership role.

The presence of a group norm is most evident when it is violated by a group member, and some form of punishment or retaliation ensues. When individuals exceed the group norm constructively, they are typically rewarded for it and allowed to alter the norm. In a well-functioning, developing group most of the norms are continually changing according to the progress of the group.

To some extent the norms of a specific group are unique to that particular combination of people, but they may be readily predicted if one understands sufficiently the characteristics of the group's members. McCanne (1977) has empirically demonstrated that member expectations prior to a group experience can be identified and that they do influence behavior in the group and the level of satisfaction derived from it. Most of the expectations of members are brought with them from their past experiences in groups.

The cohesiveness of the group will not develop until the group norms are tentatively established. Through the group norms the members understand what is expected and therefore what behaviors are safe. Only then will the original tension associated with a new experience begin to subside, which will allow some degree of spontaneous interaction.

After the first outer limits of acceptable behavior have been defined through the formation of early group norms, the group then strives toward uniformity of opinions and attitudes, particularly in relation to the purpose of the group and sometimes beyond the group itself. Cohesiveness is achieved most fully when the members of the group can reach consensus about what is true and correct concerning human behavior and relationships among people, particularly those relationships that are intimately involved in the functioning of the group. Group members do not feel safe or relaxed, even in a gamelike exercise, if they feel they do not understand each others' ideas about how people ought to relate in general social circumstances. In an ISG, a member who is suspected of holding highly deviant attitudes in regard to sexuality or interpersonal power, for example, can produce so much tension in other group members that group functioning becomes negligible. That individual's behavior must become predictable within the bounds of the dominant group norm, or the norm must be changed to tolerate the deviant attitude. If the group is unable to exert the amount of pressure adequate to this task, the leader is expected to do so.

Some exceptions to the typical responses toward deviant behavior, however, should be noted. For instance, a member who is perceived to have high status outside the group may be allowed certain deviant behaviors but not to the point of endangering the continuance of the group. Examples in an ISG might be a student who is a star athlete or one with high academic achievement or one who has held leadership positions in campus organizations (Wahrman, 1977). Low status members are not allowed this privilege.

Within-group pressures to reach agreement on certain issues may become intense and demanding. Some level of agreement is necessary in order for cohesiveness to develop and for the group to reach its fullest potential. However, if the group norms become too rigid and the conformity pressures too strong, the group cannot progress, and creative input from individuals can be stifled as well. These pressures can, in fact, lead to the gradual dissolution of the group.

Roles

Thus far in this chapter we have discussed groups as psychological entities, as if the group itself were a living, independent organism. Although a highly cohesive group does appear from outside to function as a unit (for example, to exhibit a mind of its own), close inspection will reveal that this conceptualization is not entirely valid. The group is composed of individuals, each of whom possesses unique needs and idiosyncratic behavioral patterns regardless of superficial demographic similarities with other group members. We have so far identified two forces that determine the dynamics of an ISG: (1) the structure imposed on the group by the institutional setting and that which is intentionally constructed by the group leader, and (2) the forces that arise from the group itself (cohesiveness, norms, and conformity pressures). In addition to these forces, the behavior of each individual in the group—and therefore the character of the group—is also determined by the roles each person plays in interactions with the other members, including the leader. When the interplay of roles among the group members is smooth and complementary, the individual roles are scarcely noticed, and the group functions as a unitary entity. Thus, the nature and effect of the role-taking behavior of each member should be an essential consideration of the leader.

The role behavior of people is a result of interrelated factors not readily understood by casual observation. It is not possible to ascertain which factor is predominant in any one action, sometimes not even by the individuals themselves. The roles everyone enacts in relations with others are determined partially by social identifications (such as religion, race) and partially by personal identifications (spouse, parent, teacher, student, leader, follower). Many of a person's reactions to various situations can be predicted on the basis of these identifications. Beneath these overt identifications, however, are subtle psychological influences that determine the manner in which the individual plays these roles (in an aggressive or passive manner, in an outgoing or withdrawn way, as pacifier or troublemaker, and so on). The first set of identifications are usually referred to as social or cultural roles and the second as psychological roles (Biddle and Thomas, 1966).

The role an individual plays in an ISG is also determined by past experience in groups, by what the individual thinks is expected in this particular situation, and by what the individual believes will satisfy personal needs and also be psychologically safe. In addition, the ultimate constellation of role behaviors is determined by the number of roles an individual is capable of playing in any situation. Some people have a large repertoire of roles from which to draw, while others are severely limited (Kelly, 1955). Small-group experiences are an appropriate avenue by which a member's role repertoire can be both altered and expanded, allowing for more effective social adaptation.

The psychosocial role an individual plays in a small group is typically labeled according to the impression or effect that the person's behavior has on other members of the group.

The role may imply the motivation of the role player, but the label given it designates how that role is perceived by those who encounter it.

Types of Group Roles. Following are examples of both productive and unproductive role labels that are sometimes employed in group analysis and are generally evident in ISGs. The examples are modifications of group roles as developed by Benne and Sheats (1948) and Blocher (1987). Examples of productive roles:

> *Information seeker:* Asks for clarification of suggestions made both for their factual adequacy and for their pertinence to the problem being discussed.
>
> *Opinion seeker:* Asks not primarily for the facts but for clarification of the values involved.
>
> *Initiator:* Suggests a changed way of regarding the group problems or goal, new procedures for the group, or new ways of organizing the group for the task ahead.
>
> *Interpreter:* Interprets feelings expressed by members of the group or interprets the significance of nonverbal behavior.
>
> *Supporter:* Agrees with and accepts the contribution of others; understands and accepts other points of view, ideas, and suggestions.
>
> *Coordinator:* Points out relationships among ideas and suggestions, tries to pull divergent ideas together, or tries to coordinate the efforts of the members in accomplishing tasks.
>
> *Energizer:* Prods the group to action or decision and attempts to stimulate the group to increased levels of activity or commitment.
>
> *Harmonizer:* Attempts to mediate differences between members, reconcile disagreements, or relieve tension in conflict situations through humor or denial of conflict.

Examples of unproductive group roles:

Aggressor: Attempts to deflate the status of other members, jokes aggressively, attempts to take credit for others' contributions, belittles other members' contributions.

Resister: Constantly reacts negatively to most ideas, opposes proposals for no reason, recycles rejected proposals or ideas repeatedly, is obstinately negative in general.

Recognition seeker: Frequently calls attention to herself or himself, often by boasting, bragging, or acting in bizarre or unusual ways.

Comedian: Attempts to make everything into a joke; may interrupt activities to tell jokes or humorous stories or to act in unusual ways to generate laughter.

Dominator: Tries to assert authority or superiority by manipulating members or the entire group; may use flattery, act in an authoritarian manner, interrupt others' contributions, or insist on always having the last word.

Victim: Attempts to elicit sympathy from others in a variety of ways, such as through excessive self-deprecation and expressions of insecurity or inadequacy.

Expert: Treats group members as an audience in order to demonstrate "superior" knowledge; acts as a "junior psychoanalyst" interpreting everyone's acts and feelings according to some "theory"; tends to overintellectualize all experiences in the group.

The group leader should be alert to those playing both productive and unproductive roles during the opening stages of the group. Depending on the purpose of the group, certain roles may be deemed by the leader as essential for the group's progress, while others may be perceived as being inhibiting or detracting. The leader should be able to exert some control over the emergence of desired behaviors through verbal reinforcement of individuals who assume desired roles.

Motivations for Role Behaviors. Much of the determination of roles, however, comes from the group itself. This within-group process occurs through two interacting dynamics designated as role assumption and role assignment. Shaw (1981) identifies these dynamics similarly but with a slightly different emphasis as perceived role, expected role, and enacted role, suggesting that the enacted role might be a compromise between the perceived (assumed role) and the expected (assigned role). Each group member attempts to assume those roles that feel most comfortable, that supply some degree of emotional satisfaction, and that are safe from censure or attack. At the same time, each member attempts to manipulate other members to play complementary roles that contribute to a desired group climate and equilibrium. Sometimes a group member attempts to upset the balance of the group or block the group's progress because that is the condition in which that person feels most protected or most central. This role-taking process occurs mostly at an unconscious level or, at least, is not overtly acknowledged. Within a short period of time, roles tend to fall in line with the norms of the group as they become firmly established. If this stabilization does not occur within the first two or three sessions, the group will probably remain chaotic throughout its existence. Stabilization can also occur at a nonproductive level of functioning.

These factors point up the importance of the leader's involvement in the formation of group norms during the first group meeting or even prior to it (see Chapter Seven). Although role assumption and role assignment do not occur at a fully conscious level, neither are they deeply buried. When the dynamics involved are verbalized by the leader or a group member, they are immediately recognized by nearly everyone in the group. The verbalization may take the form of an observation — "We always seem to depend on Sally to start the discussion" (initiator) — or an interpretation — "Jack, you express a lot of interest in the opinions of others. Are you possibly reluctant to state your own?" (opinion seeker). Sometimes a confrontation of the group by the leader is appropriate: "The group has allowed two or three people to do all the talking; is that really the way you want it?" In the case of unproductive roles, it is best if the group itself can exert subtle pressure on the detracting member to conform. The leader, however, may be required to confront the negative dynamics at some point. Confrontations are always risky, though, and should be used sparingly; group leaders should initiate a confrontation only if they sense that the other group members are dissatisfied.

Sensitivity to role-taking behavior in a group is an important avenue for group management and an important aspect of individual change and growth. As group leaders gain in experience they become increasingly skillful in identifying roles that are enacted in the group, in employing techniques by which roles may be shifted, and in helping individuals alter and increase the number of roles they can play.

Using Group-Dynamics Principles in ISGs

So far this chapter has set forth and explained the basic principles and concepts relating to the functioning of small groups within an organizational structure. These dynamics are applicable to any small group that is a psychological entity. The examples were chosen in an attempt to communicate the universality of the dynamics described and to show their relevance to ISGs in a college setting. Quite often some of these dynamic forces are expressed rather subtly and are not readily discernible or detected. When group leaders are aware of these basic principles, however, they can become increasingly sensitive to their presence or absence and to the particular manner in which they become manifest in any given group. The principles or dynamics remain the same, but the mode of expression may differ radically among college students as compared with factory workers or business executives.

Potential Gains. Some students have little or no difficulty adjusting to the social milieu of a college campus, while others feel lost, confused, and isolated long after the initial settling-in period. A few students remain alienated throughout their college experience. Other students achieve social adjustment through identification with a restricted set of peers, which typically results in a rather narrow world view and the elimination of important broadening experiences. All the students just described can gain something from properly designed ISGs. A new kind of personal identity may be achieved without loss of previous identifications or a sense of individuality. Students who feel confused or isolated may discover that these feelings are understood and shared by others, that such feelings are not strange or abnormal, and that change can be effected if desired. Others may discover a new world beyond the sorority or fraternity house, local pub, or residence hall. An ISG experience can also help create a bridge between the college community and the larger social order.

An ISG can provide an opportunity to learn the value of cooperative effort. Even when the purpose of the group is the exploration of individual attitudes or beliefs, mutual trust and respect develop among the group members. The achievement of mature cohesiveness becomes the total group goal. The members know they have together created the atmosphere that made such cohesiveness possible. They may legitimately take pride in both the group's achievement and their individual contribution to it.

When students feel secure and psychologically safe as members of an ISG, they are free to learn new ways of relating to each other and even new ways of relating themselves to the world at large. The nature of the group, and sometimes its stated purpose, encourages role experimentation. The group leader may facilitate the process through modeling and by reinforcing each individual's early efforts at behavioral change. Ideally, the leader's behavior will be modeled by the group members so that reinforcement of behavioral experimentations becomes a part of the group norms. It may even become difficult to resist the pressure to alter or expand one's role behavior. If the group has achieved a mature level of functioning, the pressure to change will invariably be oriented toward wellness.

Possible Negative Effects. This discussion of the positive aspects and individual gains from participation in ISGs included some important qualifiers (proper design, trust and respect, mature functioning). Obviously, ideal conditions and developments do not always hold, and when they do, they seldom if ever come about easily or accidentally. If group planners and group leaders are aware of possible negative forces that can develop in small cohesive groups, they can become alert to the early signs or clues and attempt countermeasures. As previously mentioned, a group may stabilize with its norms frozen at an unproductive level, a factor that works against the intent of the program. If the leader waits too long to intervene, it may become impossible to alter the course of the group.

The norms of a group may become extremely rigid and dictatorial, thus inhibiting individual or creative expression. The group essentially stagnates within narrowly defined modes of expression and limited subject content, resulting in discussions that are sterile and repetitive. This condition sometimes occurs because of highly homogeneous membership, which colludes against any alteration of presently held beliefs or attitudes. However, this condition is most likely the consequence of a perceived threat from outside or within the group, and the leader may need to help the group investigate what it is working so hard to avoid. Clues to the nature of the threat can usually be detected in the early development of group norms. If the group sessions have been tape recorded, a replay of previous sessions may provide the leader with the needed insights.

A group may also become overly cohesive so that the maintenance of the group and one's membership in it become more important than the pursuit of individual goals. One of the clear signs of this occurrence is the development of a sense of elitism with a concomitant denigration of nonmembers. Such a group can also reinforce prejudices that the members may have already held tenuously. Probably the most negative effect in this regard is the development of what Janis (1982) terms "group think," in which disagreement with or questioning of the group's decision or attitude becomes tantamount to treason. This condition totally blocks any spontaneous, creative expression or dissenting opinion. Leaders who wait too long to confront the development of group think may be psychologically excluded from the group. Worse yet, they may unwittingly participate in it and thereby strengthen the tendency.

Not all ISGs become cohesive, maturely functioning groups, partly because of time limitations and group size. For some ISG purposes a cohesive, tightly knit group might even be undesirable. The nature of the task should dictate the level of interpersonal exchange and attachment. Highly structured controlled groups and loosely structured psychotherapy groups can be seen as opposite ends of a structure dimension; depth of personal involvement and exposure are other measurements for this dimension. They are meant to provide points of comparison or guidelines in the construction of ISGs. Too much control inhibits the natural development of a cohesive group. Too little control can result in the emergence of highly personal issues without adequate time or leadership skill for satisfactory resolution and closure. The ultimate judgment as to the success or failure of an ISG is the extent to which its intended, pre-established goals and purposes are achieved.

The Study of Group Development

People who work with groups, in almost any capacity, come to recognize that any well-functioning unit of individuals always has a developmental history. At its inception the unit is a chaotic, loosely organized aggregate with a tendency toward being highly dependent on external direction. What happens to a chaotic, disorganized collection of people that makes it a coordinated, interdependent unit has been of interest and often of vital concern to those who work directly with people in almost every walk of life. Leaders in the military, industry, government, education, and religion have been and remain particularly concerned with understanding those factors and events that produce effective groups and those that result in unsatisfactory ones. Until the present century most of what was understood about the functioning of small groups was based on trial and error, intuition, and a kind of folk wisdom. The purpose was primarily controlling human behavior through a "disciplined subservience to leadership rather than improving the ability of group members to work together cooperatively and creatively" (Knowles and Knowles, 1965, p. 15).

Toward the end of the nineteenth and early in the twentieth century sociologists (such as Emile Durkheim and Charles

Horton Cooley) and a few psychologists (notably William McDougall) began a quasi-scientific investigation of the behavior of individuals as members of large groups, such as crowds and mobs. Some of their conceptualizations about group behavior were later substantiated by empirical investigations, but their observations were couched in a language that proved to be unacceptable to the dominant force in American psychology of that period and therefore had little impact on the psychological community. Early in the 1930s scientific interest shifted from large groups to the psychology of behavior in smaller units of people. There was also a shift toward an interest in the development of groups that were relatively free of administrative control.

As succinctly pointed out by Cartwright and Zander (1968), it was not accidental that this upsurge of scientific interest occurred in the United States during this period of history. "By the end of the 1930s cultural and economic conditions in the United States were favorable for the emergence and growth of group dynamics. Great value was placed on science, technology, rational problem solving, and progress. There was a fundamental conviction that in a democracy human nature and society can be deliberately improved by education, religion, legislation, and hard work" (p. 7). During this period several researchers, working independently of one another, established empirically some rather firm principles of small-group behavior. Predominant among these were Sherif (1936), with his work on group norms, and Lewin (Lewin, Lippitt, and White, 1939), with his research on the effects of group atmosphere and leadership styles. The field theory of Lewin (1951) has continued to have an impact on all the social sciences.

The impetus provided by the researchers of the 1930s resulted in establishment of the National Training Laboratories (NTL) immediately following World War II, initially under the direction of Kurt Lewin. The focus was primarily on research of small groups, but NTL also provided training in group processes for business, industrial, and educational leaders. The emphasis in the training programs was on awareness, open and direct communication, and the creation of a democratic atmosphere. By 1950 some clear, well-formulated principles of the dynamics of small groups had been established. Also, increased understanding had been achieved of the psychology of the individual in reaction to a group experience.

Stages of Group Development

The stages or phases of group development loosely parallel individual development, greatly telescoped. The stages parallel, even recapitulate, individual needs and fears in relation to inclusion in the group (or acceptance by others) and the prediction of and control over one's psychological well-being. The needs stem from the natural social interest in belonging, the security provided by group membership, and the use of the group as a source for validating one's social reality. The fear is of rejection and inadequacy. The apprehension that one will be unable to predict what will happen in the group and how one ought to behave becomes intense if the nature of the group or its members are unfamiliar. The more ambiguous the purpose and process of the group, the less predictable it appears and the higher will be the anxiety (Neimeyer and Merluzzi, 1982).

The group leader should always keep in mind that individuals differ widely in their tolerance for ambiguity. One person in a group may find the ambiguity of a situation intolerable, while another may respond to it as intriguing and exciting. Some of the signs of ambiguity intolerance are anger, confusion, and withdrawal (Norton, 1975). Excessive control or absence of ambiguity will likely be interpreted by the group members as lack of freedom and thereby lack of trust or even disrespect of the membership by the leader. Reactions to this condition may take the form of nonparticipating resistance, attacks on the leader's authority, or sullenness. An ISG, as we have conceived it, is an attempt to establish a balance between a group tightly controlled by the leader and a group that has too little control because of the absence of intentional structure and leader guidance. We have made references to authoritative groups and therapy groups as anchors of comparison for leaders of ISGs. The group leader may be tempted to move too far in either direction and lose the essential value of the group as a creative learning experience.

Representative Models. Bach (1954), a student of Lewin and a group psychotherapist, was one of the earliest authors to postulate defined stages of group development (Bach, 1954, p. 269): (1) initial situation testing, (2) leader dependency, (3) familial regressive, (4) associative compeering, (5) fantasy and play, (6) in-group consciousness, (7) the work group. Although his developmental phases were based on observations of intense therapeutic experiences of long duration (over 100 sessions), other systems based on groups with much shorter time periods and with different interests do not differ greatly in the kind of stages postulated or in the order of their occurrence (although some of Bach's terminology is unique).

Bach, like most others who promote the stage concept in therapy groups, cautions that the developmental sequence is seldom neat or tidy. There is always some overlap, and regressions to former levels are not uncommon. He also stresses the importance of allowing the natural process of group formation to take place. "The group medium should be the stage for the recognition of the previously unconscious condition of leader dependence and of weaning past due. Going beyond insight, the group makes it possible for the . . . [member] to have the new experience of actually participating in the shaping of his own social field" (Bach, 1954, p. 272). The shaping of one's social field should have importance for the development of young adults, who may not have previously experienced such a clear opportunity as may be afforded by participation in an ISG.

Schutz (1958) in his theory of interpersonal behavior proposes three stages of group development: inclusion, control, and affection. He states that the development of a group always follows the same sequence, which may be repeated. The sequence is reversed when the group anticipates its termination. Schutz based his observations on groups of much shorter duration (thirty to forty sessions) than Bach's and of less emotional intensity. In the *inclusion* phase, members are concerned with acceptance, individual status in relation to others, maintaining personal identity, and extent of commitment. The topics of discussion are referred to as *goblet issues*, taken from the discussions at cocktail parties. The topics are not important in themselves but serve as vehicles for sizing up the other members of the group. In the *control* phase, decision-making procedures are determined, ground rules are established, and the distribution of power and control is begun. People attempt to determine where they fit in relation to control, influence, and responsibility. In the *affection* phase the group members become aware of each other on a social/emotional plane. "Each member is striving to obtain for himself in the group his most comfortable amount of affectional interchange and most comfortable position regarding initiating and receiving affection" (Schutz, 1958, p. 171). Schutz states that these are not distinct phases but are a matter of emphasis at any particular point. Not all members will be involved in the current phase of the group, as some individuals may not have resolved their problems at the previous phase.

Tuckman (1965) reviews fifty articles based on stages of group development with varying time periods. He separates the stages identified in these articles as social/interpersonal activities or as group task activities. He states that some confusion in the literature on groups was created because this separation was not clearly identified. From his review he proposes four general stages of group development. "In the social realm, these stages. . . are testing dependence, conflict, cohesion, and functional roles. In the task realm they are orientation, emotionality, relevant opinion exchange, and the emergence of solutions" (p. 384). Tuckman contends that in any small cohesive group a task always exists, and the task is accomplished through interpersonal relations. In a therapy group or a training group it is often difficult to distinguish the two realms because they are interdependent. The pursuance of the group goal must involve the resolution of interpersonal difficulties. In a sense, that becomes the group goal. In what appears to be a strictly task group—an administrative committee, for instance—interpersonal issues must also be dealt with in order for the group to reach an optimal level of functioning.

At the conclusion of his review Tuckman reduces his model to four words: forming, storming, norming, and performing. He then relates each of these group stages to stages of childhood development. Orientation, testing, and dependence are typical of the group's *forming* stage and the first year of an infant's life. The *storming* stage is characterized by conflict, emotionality, and resistance to influence and task requirements, which typifies the rebelliousness of the young child ("the terrible twos"). In the *norming* stage of the group "in-group feelings and cohesiveness develop, new standards evolve, and new roles are adopted. . . . This sensitivity to others is mirrored in the development of the child and represents an essential aspect of the socialization process" (p. 396). In the *performing* stage, "finally, the group becomes a functional instrument for dealing with the task" (p. 396) and present reality, which is characteristic of the mature human being. In these comparisons the author refers to the developmental theories of Piaget (1932), Mead (1934), Erikson (1950), and Fromm (1941). In a later review Tuckman and Jensen (1977) added a fifth stage, which they titled *adjourning*.

Bonney and Foley (1963) propose a modification of Bach's (1954) phase model with the addition of a *transition* stage. This stage is a movement from a condition of leader dependence and socialization to a commitment to work or therapy. During the transition stage the underlying concern of the members is their capacity as a group to fulfill their original intended purpose, which they now realize will demand cooperation and mutual trust and respect. The concern is often expressed as interpersonal conflict, testing the limits of the group norms and challenging the authority and skill of the leader. The conflict is the result of dissonance or incongruity between learned, appropriate social behavior, which prohibits self-revelation in social groups, and the expectation in counseling groups of intimate self-disclosures. The dissonance may be partially resolved by the leader's redefining the counseling group as basically different from other groups the participants have experienced and accepting their misgivings and anxieties as normal and understandable. If this resolution can be accepted, it allows the group to cope with other obstructions to progress.

The concept of the transition stage as a unique period in the life of a group was supported in a research study by Foley and Bonney (1966). A full sequential model of counseling groups, with the transition stage as pivotal, was developed by Bonney (1969, 1974). A rating scale based on this model was constructed for research on group processes. The pertinence of the scale has been demonstrated in a research study of a counseling group of psychiatric residents (Sisson, Sisson, and Gazda, 1977).

The Foley and Bonney model begins with the *establishment stage*. The participants attempt to establish themselves as a group at some level of functional significance. For descriptive convenience this stage may be somewhat artificially divided into two parts: In the exploratory phase, "each member of the group attempts to estimate how he or she is received by the others and how he or she can expect each of them to behave. The form in which the exploration occurs will depend on the kind of people involved, their customary ways of relating in groups, the behavior of the counselor, and the setting" (Bonney, 1974, p. 457). In the socialization phase, member roles have been established, and a sense of comfort and congeniality has developed. In some instances a group may not move beyond this point because it feels pleasant and safe.

In the *transition stage*, through self and interpersonal confrontations the group, including the leader, seriously encounter the issue of therapeutic goals. The degree to which the problems arising in this stage are resolved determines the relative success of the group endeavor and therefore how much each member is likely to profit from it.

In the *experimental stage*, the group can go in one of two directions. If the first tentative efforts at self-exploration are honestly pursued and empathically received, the group can move forward; if not, they may have to return to some of the problems of the transition stage and reconsider the depth of their commitment.

In the *operational stage*, the group members have achieved a level of trust and respect that allows for genuine self-exploration and therapeutic change to occur. They feel confident that the group will be supportive and helpful regardless of the nature of individual self-disclosures.

The termination of a group is obviously an end of its progression and cannot logically be termed a developmental stage. Schutz (1958) suggests that the progression of inclusion, control, and affection is reversed toward the end of the group's life. When termination is recognized by the group as imminent, new material is not likely to emerge, and intense involvements are avoided or played down. The importance of the termination process depends on the intensity of the previous involvement. If the level of emotional intimacy within the group has been minimal, the termination can be quite casual and managed at a cognitive level. In groups with intense emotional interaction, the end of the group may be experienced as a significant loss (Yalom, 1985).

Although termination may be logically inconsistent as a developmental stage, the manner in which the group is concluded should always be a matter of concern if the intent of the group is to provide growth experiences to individual members. Insights gained during the group that transfer to other situations can be identified and discussed with the help of the leader. There are more and less appropriate ways to bring the group to a close. (These concerns are dealt with later in this chapter and in Chapter Seven.)

Stages of development are typically viewed as a linear progression toward an advanced and presumably mature level of group functioning. Some theorists suggest that the group life is not a steady progression of increasingly complex stages but rather a series of recurring cycles (Schutz, 1958; Bion, 1961; Ivey, 1986). Both conceptualizations can be encompassed by overlaying a spiral effect on the developmental-stage paradigm. Thus, in Bonney's model, if the group endures long enough, the transition stage will reoccur, perhaps several times. Each occurrence would appear to be a regression, but each succeeding work stage would be more advanced than the preceding one. Caple (1978) also notes the spiral effect in groups, with the following commentary: "Problems or conflicts experienced within a group are never totally resolved. . . . When the conflict does reappear, members often feel disillusioned. The effective group learns to accept the reappearance of problems or conflicts and, each time, work through them to a deeper, more satisfying level. This is the spiraling phenomenon often observed in groups" (p. 475).

Research on developmental stages is scarce and rarely replicated. Most of the research that has been done (Tuckman, 1965; Tuckman and Jensen, 1977; Sisson, Sisson, and Gazda, 1977; Foley and Bonney, 1966; Lundgren and Knight, 1978; Cissna, 1984) tends to support the progressive nature of process changes over time but only when the natural processes of group dynamics are allowed to develop without authoritarian or experimental controls. Laboratory or analog groups typically do not follow the sequence (Cissna, 1984); neither do highly structured groups with authoritarian leadership (Lewin, Lippitt, and White, 1939). When natural groups deviate from the expected sequence, it is usually due to the duration of the group, the composition of the group, or leader behavior that prevents the occurrence of one or more stages (Foley and Bonney, 1966; Cissna, 1984). The group worker should understand clearly that models of sequential development are generalizations; each group has its own peculiarities. This important consideration is adroitly condensed by Cissna (1984). "Every group is like *all* groups in some respects, like *some*— or perhaps even most— groups in some respects, and like *no* groups in other respects" (p. 25). An understanding of the expected sequence and the nature of each stage provides the group leader with a sensitivity to any deviation or alteration that may occur.

Summary. The professional literature since the 1930s contains several hundred references to the dynamic processes of small groups. Many of these focus on developmental sequences or imply the existence of some similar processes. Most of the approaches to stage or phase development are theoretical with relatively few empirical research studies. Most of the research that has been done is flawed with methodological problems (Lundgren and Knight, 1978; Cissna, 1984). In addition, much of the work has been done with laboratory groups, training groups, and therapy groups, all of which employ somewhat different semantics and have differing foci. Translating from one system to another is difficult but not impossible. We believe that the four models presented here adequately represent the numerous approaches and developmental models that have been employed. There are commonalities among them. In the next section, Bonney's model is modified and a termination stage added to provide a better image of the dynamics of ISGs.

A Developmental Model for ISGs

As pointed out previously in this chapter, it is essential that the leader of an ISG understand the natural dynamics of a small group (particularly, cohesiveness, group norms, and conformity pressures). It is equally important for the group leader to comprehend, and be sensitive to, the sequential stages of a group's development from a loose collection of individuals to a maturely functioning unit. Events and progressions within a group do not just happen; they are the consequences of identifiable forces and the structural elements of that group of individuals. These two major aspects of a group are essentially different views of the same process, but the relationship between them is not always obvious. For instance, the group may have achieved a high level of cohesiveness, but the quality of that cohesiveness cannot be fully understood without reference to the present stage of the group's development.

When the group progresses in an orderly fashion according to the expected developmental sequence, the leader may be relatively confident that this particular group will attain its intended purpose. However, groups do not always follow the predicted course of development. A group may move too rapidly, too slowly, or not at all, and a group may also regress from a higher or more mature level to a lower one. All these events are clues to the leader that something requires attention and possible resolution if the group experience is to be a successful one. The divergence of a group from the expected sequence is not necessarily counterproductive. Something unique about the composition of a given group may account for its unusual mode of progression. There are generally understandable reasons why a group has deviated from the normal course, but the discovery of those reasons in time to redirect the progression of the group may prove to be a difficult task. On rare occasions the composition of a group may be such that rescue attempts are futile. Still, something may be learned for future efforts.

We have developed a model of group development that is specific to ISGs. We now present an outline of each stage of a typical ISG, followed by amplification of the points stated, a generalized timetable, and a discussion of possible deviations and corrective measures. References are also made to other chapters (especially Chapters Four, Six, and Seven) where additional explanation is provided. The stages identified for this model are establishment, exploration, transition, working, and termination.

Establishment Stage. The following events are generally characteristic of those that occur during the establishment stage.

1. Group members learn each others' names and superficial information about their backgrounds.
2. The leader presents ground rules for the group.
3. The leader explains the goals and purposes of the ISG.
4. Group members begin to sense a group focus or group identity.
5. Members begin to identify appropriate group norms (primarily from observation of the leader's behavior).

The getting acquainted process may be accomplished by simply going around the group and having members state their names, hometowns, academic majors, and class status. Usually some embellishment will serve the purpose better than this simple process and also help relieve the tension of a new experience. Each person in the group may be asked to include in the introduction previous experiences in small groups in college and high school. This addition allows the participants an opportunity to express anticipations (positive or negative) in regard to this experience and also allows the leader to anticipate some individual reactions. Other, gamelike warmup exercises may also be initiated by the leader if the group appears to be receptive. The leader must participate in all these activities. The expectation is set that this collection of individuals will become a group.

The ground rules may be imposed by the leader on the basis of experience and group purpose or may be determined by group consensus. Typically these issues have to do with meeting times and the importance of regular attendance. Other ground rules discussed should include the importance of confidentiality, the right of a group member not to participate in some activities, how necessary absences and tardiness will be handled (notify in advance), and any other procedural matters peculiar to the given ISG. The goals and purposes of the group should be carefully explained and reactions elicited from the members. The importance of active and cooperative participation should be stressed, with the hope that a sense of group responsibility will be initiated. (See Chapter One for a detailed discussion of ground rules.)

The process of building group identity and commitment to group goals is the beginning of group cohesiveness and norm formation and should be addressed from the first session of the ISG. Leaders influence this process more by their manner of relating to members than by any formal presentation. During the first meeting leaders set the tone by the seriousness with which they take the leadership function, the degree to which they actively participate, the casualness of their attitude and attire, the degree of levity they promote and allow, and the level of intimacy they encourage.

Most of the establishment-stage tasks can be accomplished during the initial group meeting. If the suggested process is blocked or diverted into issues irrelevant to the group purpose, the leader must evaluate carefully the dynamics of the meeting and the composition of the group. The participants may have anticipated something different from what was offered; the purpose may not have been clearly understood; or the leadership style may have been inappropriate. Conflicts among the participants may also have prevented progress. Whatever the reasons, the group should be redirected at the opening of the second session, ideally with the help of the participants. Failure to take action then will probably result in the ISG's never accomplishing its preestablished goals.

Exploration Stage. The exploration stage has these dimensions or components:

1. Members begin to identify roles for themselves and to assign roles to other members of the group.
2. A status hierarchy is established.
3. Ground rules are tested, accepted, rejected, or modified.
4. Norms emerge from the group and blend with or modify those proposed and modeled by the leader.
5. An atmosphere of trust begins to develop (limits of trust widen).
6. The leader's competence is evaluated by group members.
7. Members recognize the value of participating in the ISG and accept the goals as personally relevant.

The processes of role assumption and role assignment were discussed previously in this chapter. The identified roles tend to remain relatively fixed unless some action is taken to alter them. These actions become part of the dynamics of the transition and working stages of the group. Status assignments are even more stable than role assignments and therefore are less likely to be altered. Both of these processes occur without overt acknowledgment and probably at a partially unconscious level.

The difference between roles and status position is an important distinction for the group leader to understand. Although the two are not totally unrelated, they originate differently and should be given consideration by the leader. Status assignment determines the extent to which each member has the capacity and the right to influence other members and the functioning of the group as a whole and has the privilege of expressing opinions that differ substantially from those of the majority. Hollander (1964) refers to this type of status in a group as "idiosyncrasy credit."

Hollander did most of his work on the dynamics of emergent leadership (neither elected nor appointed) within small groups. He defines leadership as the capacity of an individual to influence others and to alter the norms of the group, positively or negatively, in relation to group goals. He discovered that an individual may be allowed to alter the direction of a group only if the individual has first demonstrated a willingness to conform. Hollander's contention has been supported by Katz (1982) based on laboratory research. The situation, however, is not as simple as it might first appear. ISG leaders should also be aware of the difference between nonconformity as a characteristic trait and independence of judgment (Kimball and Hollander, 1974). Independent thinkers are capable of accepting or rejecting the majority opinion depending on whether they consider it to be correct. Nevertheless, an attempt to alter the norms of the group by a member who has not demonstrated a commitment to the group and its purpose will likely be rejected. An early innovator is typically rejected regardless of the value of the ideas presented. What may be considered unacceptable nonconformity at one point in the life of a group may not be considered so at a later time.

At this stage the leader's competence is evaluated at two levels, task and interpersonal. As pointed out in a classic study by Fiedler (1967), the task-relevant skills of the leader are relatively unimportant if the interpersonal skills are perceived as either lacking or negative (for instance, hostile or fawning). For most ISGs the task-relevant skills of the leader include knowledge about the content and goals of the group and the processes by which they may be achieved. If the group's purpose is career exploration, for example, the leader should be familiar with available resources and the sequence of decision making by which both good and poor career choices are made. If the group goal is the development of interpersonal skills, the leader should be able to serve as a model and also understand why these skills are difficult for some people to achieve.

The ground rules as originally proposed by the group

leader may become modified as the group norms begin to emerge from within the group itself. The alteration should be allowed to occur if the new development does not seriously deflect from the basic intent of the group or create difficult ethical dilemmas. This process is most likely to become troublesome if it represents a threat to the leader or if the effort at modification arises from a deviant member (Gleason, Seaman, and Hollander, 1978).

Most of the dynamics in this stage should have become evident by the second or third group meeting. If leaders cannot detect a sense of personal involvement and trust by then, they must assume that the group is not moving toward becoming a cohesive unit. Through the assistance of the members the leader may be able to identify the problem and reorient the group. At times the problem is either unidentifiable or unsolvable, in which case the group experience will be something less than optimal but not necessarily totally ineffective.

Transition Stage. The following characteristic behaviors and activities are evident during the transition stage:

1. Group members confront themselves in relation to commitment to the task and to each other.
2. Limits and ground rules are tested, and the leader's authority may be challenged.
3. Some members may experiment with violating group norms to determine consequences.
4. Members envision the potential of a cohesive and productive group experience.
5. Noncommitted members may experience pressure from others and the leader to become involved or leave.
6. The importance of accepting and projecting influence is recognized.
7. The power of the group and the leader's limitations are recognized by most group members.

Transition, as used here, implies a critical movement from one developmental stage to another. If the transitional move-

ment is successful, it almost always involves some level of conflict. The conflict may be direct and obvious, or so subtle that an
inexperienced leader may not be able to detect it. "If the group
has maturity potential (as a group), it will reevaluate its purpose,
reform its norms, and determine to try again at a deeper and
more intentional level" (Bonney, 1969, p. 170). The transition
from the exploration stage to the work stage can be a significantly different experience for the members; therefore it deserves recognition as a stage in itself.

     Some conditions can prevent or obviate the occurrence of
a transition stage. If members of a particular ISG know and
accept each other prior to the inception of the ISG, they may be
capable of moving smoothly from exploration to work stage
without overt conflict or problem resolution. An exceptionally
high level of task orientation can produce a similar effect. Members of another ISG, however, may not perceive the group as any
different from an academic class and may therefore remain
individually task oriented. An ISG can also become so socially
and emotionally oriented that its members never accept the
necessity of working toward goals. In either case, the leader is
involved to some extent. The potential of the group may also be
thwarted by a severe dyadic conflict or a powerful deviant member (Kimball and Hollander, 1974).

     Most of the activities of this stage are explained in other
chapters (especially Chapter Seven). However, a few additional
comments might be helpful. The central problem during this
stage is to combine the goal intentions (task dimension) with the
dynamics of a cohesive group, which demands a level of interpersonal respect and commitment beyond interpersonal liking
and individual goal achievement. The leader's efforts to empower the group by transferring responsibility for further movement initiate and sustain the transition toward a work stage (see
Chapter Six). This process may also be initiated and assisted by
one or more group members who have either an intellectual or
intuitive understanding of what is needed. It is vitally important
for the leader to be sensitive to such indicators as leading
comments, nonverbal expressions of annoyance or frustration,

eagerness to move forward—and to reinforce them. The leader's timing during this stage is crucial to a successful transition.

Members must come to the following realizations to achieve a fully functioning group and optimal individual gain: (1) We can help each other achieve our individual goals and are willing to accept each others' ideas. (2) The leader cannot achieve goals for us; we must accept responsibility for total group movement toward goal achievement. (3) We must accept the power of the group and the leader's limitations (we can create our own social environment). (4) We must exhibit respect for individual opinions and needs. (5) We can trust that personal attitudes and feelings will be accepted and not disallowed or attacked.

If all or most of these attitudes are present, the norms of the group will most certainly have changed and group maturity will have been achieved. The key words for the transition stage are *group responsibility*, *trust*, and *respect*.

Working Stage. The working stage has these characteristics:

1. Goal-related activities become a cooperative effort with a high level of individual involvement.
2. Group members practice new behaviors and experiment with new interpersonal roles.
3. Members provide and receive feedback.
4. Personal risk taking increases and is supported by the group.
5. Members express concern about each others' progress and general welfare.
6. Communication is no longer directed primarily to or through the leader; there is direct communication among the members.
7. The leader acts as a consultant.

The group has accepted that only through cooperative effort can they achieve optimum gain from the ISG experience. The discovery that they are capable of creating an experience beyond their original expectations increases their enthusiasm and their sense of commitment. The realization leads to an emotional identification with the group and to specific task-related efforts toward goal accomplishment.

When the focus of communication becomes other members and no longer the leader, feedback between members is a natural consequence. By this time, the leader's role modeling should have provided a positive feedback style, although an occasional need to intervene to divert negative confrontation may arise. It is important that the group feel confident that the leader is always available to serve as a protector, particularly during moments of high group emotionality. With these conditions the group members should experience a sufficient amount of group and leader support to risk new behaviors and to experiment with new roles. The leader has now become relatively inactive in any directive sense but active in a consultive capacity when expertise is required.

Termination Stage. The termination stage has the following characteristics:

1. Members project into the future and make plans for applying new learning or skills.
2. Goal-related closure is achieved (goals or purposes of the ISG are evaluated).
3. Psychological closure is achieved (members begin to view the group as a past event).
4. The total experience is evaluated subjectively.
5. Members say good-bye to each other.

Projecting into the future from the ISG experience is not likely to occur spontaneously. It will probably need to be initiated or suggested by the leader. Ideally, most members will already have begun the process privately, but much can be gained through an open discussion. If the task and its related goals are appropriate for an ISG, we can assume that it will have transfer value in the present or near future to other aspects of each individual's life. In an assertiveness-training group, for example, members can estimate how much they have learned about assertiveness and the extent to which their behavior has changed. Feedback from other members can be most helpful. The same criteria and discussion process can be applied to most any skill- or knowledge-based ISG. The total process by which the goals have or have not been accomplished should also be evaluated, and a final determination of the effectiveness of the process should be made. This final determination is intended to reduce members' ambivalence or self-doubts.

Psychological closure is concerned primarily with interpersonal and individual issues that have arisen during the group and that remain unresolved. Although these issues may not be totally resolved, and some of them should not be, they should at least be identified and discussed if the concerned individuals wish to do so. The members may also wish to evaluate how they functioned as a group in relation to other group experiences and the potential that was present. Whatever the members decide to do as far as continuing their relationship with each other should be left to their own discretion and need not become a concern of the group leader.

The final good-byes can range from some simply stated and casual farewells to a group party or dinner, depending on the depth of personal involvement in the group experience. If the involvement has been intense, a social event can help the members return to a normal mode of relating. Whatever the nature of the final meeting, the members should feel comfortable terminating the experience.

Summary. From the professional literature on the sequential development of small groups we have constructed a conceptualization of group developmental stages that we believe best fits the typical operation of an ISG. As we have proposed, an ISG is structured to fit college-student needs and time limitations but with sufficient flexibility to allow for the spontaneous creation of a group climate. Our construction has some elements that are consistent with a task-oriented group and others that are characteristic of counseling or therapy groups. Readers are encouraged to employ any of the schemes presented here that suits their purposes, talents, and previous experiences. The knowledge and research in this area of practice are much too incomplete to derive any absolute truths.

ЮI THREE ЮI

Using Intentionally
Structured Groups
in Student Development

In most of American higher education, students' growth is not viewed as being limited to academic and intellectual development alone. Although intellectual development receives primary attention, one of the unique aspects of collegiate life in the United States continues to be concern for the personal development of students as well. The "collegiate way of life," which focuses attention on all aspects of student life, was identified by historians such as Brubacher and Rudy (1976) and Rudolph (1962) as a major factor in the unique development of higher education in the United States. Although scholars such as Bloom (1987) might contend otherwise, viewing the out-of-class lives of college students as having coordinate educational status with the acquisition of academic knowledge and related scholarly activities is a unique American perspective and, in fact, one of its educational strengths. Higher education, from this viewpoint, is concerned with enhancing the quality of life through the development of personal survival skills essential for successfully negotiating an increasingly complex world. In American higher education, the personal and social development of students, as well as their intellectual and scholarly development, is commonly viewed as being an essential characteristic of the quality of education.

From this perspective, then, the higher education enterprise has responsibility for attending to the total development of its various student clients, no matter what their ages, educational aspirations, initial level of academic preparation, career goals, or cultural heritages. There can be little doubt that much of this comprehensive growth and development occurs spon-

73

taneously and naturally as a direct result of student participation in the numerous social, cultural, and physical activities common to an educational environment where people come together for intellectual stimulation and social interchange. For instance, the level of active participation and involvement is one of the most significant factors influencing the higher education experience (Astin, 1977, 1985; National Institute of Education, 1984; Hood, 1984). The quality of that experience, however, is greatly influenced by the types of opportunities and resources available to students, the challenges and stimulation provided students, and the attitudes of those with whom students come in contact. The characteristics of an institution of higher learning—its student support programs and services, faculty and staff members, and educational programs and curricular offerings—all influence the quality of the students' growth and development. Likewise, each student is unique and enters higher education at a certain developmental level, with reasonably determinable potential. Ascertaining where students are, developmentally, on entrance is useful for assessing the developmental changes that occur as a result of attending college (Pace, 1979). All these factors are germane to an examination of the growth and development of college students.

For our purposes, the ISG approach is an excellent vehicle for positively influencing the total development of college students, especially in the eight developmental areas identified in the ISG conceptual model presented in Chapter One (see Figure 1).

Use of this model increases immeasurably the opportunities for life-skills development, cultural sophistication, and psychological maturity as a normal part of the higher education experience. If student development is defined, in part at least, as the process by which individuals move from simpler to more complex modes of functioning, then the three ISG intervention foci identified in the model are extremely relevant to the overall mission of higher education.

It is the purpose of this chapter (1) to summarize what is known about the growth and development of college students by presenting thematic developmental models, (2) to identify basic processes and principles that underlie students' development, (3) to explore in detail the developmental domains identified in the ISG model, (4) to give examples of how the ISG conceptualization model can be used to guide the creation of ISGs, and (5) to describe both spontaneous and institutionalized groups that influence students' attitudes and behavior.

Themes of College-Student Development

The developmental themes common to the college experience must be assessed in light of variables that influence life changes during the college years. Factors such as age, gender, developmental needs, native intelligence, socioeconomic status of the family of origin, and cultural background are each important in the lives of college students and should not be overlooked when attempting to examine the relationships between the college experience and personal development. For example, a seventeen-year-old and a twenty-five-year-old may be of the same sex, register for the same classes, live in the same hall, possess similar entrance test scores, have a common academic major, and come from a similar sociocultural background, and yet their development can be affected in extremely different ways. Most would agree that even though both of these individuals are being exposed to relatively similar environments, their developmental needs are dissimilar, thereby causing their development to be different. Whereas the seventeen-year-old may be seeking to establish a personal identity, the twenty-five-year-old may have previously accomplished this task to a reasonable degree and now be seeking to establish intimacy in relationship with a significant other. Likewise, although they both may be exposed to the same basic academic subjects, the seventeen-year-old may view them largely as class assignments required by professors, whereas the twenty-five-year-old may view them as validating previously established hypotheses or clarifying the meaning of life experiences that had heretofore been vague feelings because his or her reasoning processes are more intellectually complex than those of the seventeen-year-old. In effect, the same environment is interpreted and responded to differently by these different individuals. For one, the person-environmental fit may be exceptionally appropriate, while for the other it may be poor. In light of these factors it is important to understand that although we can identify developmental themes common to most students, personal development may be manifested in different ways by different people, depending on the interactions that occur between and among variables. It is imperative, therefore, that those planning to offer ISGs on campus take such factors into account.

Developmental themes relevant to the college experience or life in general can be organized and categorized in a number of ways. One of the simplest holds that the three areas of cognitive, affective, and psychomotor development adequately encompass the essentials required to describe development for any age range. Chickering (1969), in his seminal work on student development using Erikson's (1968) identity stage as a foundation, proposed a vector model that can be viewed as thematic. His model incorporates seven developmental vectors: developing competence, managing emotions, developing autonomy, establishing identity, freeing interpersonal relationships, developing purpose, and developing integrity. Another authority identifies five primary tasks of the developing college student as being resolution of the child-parent relationship, resolution of one's sexual identity, establishment of a personal value system, development of the capacity for true intimacy, and choice of a life's work (Coons, 1971). Drum's (1980) model is another way of organizing the developmental dimensions common to young-adult college students. The seven dimensions are cognitve structures, esthetic structures, identity formation, physical health, moral reasoning, interpersonal relatedness, and social perspective. Likewise, Miller and McCaffrey (1982), who focused attention on developmental academic advising, propose the "SPICE of Developmental Life" model, which identifies five primary components that can be readily influenced through the academic advising process: the self, the physical, the interpersonal, the career, and the educational aspects. Each developmental dimension has relevance for most students, no matter what their age, stage, gender, or other characteristics.

Developmental Principles

Since the late 1970s several authors have attempted to identify and describe the various schools or families of theories that explain the process of development in college students and other adults (Knefelkamp, Widick, and Parker, 1978; Drum, 1980; Rodgers, 1980, 1984). These presentations are especially helpful for obtaining an overview of the many theories, approaches, and models, and for identifying their commonalities and differences. Application has been complicated by incomplete knowledge of the relevant environmental forces operating, lack of sophisticated and precise measurement tools, incomplete knowledge of the effects of background variables, and lack of sufficient controls to accurately assess and compare the effects of different interventions.

The different developmental theories can be categorized into several relatively distinct clusters. Those most commonly identified are psychosocial-development theories, cognitive-development theories, theories of person-environment interaction, and typological theories (Knefelkamp, Widick, and Parker, 1978; Rodgers, 1980, 1984). *Psychosocial-development theories* are concerned principally with describing the content or substance of personal, emotional, career, educational, and social development. The works most closely associated with this cluster are those by Erikson (1963, 1968), Sanford (1966, 1967), Heath (1968), Chickering (1969), Havighurst (1972), Levinson and others (1978), and Chickering and Havighurst (1981). *Cognitive-development theories* focus primarily on the sequence of stages and structures involved in the intellectual processes of thinking, reasoning, evaluating, and making meaning of life experiences. Theorists associated with this cluster include Piaget (1952, 1969), Perry (1970), Kohlberg (1972, 1975), Loevinger (1976), Gilligan (1982), and Kegan (1982). Theories of *person-environment interaction* deal primarily with the campus ecology and the way change occurs in individuals and organizations as a result of the many interactions involved. Works associated with this cluster include those by Lewin (1936), Stern (1970), Pace (1979), Astin (1977, 1985), Clark and Trow (1966), Morrill, Hurst, and Associates (1980), Moos (1976, 1979), Banning (1978), and Huebner (1980). The fourth cluster, *typological theories*, is probably equally relevant to all those in higher education institutions who are concerned with the growth, change, and quality of college life experienced by students, for it focuses attention on the individual differences that students possess and exhibit, which influence, guide, and interact with the developmental processes. Because theories associated with this cluster tend to emphasize the complexities of personality, psychological, and sociological typologies as they interact to influence individual development, they tend to be more individualized and less generalizable than theories associated with the other three clusters. Consequently, typological theories have less direct utility for the purposes of this book than do the others. Representative theorists in this cluster are Heath (1964), Myers and Briggs (1962), Holland (1973), Kolb (1976), Cross (1976), and Aslanian and Brickell (1980).

The following discussion identifies the four most significant principles of development postulated by proponents of the various theories and explores their implications for those working with college students.

The first principle is that development is a continuous and cumulative process that occurs throughout the life cycle as the individual tends to move from simpler to more complex modes of behavior. This fundamental principle suggests that individual college students, no matter what their age or life experience, have potential for change from present levels of functioning to increasingly complex levels. In fact, the term *development* itself, according to Sanford (1967, p. 47), "means, most essentially, the organization of increasing complexity." Although this movement is experienced differently by individuals in that it does not take precisely the same form for all, it does appear in most people. As students grow and change, they accumulate new experiences and learnings that are additive. In effect, students grow more mature and able to function more successfully at higher levels of abstraction and complexity as they interact with the educational environment and acquire a wide range of experiences.

Second, development is a natural process influenced by the environment, biological maturation, and personal values and aspirations. Erikson (1968) postulates the concept of *epigenesis*, which underlies the complete process of personality development throughout the life cycle: "Anything that grows has a ground plan, and. . . out of this ground plan the parts arise, each part having its time of special ascendency, until all parts have arisen to form a functioning whole" (p. 92). This principle views human beings as dynamic entities constantly interacting with their external environments, which they interpret through unique sets of internal filters. "Research studies of adults aged eighteen to eighty confirm the broad hypothesis that human personality does change perceptibly as people grow older. These changes in personality are caused not by the passage of time but by the various biological and social events that occur" (Chickering and Havighurst, 1981, p. 19). In effect, human development is a process of adaptation, assimilation, and accommodation in which the individual's personality and thinking patterns are key elements and for which those who desire to influence the direction of student development can plan.

Third, development is characterized by qualitative change, which results from individuals' exposure to experiences, challenges, and crises. There appears to be little doubt that development is influenced significantly by exposure to challenges, which require new adaptive behaviors or qualitatively different intellectual and emotional responses. Numerous theorists have defined the responses that occur as a consequence of an individual's facing and dealing with new and challenging experiences, ideas, and concepts as the essence of development. Sanford (1966, 1967), for instance, identifies challenge and response as extremely important factors in the development of college students. From his perspective, response to challenges stimulates development—that is, the capacity to deal with increased levels of complexity. He recommends that colleges purposefully provide students with strong challenges of various types and appraise students' responses in light of their abilities to cope, being sure to provide adequate support when the challenges become overwhelming. Erikson (1963, 1964, 1968) identifies crises as important to development as individuals seek to resolve the basic conflicts they face. He postulates that individuals reach periodic and predictable crisis points, where the challenge and conflict reach such a level that they feel compelled to act. "A crisis is not a time of panic or disruption. It is a decision point — that moment when one reaches an intersection and must turn one way or the other" (Widick, Parker, and Knefelkamp, 1978). Resolution of these crises is reflected in movement to new levels of consciousness, competence, and capacity to cope with future crises.

Piaget (1952, 1969), recognized by many as the father of cognitive-development theory, first conceptualized the qualitative differences in development that result from exposure to cognitive conflict or dissonance. His interrelated concepts of equilibration, assimilation, and accommodation provide explanations for the ways that people develop their capacity to think and "make meaning." Cognitive development is a sequential process based on the human need to achieve balance or *equilibrium*. When challenged by cognitive conflict, individuals are thrown out of balance by the dissonance involved. People, in effect, are forced into a period of transition of reasoning processes; they are caught between the way they had previously thought and the conflicting data and confusing ideas that no longer seem to fit their cognitive universe. In an attempt to achieve a comfortable balance and to overcome the confusion, they may initially seek to force the new data to fit their current way of thinking and structures of reasoning. This process is referred to as *assimilation*.

At some point, attempts to resolve cognitive conflict and confusion by assimilating new data into old constructs will probably not provide the balance necessary to function comfortably. Individuals, in an attempt to achieve that balance, may then change their way of thinking and reasoning to accommodate the new and conflicting data. This *accommodation* process, according to cognitive-development theory, reflects a new stage of development represented by an increased level of cognitive complexity. Kohlberg (1972, 1975) postulates that accommodation can be encouraged or even brought into being if the level of challenge is only one developmental stage above the individual's current level of reasoning. This idea has been referred to as "Plus One" challenge and is the optimum level of challenge that promotes a qualitative change in the reasoning of the individual.

Psychosocial theories, which focus attention on both the content and the process of developmental change, suggest that young-adult college students are likely to be involved in personal development related to, among other goals, achieving increasingly high levels of academic, interpersonal, and physical competence (Chickering, 1969), establishing an increasingly mature sense of personal identity (Erikson, 1968), achieving increased esthetic appreciation, physical health, and social perspectives (Drum, 1980), and developing vocational maturity (Super and Kidd, 1979).

Cognitive-development theories, in contrast to psychosocial theories, focus more on the process of intellectual development, particularly the thinking processes concerned with interpreting data, reasoning intelligently, and "making meaning" from life experiences. The view of development emphasized by cognitive theorists emphasizes increasingly complex levels of critical thinking and reasoning. From this perspective, students are viewed as moving from basic dualism through multiplicity and relativism to commitment (Perry, 1970), as learning to function at increasingly complex levels of moral development (Kohlberg, 1972, 1975), and as going from the conformist stage to the conscientious stage by becoming increasingly self-aware (Loevinger, 1976).

Theories of person-environment interaction emphasize the institution as well as the individual student. Banning (1980) and Banning and McKinley (1980), following the leads of Walsh (1973), Lewis and Lewis (1977a), Aulepp and Delworth (1976), and Blocher (1974, 1978), postulate an ecological perspective, which approaches student development and institutional development on a concurrent basis, acknowledging that both individuals and institutions grow, adjust, develop, change, and interact. Three environmental dimensions common to all higher education environments are identified by Moos (1979). These are the environment's purposes, its human relationships, and its administration or management. Using these dimensions as a base, Pace (1979) developed an environmental questionnaire designed to assess the nature of larger institutions' subenvironments. He included sets of items that dealt with educational purposes — emphasis on the academic-scholarly, emphasis on the esthetic-expressive, emphasis on the critical-evaluative, and emphasis on the vocational. In addition, he developed scales for measuring relationships among students and their peers, faculty members, and administrators. Finally, Pace included several measures of the institution's environment as a whole.

Those wishing to influence student development through programming efforts such as ISGs must be responsive to the broad context of society in general and to the unique characteristics of the institution in particular (Hurst and Jacobson, 1985), and give special consideration to the psychological environment as perceived by the student (Walsh, 1973). Further, the core conditions for fostering learning and student development, according to Blocher (1978), include involvement, challenge, support, structure, feedback, application, and integration. Each intervention needs to be structured in such a way that participants go through all seven aspects of this process.

Advocates of typology theory suggest that because individual differences are both evident and influential, they must be accounted for if human growth, development, and maturity are to be truly understood and guided in positive directions. Consequently, when developmental change is examined, theorists such as Heath (1964, 1973) believe that students who represent different types respond differentially to different challenges and sources of environmental support. Katchadourian and Boli (1985), for instance, identified a student typology with four basic academic orientations (Careerists, Intellectuals, Strivers, and the Unconnected). Their research indicates that typologies may be more usefully viewed as vehicles to be used to understand and guide developmental processes than to describe development as such.

Finally, the fourth principle of development is that developmental tasks and the mastery of new knowledge, skills, and behaviors correspond with each phase, stage, or level of development. From the psychosocial perspective, the concept of developmental tasks has proven a concise means of describing behavior and conceptualizing change processes. Although Blos (1941) is credited with being the first to use the term in print, Tryon and Lilienthal (1950) and Havighurst (1952) were the early human-development theorists to emphasize developmental tasks in relation to learning and life changes. A *developmental task*, defined simply, is an activity that arises at or about a certain time in life and that, if successfully accomplished, brings the individual to the threshold of a new phase, stage, or level of development. Failure to accomplish or achieve a developmental task creates impediments to future development.

Developmental tasks are typically associated with or emphasized during a particular life stage. For example, Chickering and Havighurst (1981) identify achieving emotional independence, preparing for marriage and family life, choosing and preparing for a career, and developing an ethical system as the primary developmental tasks of late adolescence and early adulthood. Previously, Chickering (1969) had identified the seven developmental vectors that we have already mentioned. Each vector represents both the nature and range of the developmental tasks with which it is associated. By identifying relevant developmental tasks, it is possible to both map and influence development. The more that is known about the relationship of developmental tasks to vector and stage development, the greater the likelihood of influencing that development in positive ways.

A *developmental stage* is a particular level or phase of development common to most individuals. It is often associated with a time period during which an individual is experimenting with new behavior patterns and ways of responding. Some theorists (McCoy, 1977; Levinson and others, 1978) postulate the existence of transition stages between major life stages; in transition stages the individual is, in effect, preparing for the next, more advanced stage. One must, as Montagu (1981) suggests, beware of the "age-stage dilemma" when considering developmental stages. He asserts that people often make the false assumption that a given stage of development is related to a certain chronological age. Even though many theorists postulate a relationship between chronological age and life stages, there is danger in viewing them as synonymous because research has been able to establish only moderately low correlations between them.

Probably the theorist who most influenced the construct of life stages was Erikson (1959, 1963), who postulated the "eight stages of man" from a psychoanalytic perspective. Although not referring to them as developmental tasks, Erikson does identify a number of objectives that must be achieved by an individual in order to complete a particular life stage and thereby move on to the next stage. Within his stage of youth, puberty, and adolescence, for instance, he postulates the life crisis of identity versus role confusion, popularly referred to as the "identity crisis." According to Erikson (1963), certain essential acts (or tasks) must be accomplished to resolve this life crisis. These include learning a gender-appropriate social role, accepting one's body, achieving emotional independence from parents and other adults, selecting and preparing for an occupation, and developing an ethical value system. As these objectives are accomplished, the individual moves to a point where the next developmental stage, young adulthood, with its crisis of intimacy versus isolation, comes clearly into focus.

In cognitive-development theory, developmental tasks are little emphasized, but developmental stage has critical importance. Piaget (1965), Kohlberg and others (1978), and Loevinger (1976) all refer to developmental stages in their work; Perry (1970, 1981) refers to positions rather than stages, but all are postulating basically similar constructs. The stages in cognitive-development theory are viewed as invariant sequences that are hierarchical and universal in nature, whereas psychosocial theory views stages as being cyclical and potentially influenced by the environment and prevailing culture. A stage to the cognitive theorist reflects how the individual finds meaning in an experience, while a stage from a psychosocial perspective reflects both what the individual is seeking to achieve and the activities associated with satisfactory achievement. From the person-environment theoretical perspective, stages and tasks are not viable constructs, except to describe people and how they are likely to respond to the environment.

Neither person-environment interaction nor typology theories recognize developmental tasks and stages as do cognitive and psychosocial theories. Rather, they tend to focus attention upon the processes of change as influenced by the interactions between individuals and their environments. Levels of development may be recognized (Heath, 1964), but it is the personality type or social orientation that is viewed as most influential on the process of change. Rather than focusing upon stages as such, typology theories deal more with levels of maturity or effective functioning while person-environment interaction theory focuses on person-environment fit and the developmental consequences resulting from it.

Developmental Domains

Although there are numerous ways of organizing the developmental tasks of college students, for our purposes the eight developmental domains incorporated in the ISG conceptualization model (see Figure 1) presented in Chapter One are the most relevant developmental dimensions. These domains are the physical, social, emotional, career, intellectual, academic, esthetic, and moral. From that model, we also use the process foci—intrapersonal functioning, interpersonal relationships, information, and task skill development—and the intervention foci—remediation, prevention, and enhancement—when we discuss here the ways that ISGs can be designed to be responsive to students' developmental needs.

We present examples of ISGs to aid readers in understanding the relationship between the developmental tasks of college students and alternative intervention strategies that can be provided using our ISG model. A particular developmental task (for example, stress management, child-parent relations, vocational choice, or creative problem solving) can be approached from a number of different directions by placing emphasis on different aspects, like taking photographs of the same subject from different angles. This emphasis may change as the ISG develops. In an ISG designed with the primary process focus of interpersonal functioning, with a remedial intervention focus, directed at the physical developmental domain, it is likely that some overlap with other processes, interventions, and domains may occur. It is, for instance, likely that some form of new or relevant information will be presented during the course of most ISGs, but unless the primary process focus of a particular ISG is to provide information, that process focus is viewed as secondary. Although it is usually undesirable to attempt to rigidly limit a comprehensive ISG to a particular segment of the ISG model, the examples provided in this chapter emphasize a primary process, intervention, or domain in order to simplify the ISG model and make it easy for readers to understand the relationships between the examples and the model. In all likelihood, practitioners will discover a need to shift from one process focus to another during the course of the ISG. Such shifts are not only acceptable but probably essential for success. They will occur less often between developmental domains than between process foci, although there is bound to be some overlap there as well. It is not recommended, however, that one plan to shift among the intervention foci during a given ISG because the selected focus is determined by the developmental level of the participants being targeted.

Physical Development. Although most college students have reached physical maturity, the need for continued attention to physical functioning and well-being remains, and for some takes on increased significance. Chickering (1969) identifies the development of physical and manual competence as an important area during the college years. Typically students are faced with the need to learn to manipulate their physical environments, improve their skills in sports or recreational activities, master new skills unique to the academic environment (such as manipulation of laboratory apparatus), handle increased levels of stress, and, in many instances, learn to deal with their maturing sexuality. Programs such as Outward Bound and "ropes courses" increase feelings of personal confidence and trust through group activities and team training. The ability to use one's body well in sports and athletics, arts and crafts, recreation, and physical exercise is self-enhancing and tends to foster a sense of psychological and physical well-being.

Wellness has become increasingly important to many college students. More and more, students show interest in participating in physical-fitness programs, whether through individualized walks, jogs, weight lifting, and bicycle rides, or group activities such as exercise classes. Intramural and club sports appear to have achieved a new level of popularity on many campuses. Conscious efforts to enhance and maintain physical well-being appear to be viewed with growing favor by many students. It is not uncommon, for instance, for students to be interested in becoming informed about or participating in programs designed to provide them with guidance about body image, nutrition, weight control, substance abuse, AIDS and other socially transmitted diseases, birth control, and stress management. Older students are faced with adjusting to the biological changes of middle age (Chickering and Havighurst, 1981). Although higher education is concerned primarily with the development of intellectual competence, no matter what the student's age or stage, there is need to be concerned with physical development or maintenance as well.

Interests in physical development manifest themselves on campuses in two principal areas: wellness and recreational sports programs. These programs provide both education and participation opportunities that can lead to a sense of well-being (Leafgren and Elsenrath, 1986). According to Hettler (1980), wellness is directly related to emotional, intellectual, physical, social, occupational, and spiritual development. From this perspective, programs designed to inform students about health enhancement, instruct students in skills and practices that can be used to promote wellness, and provide students with opportunities for participating in physical activities will be developmental in character and purpose and will promote positive changes in those who become involved. Leafgren and Elsenrath (1986) suggest that healthy change in students' behavior can be influenced by providing positive role models, institutional programs and groups with which to identify and associate, oral and written information, and direct interventions (ISGs that focus on physical development or wellness, for example).

An example is an ISG on stress management. From the perspective of the ISG conceptualization model presented in Chapter One, such a group might have an intervention focus on remediation, a process focus on skill development, and the physical development domain. From this "camera angle" the ISG would be aimed at individuals who experience high levels of distress when faced with situational pressures and whose coping-skill deficits deny them the capacity to handle the resulting stress effectively. Likewise, the primary process of the ISG itself would be to help participants identify the situations that cause anxiety and to teach them the requisite skills (perhaps through behavioral restructuring, self-hypnosis, or systematic relaxation training) to handle those situations effectively. As previously discussed, other ISGs concerned with stress management could be designed to emphasize different intervention levels or process foci or developmental domains. As Deffenbacher and McKinley (1983) note, numerous intervention strategies can be used to help students effectively manage stress. Likewise, numerous ISGs can be designed and implemented to respond to this important need, which often manifests itself in the physical domain of development. We, however, must emphasize that in order for the intervention to be considered an ISG, more must be involved than simply teaching stress reduction to a collection of students; it is important to structure the intervention so that the group itself becomes part of the treatment. (See Chapters Two and Seven.)

Social Development. Interpersonal relationships, group-interaction skills, and the capacity for mature intimacy are especially important areas of social development for young adults. Chickering (1969) identifies both the development of social competence and the freeing of interpersonal relationships as important parts of his vector model and also includes the concept of interdependence as important to the development of autonomy. Functioning effectively in both social and work groups is an extremely important skill for any educated person to possess, as the inability to function well in groups can haunt an individual's entire life. The capacity to view one's relationships from the other person's perspective creates comfort and self-confidence when interacting with peers and authority figures in the academic environment. Developing the capacity to exhibit empathy for others enhances the ability to form meaningful social, work, and intimate relationships.

Tolerance for others' life-styles, beliefs, and behaviors is also important if one is to function without undue stress. Being comfortable with those who have different cultural patterns and styles is especially important in today's shrinking world, where global interaction is becoming increasingly common and necessary. (We believe that bigoted and prejudiced students cannot fully realize their potential and are the antithesis of "educated" people. These irrational and personally damaging beliefs and behaviors should be directly confronted as part of the educational process.)

Likewise, as Coons (1971) notes, it is important for individuals to develop the capacity for true intimacy during the young-adult years. If the ability to establish truly intimate relationships is lacking, the years of maturity will probably be much less fulfilling than they can be. People do need people, and the more one has developed the capacity to relate effectively to others in a social sense, the greater one's chance of happiness in life.

Social development is a process that continues as long as an individual is involved with others. As noted previously in this chapter, at certain turning points individuals appear to be faced with conflicts and challenges that require action in order to be resolved. Resolution represents movement toward advanced levels of consciousness and competence. If we combine this process with Erikson's (1968) concept of epigenesis, it appears that human beings are typically faced with a series of reasonably predictable circumstances that demand attention and promote change. Within the social-development domain these changes are related largely to the interpersonal-relationship dimensions previously mentioned (for example, social competence, human-relations skills, and tolerance). Essential changes in one's social development occur largely as direct consequences of interaction with others and the feedback obtained from them. According to Capelle (1979), the change process involves these steps: (1) analyzing the situation, (2) assessing change potential, (3) setting outcome criteria, (4) generating alternative solutions, (5) making decisions, (6) developing plans, (7) implementing plans, (8) evaluating performance, and (9) rewarding performance. He notes, however, that change is a continuous process that occurs over time, that one need not progress through all nine steps of the model all the time, that people often tend to select the first satisfactory alternative or solution available rather than persisting in the process until the maximum (most effective) solution has been found, and that the change decisions people make regarding their social behavior are often more subjective than objective. Thus, an ISG concerned with enhancing students' social development will affect participants in different ways, depending on individual differences, past experiences, and other personal characteristics. Usually, individuals cannot be expected to change their social behavior radically over short periods of time; even long-term change efforts require considerable personal investment of energy and support from others.

Numerous ISG possibilities available in the area of social development would be relevant and appropriate for responding to the developmental needs of young-adult college students. For instance a preventive ISG on date rape with a primary process focus on interpersonal relationships would be useful on most campuses today. Such a group could help students explore gender differences in interpersonal relationships, strategies for avoiding being placed in compromising positions, ways of controlling physical aggression and sexual impulses, and ways of saying "no" that are clear and that will be correctly interpreted by one's partner. Another example of an ISG designed particularly for this developmental domain would be a new-student orientation for the culturally different (for example, minority or international students). An ISG leader could select information as the primary process focus with interpersonal relationships as secondary and enhancement as the intervention focus. This group could provide entering students with an opportunity to learn about the new culture of the college environment, the social expectations that exist, and strategies for interacting with students from different cultural backgrounds who possess different value systems. In such an ISG it would be important to include students from the prevailing culture as well; for those students the ISG might be viewed as a means of helping them develop tolerance.

Emotional Development. The ability to manage emotions effectively is a sign of maturity and influences self-concept, personality, identity, and character development. The human-development literature is replete with references to the importance of developing the ability to manage emotions. In psychosocial theory, Erikson (1968) established the importance of developing a personal identity. This developmental task is not complete unless or until emotional autonomy has been achieved. Erikson postulated that during adolescence and youth, a period when many individuals are attending college, concern for personal identity is in its ascendency, and individuals begin seriously to seek resolution of questions such as Who am I? Where am I going in life? What am I to become? Where do I belong? Without resolving these important questions, the individual is faced with role confusion, the polar opposite of identity, which results in failure to move easily to advanced levels of development.

Chickering (1969), following the lead of Erikson, determined that establishing identity was a core construct in his seven-vector model. Establishing identity "involves an increased ability to integrate the many facets of one's experience and negotiate a realistic, stable self-image. It occurs as an inner sense that there are core qualities which comprise one's being in the world" (Widick, Parker, and Knefelkamp, 1978, p. 24). In addition, Chickering postulated that certain conditions are necessary if a sense of identity is to be established. These conditions include the ability to manage one's emotions and the development of emotional autonomy. Establishing a sense of identity requires a high degree of self-awareness of feelings.

A well-established sense of identity is the essence of a mature self-image and provides a foundation for moving forward in life with a sense of confidence. Without a sense of identity, one cannot effectively achieve character development, which reflects an individual's capacity to both understand and act on what is "right" (Whitely and Associates, 1982); freed interpersonal relationships, purpose, and integrity as postulated by Chickering (1969); and intimacy as identified by Erikson (1959). In many ways, achieving a sense of identity is a major accomplishment; it provides a sense of self that is the keystone for mature adulthood.

According to Chickering (1969) individuals must learn to manage two basic emotional impulses if they are to achieve mature development: sex and aggression. Gender identity is a primary developmental theme in this domain; it results from interaction with parents, peers, siblings, and surrogate caregivers. Individuals must first, usually during adolescence, come to understand and accept their secondary sex characteristics and ultimately, as young adults, come to fully participate in intimate sexual relationships (Gazda, Childers, and Brooks, 1987). This developmental process is, however, fraught with emotion as parents, peers, and society at large pressure the individual in often confusing and contradictory fashions. Attempts to resolve the conflict between biological desires or urges and established social limitations create a volatile and emotion-charged roller coaster in many students' lives. Dealing effectively with these experiences, sensations, feelings, and demands in socially responsible ways is a sign of maturity and the foundation for achieving true intimacy.

Likewise, dealing with feelings of anger, hostility, and even hate are essential aspects of managing emotions. In many instances, learning to accept and own these often frightening emotions as a natural part of life and living is another sign of emotional maturity. As Chickering (1969, p. 11) notes, "*Until lust and hate are admitted as legitimate emotions, as legitimate as love and*

*admiration, their motive power is not likely to be harnessed to produc-
tive ends."*

Because the individual is moving increasingly into the
adult world of work and responsibility, the adolescent and
young-adult years form an important transition period. Learning to deal effectively with authority figures, to manage the often
excessive demands of peers, and to resolve child-parent relationships are all areas of concern for most young adults. All
maturing students are exposed to conflict-loaded situations that
stimulate affect (for example, sexual interactions and opportunities, instructional and supervisory relationships, parents
attempting to maintain the status quo, and peers applying
pressure toward conformity). The emotions that these interactions evoke, sometimes at relatively unconscious levels, require
that young adults become sensitive to new subtleties and acquire
new, different, and mature response modes for dealing with
them. Effective management of emotions does not mean that
their existence is denied, that they are repressed, or that attempts are made to control them. Rather, it implies the ability to
recognize the various emotions that arise from day to day and
the capacity to make intelligent judgments about how, when, and
where to express them.

Developmental change in managing emotions is largely a
result of bringing one's emotions and feelings to a conscious
level, owning them, analyzing the factors that brought the emotions into existence, thoughtfully considering the alternative
responses, and expressing them in the most socially acceptable,
yet personally satisfying, ways possible. This considered approach is an effective, therefore productive, way of responding
to the frustrations, irritations, and personal pain that everyone
experiences from time to time. It tends to bypass the impulsive,
thoughtless, or conditioned responses of childhood and provides the individual with a mature, considered response style
that will satisfy societal demands and gratify individual needs.

Because ISGs are themselves social situations in which
norms are often established to allow for greater expression of
emotion than in conventional social groups, they are especially

effective interventions in this domain. An ISG in the emotional developmental domain would probably have intrapersonal functioning as its primary process focus, largely because emotions are so highly personal and internal in nature. The intervention focus, however, because it depends largely on the target population's level of development, might well be any of the three. For illustrative purposes we have selected remediation as the intervention focus; the ISG would be aimed at students who exhibit ineffective modes of managing affect or who believe that they need special help in learning to express themselves in socially acceptable or health-engendering ways. Although secondary process foci would, in all probability, be acquiring knowledge about and strategies for managing emotions (that is, information and skill development), the primary focus would be on intrapersonal views and response patterns that cause or promote the difficulties being experienced. Group sharing of the various responses that participants have exhibited and exploration of why individuals function as they do when dealing with emotional issues and concerns might be a first step. Willingness, or unwillingness, to recognize and own feelings of hate, hostility, anger, irritation, fear, love, and affection might be explored, and practice in public admission of such feelings in the ISG forum might be encouraged. Strategies for effective social expression of emotions might then be introduced, followed by modeling and skill-building practice. Such an ISG would call for a leader who is skilled in the area of intrapersonal dynamics, knowledgeable about emotional dysfunctioning, and well experienced in working with groups where high levels of volatility can occur. From the perspective of the ISG model, the remediation intervention focus is probably the most problematical for most leaders because it is designed to help individuals who are functioning at especially low developmental levels. Students with developmental deficits in any of the developmental domains are especially difficult to work with and often require individual attention before they are ready to participate fully in an ISG.

Career Development. Needs related to choosing a career are the single most frequently expressed needs of college students (Weissberg and others, 1982; Ragan and Higgins, 1985). Although many institutions of higher learning emphasize the values of a liberal education and therefore do not expressly promote a vocational emphasis, almost all students are concerned about making career decisions during college.

Career development goes well beyond vocational concerns alone. The term *career* implies much more than a vocation or a job; it may in fact be viewed as a way of life. Although choosing a life work (Coons, 1971) is an important developmental task for college students, Chickering's (1969) vector of developing purpose— personal interests, educational and career options, life-style preferences— is probably a more appropriate way to view career development. Developing purpose results in setting a coherent, if general, direction for one's life (Widick, Parker, and Knefelkamp, 1978). Career maturity, according to Super (1983), is a cyclical process that includes several principal dimensions including planfulness, exploration, information, decision making, and reality orientation; in this view, vocational development is essentially the development and implementation of a self-concept. From this developmental perspective, work satisfaction and life satisfaction depend on the extent to which individuals find adequate outlets for abilities, interests, personality traits, and values as well as on the role one finds most congenial and appropriate (Crockett, 1978).

Higher education administrators and faculty members often assume that students who enter college with declared majors do not need career assistance, unlike those who enter as undecided majors. Evidence indicates, however, that such assumptions are often erroneous and can lead to failure to provide students with the support they need (Goodson, 1981; Titley and Titley, 1980). In fact, Titley and Titley (1985) report that even to assume that a given entering freshman is either decided or undecided about a major is a serious error because the degree of certainty involved is highly variable. Gordon (1984) points out that there are many types of undecided students and that an understanding of the nature and cause of the undecidedness is essential before an intervention is attempted.

Career indecision is relatively common in young-adult

college students in particular and in older, nontraditional students to some extent as well. Many students choose a career because of the opportunities it provides for self-expression or for accomplishing a desirable social outcome or because of the economic security it offers without any understanding of the kinds of tasks and stress that are involved (Johnson and Figler, 1984). Therefore, it is important that students have ample opportunity to consider and then reconsider their career decisions carefully and systematically if they are to be reasonably sure that their choice is the most appropriate one for them. Even then there is reasonable likelihood that career changes will occur in the future.

Osipow (1973) identifies four major reasons for misdirected career development: making career choices that are not consistent with self-information, being developmentally retarded or a late bloomer, being emotionally unstable, and being caught between two equally desirable choices.

An ISG concerned with the career developmental domain might well have a remediation intervention focus, for, as Osipow (1973) notes, retarded development is probably the single most likely cause for vocational indecision on the part of college students. The primary process focus for the ISG could readily be information because many individuals know little about career alternatives and have even less access to accurate and up-to-date career information. With these three dimensions from the ISG conceptualization model, it would be possible to create a number of different ISGs depending on the type of information to be emphasized. If information resources are emphasized, the ISG might introduce students to the various career libraries and other campus and community agencies and programs that provide career-related information through publications, films, and videotapes. Other avenues for obtaining information, such as interviewing individuals employed in a particular field, observing work settings, or preparing for short-term, part-time, or cooperative-education work placements, might also be used. If the process focus were shifted to task skill development, an ISG on building decision-making skills could be initiated to help individuals overcome deficits in this important aspect of the career developmental domain. Any ISG in the career domain usually requires some attention to the intrapersonal-functioning process focus because an understanding of interests and other personality characteristics is essential for using career information.

Intellectual Development. Intellectual, or cognitive, development focuses on the reasoning processes used to deal with the world of ideas, to "make meaning" from life experiences, to interpret data, and to solve problems; cognitive development encompasses the intellectual changes that can occur as a result of attending college.

A major factor that promotes change in students is their exposure to new and stimulating ideas, concepts, and theories. Perry (1970, 1981), in his research, identified a series of "positions" common to the intellectual and ethical development of college students. Perry determined that young-adult college students tend to move from the dichotomous position of "basic dualism," in which they view the world largely from an either/or, right/wrong, or good/bad perspective, to one of "relativism," in which they view the world from an open-ended, less rigid perspective. (See Table 1 for an overview of Perry's scheme of intellectual and ethical development.) A parallel process, not unrelated to changes in reasoning, is the way students respond to significant others who are viewed as the authorities in their lives. Initially, students tend to view their professors as all-knowing authorities who possess the "right" answers. As their intellectual development progresses, they come to realize that authority is largely in the eye of the beholder and that no one is all-knowing. As a result, their relationships with college faculty and staff members tend to shift from a superior-subordinate (similar to parent-child) framework to one of equality (adult-adult) in which the experienced person is the means by which new information and ideas are introduced. It then becomes the students' responsibility to "make meaning" from these data for themselves.

Understanding the cognitive developmental processes that commonly occur when students attend college or deal with

Table 1. Perry's Model of Intellectual and Ethical Development.

Dualism: Knowledge is quantitative. Meaning is divided into two realms—for example, good versus bad or right versus wrong, we versus they or success versus failure. Right answers exist somewhere for every problem, and the authorities know them. Right answers are to be memorized by hard work. Locus of control is founded in external authority.

Multiplicity: Diversity of opinion and values is recognized as legitimate in areas where the right answers are not yet known. Opinions remain atomistic without defined patterns or system. It is not possible to make distinct judgments among all the alternatives, so people have a right to their own opinions; none can be called wrong.

Relativism: Knowledge is qualitative, dependent on contexts. Opinions, values, and judgments are derived from coherent sources, evidence, and patterns that provide the bases for analysis and comparison. Although some opinions will be judged worthless, on some matters reasonable people will reasonably disagree.

Commitment: Reasoned and consciously affirmed choices and decisions (career, value, political, relationship) are made in the full awareness of relativism. Locus of control is found within the individual.

Source: Adapted from Perry (1970, 1981).

any new, previously unexperienced life challenge can be useful in working with students and stimulating them to think and reason at increasingly complex levels. The concepts of cognitive dissonance and equilibration (Piaget, 1952) as well as those of challenge, support, and response (Sanford, 1967) are of particular relevance here because they describe the processes by which individuals move from simpler to more complex modes of reasoning. Chickering (1969) notes that change occurs through cycles of differentiation and integration, and the higher education environment provides many opportunities through which these processes may become manifest. As Miller and McCaffrey (1982) describe it, there are numerous ways in which college faculty and staff members can influence development in this important area, in some cases by using the ISG approach in direct and practical ways.

Because intellectual development is concerned primarily with cognitive processes as opposed to content, an ISG designed to enhance the intellectual-development domain that has an enhancement intervention focus might well incorporate skill development as its primary process focus. Such an ISG might provide students who have exhibited high levels of academic competence with an opportunity to learn creative problem-solving methods and skills incorporating both traditional scientific and intuitive styles.

Because development in this domain is stimulated principally through confronting situations in which past strategies of making meaning are challenged, an ISG that deals with dilemmas (in the context of problem solving) that do not have "correct" answers could stimulate development. The group aspect of the ISG would be enhanced if it purposefully included some members who were operating at approximately one position or stage above the majority. The interchange between students operating at qualitatively different levels should produce enough dissonance to stimulate growth.

Academic Development. Students' development of academic skills and mastery of a body of knowledge are generally acknowledged as the principal goals of higher education. Some, such as Bloom (1987) and earlier Hutchins (1936), have argued that those are the only appropriate goals for higher education. Student-development advocates do not argue against the importance of academic development but emphasize that personalizing the academic experience and humanizing the educational environment are important.

One challenge that typically influences this domain of student development is the requirement that students decide on an academic major, select a course of study, and establish an educational plan prior to moving to upper-division coursework. Individuals faced with making important decisions tend to grow from the process of coping with the challenges such requirements present. Charging students with this important responsibility, and providing a support system to aid them in the process, can be most beneficial in helping them establish patterns of self-directed learning.

Another challenge in this domain for college students is that they must successfully master the academic curriculum if they are to complete their formal educations. Students must not only register for courses, complete class assignments, and pass appropriate courses, but must know how to learn, to organize materials, to study effectively, to prepare for and take examinations, and to manage time well. It is not sufficient to assume that students will have developed these essential skills prior to attending college. It is the responsibility of higher education to assess the extent to which such skills have been developed and to help students strengthen them as needed. Significant numbers of students have developed defensive reactions to or near phobias about academic performance (such as debilitating anxieties related to mathematics, public speaking, and test taking), which severely limit the academic areas they may pursue and which may even prevent them from graduating.

An ISG designed to respond to students' manifest needs in the academic developmental domain with a remedial intervention focus and task skill-development process focus would be a group on test-anxiety reduction. Such an ISG would probably begin by providing students with an opportunity to identify the factors that cause them difficulty when preparing for and taking an examination (that is, using intrapersonal functioning as a secondary process focus for this ISG). Once these factors are identified, the process focus would shift to skills that individuals can use to help them deal with test-taking stress. Such skills could include almost everything from taking and reviewing notes to establishing systematic study patterns, using mnemonic devices, and learning relaxation techniques.

Esthetic Development. Exposure to, knowledge about, appreciation for, and involvement in the esthetic aspects of culture have long been an important part of being a liberally educated person. As society has become increasingly complex and as higher education has become increasingly egalitarian and utilitarian, there has often been a tendency to decrease the emphasis placed on the esthetic. Bloom's (1987) treatise on the current lamentable status of philosophy and literature in American higher education maintains that educational institutions have failed to provide students with sufficient exposure to a cultural heritage or tradition. From this perspective, today's college students are becoming increasingly unaware of and unfamiliar with, and thereby uninterested in, those historical and cultural antecedents so important to a fully developed person. Likewise, there has been a failure to introduce students to non-Western cultures and art forms.

Beauty is, indeed, in the eye of the beholder, but it is necessary for one to be exposed to and understand that which exists in order to establish the capacity to appreciate it. Having the capacity to be sensitive to beauty is one of the unique ways that humans differ from the lower species. Esthetic development — development of the capacity to create, perform, critique, or observe a particular art form (Gardner, 1973) — is an especially important part of this process. As Drum (1980) indicates, one who has reached the stage of enhanced sensitivity is someone capable of being sensitive to beauty and of understanding its personal meaning and value. Not unlike tolerance for others' ideas, ways of viewing the world, or cultural differences, esthetic development implies an openness to the world, and the college years are a particularly good time for becoming exposed to the world.

Members of the academic community have ample opportunity to provide ISGs designed to promote esthetic development in students. They do, however, need an understanding of the factors that serve to stimulate interest and involvement in the arts and that stand as obstacles to esthetic education (Brown and others, 1982). An ISG designed for the esthetic developmental domain with a remedial intervention focus might be created to emphasize the intrapersonal-functioning process focus. This process focus would have utility if the intent were to broaden esthetic appreciation in students. This level of esthetic development is viewed as being more advanced than the most basic position, instilled esthetic preferences, but less complex than the most advanced level, enhanced esthetic sensitivity, by Drum (1980). From his perspective, broadened appreciation occurs when "students' esthetic judgments and preferences are built less on imitation of others' tastes and more on the basis of personal experimentation in which they have sampled new cultural stimuli" (pp. 28–29). An ISG designed to focus attention in this area would likely provide students with opportunities for exposure to a variety of art forms or cultural experiences, for examining their own special preferences, for adopting their newly defined preferences into their life-styles, and even for expressing themselves through several media.

Moral Development. Moral development is a multifaceted and complex process closely related to the cognitive developmental domain. This connection is reflected in the fact that those concerned with moral education are usually less concerned with the specific content of the judgments that individuals make about issues and dilemmas than with the processes involved in making those judgments. Although Kohlberg (1971, 1972, 1975) is probably the best-recognized proponent of moral-development theory, others are also well recognized (Durkheim, 1961; Piaget, 1965; Rest, 1979, 1985; Staub, 1978, 1979). (An overview of Kohlberg's stages of moral development is presented in Table 2.) These authorities all view moral development as important to human maturation and provide a wealth of information to guide those interested in devising relevant educational programming in this area. Specifically, Coons (1971) contends that one of the developmental tasks of the college years is the establishment of a value system to guide one's life. Such a value system is important to the development of identity and personal integrity (Chickering, 1969; Erikson, 1963, 1968), and is closely linked to moral development. Excellent resources for those interested in values development in college include Simon, Howe, and Kirschenbaum (1972), Smith (1977), and Dalton (1985).

The processes by which moral and character development occur are important for those wishing to create ISGs designed to enhance students' development. In a report on the Sierra Project at the University of California, Irvine, Whiteley and others (1985) identify five factors that students perceive as influencing their character development while in college: interaction with faculty and staff members, involvement in a supportive community, exposure to diversity, interpersonal relationships, and establishment of personal and instrumental

Table 2. Levels and Stages of Moral Development.

Preconventional: Founded in an individual context (judgment is egocentric)

Stage 1. One feels vulnerable to the retribution of powerful external authorities and seeks to survive by staying out of trouble. Moral judgment based on punishment or reward with obedience and subordination to authorities.

Stage 2. Individual recognizes through experience that rules often conflict, justice is not always assured, bad is not always punished, and good is not always rewarded. Moral judgment based on fairness and initially on reciprocity or even exchange.

Conventional: Founded in a societal context (judgment is socially shared)

Stage 3. One is concerned about others and can see their perspectives as different from own; individual seeks agreement, conforms, and subordinates individual needs to group relationship. Moral judgment based on shared assumptions that underlie mutual trust.

Stage 4. One's perspective is expanded to include society as a whole and the rules and roles to which members adhere to preserve social order. One understands that individual welfare is inextricably tied to preservation of society. Moral judgment based on societal rules that prescribe the nature and extent of moral obligation.

Postconventional: Founded in a prior-to-society context (judgment is universal)

Stage 5. One acknowledges that the limits of societal morality are transcended through the discovery of ethical principles. Moral judgment based on principles of equality and reciprocity generated through an understanding of social contract and individual conscience.

Stage 6. One understands that the foundation for a universal conception of justice is an abiding respect for persons. The social unit expands to include all human beings as the individual discovers the moral capacity to take the role of the other. Moral judgment based on principles of justice, which becomes autonomous in its function and universal in its impartial application to everyone.

Sources: Adapted from Kohlberg (1971, 1975), and Gilligan (1981).

autonomy. According to Rest (1985), those wishing to provide moral education to students need to consider four major processes related to the establishment of moral behavior: "(1) The person must interpret the particular situation in terms of recognizing who is involved, what lines of action are possible for the actor, and how each of those lines of action would affect the welfare of each party involved. . . . (2) The person must judge which of the alternative lines of action is most just or fairer or morally right. . . . (3) A person is usually also aware that other values besides *moral* goals can be served by alternative courses of action. . . . (4) The person must have actually carried through on the decision to do the moral action, persisting and not wandering from the goal, and must have been able to implement that intention" (pp. 76–77).

Whether the process of moral development is similar for both genders is currently a debatable issue because some authorities contend that there are characteristic differences between the two (Gilligan, 1981, 1982; Miller, 1976). For instance, Gilligan sees the sequential development of first identity and then intimacy in men while women tend to develop the two simultaneously. From her perspective, moral development for women is predicated on an understanding of fairness, as it is for men, but she sees affiliative and caring relationships as essential components as well. Thus, those concerned with providing students with opportunities to enhance their moral development may need to provide men and women with different interventions, especially in the early college years. According to Gelwick (1985), different programs are necessary in order to help women come to understand that care encompasses concern not only for others but for oneself as well.

Because moral development and human values are so closely intertwined, it is important to consider the possibility that students from different cultural backgrounds—such as blacks, Hispanics, native Americans, and international students—may respond differently to some moral-development interventions because of cultural differences. As Wright (1987) notes, most developmental theories have been created by nonminority persons who neither recognize nor understand minority values concerning such issues as achievement and competition. Because of these circumstances it is important that practitioners seek to take such factors into account when designing ISGs and other developmental interventions. For example, if one desires to provide a moral-development ISG that may involve international students or cultural minorities, then it would be essential to consult with a member of the target group or, better yet, allow that person to help design the intervention.

Basically, this recommendation holds true for ISGs concerned with all developmental domains.

An example of an ISG in the moral developmental domain with a remediation intervention focus and a process focus of interpersonal relationships would be antiracism training. Such an ISG could be designed to provide white students with an opportunity to examine their awareness of and to take appropriate ownership for both personal and institutional racism as it currently exists. Other antidiscrimination ISGs can be developed around issues such as sexism or religious differences.

Summary. Each of the eight developmental domains identified in the ISG conceptualization model—physical, social, emotional, career, intellectual, academic, esthetic, and moral development—has great value for those who are responsible for enhancing students' development. Both developmental theory and practical observation have been used to ascertain that the developmental domains are important in the lives of college students. By focusing attention on them, practitioners can create many effective ISG intervention programs and processes designed to influence the lives of students and the quality of their development. Use of the ISG conceptualization model as a developmental intervention guide provides campus programmers with both a content and process framework to assure that students' developmental needs are being appropriately addressed. Using this model's components as criteria, programmers can also assess the extent to which the institution's developmental program is accomplishing its purpose and goals.

Tapping the Power of the Peer Group

At least two types of groups in the higher education environment have potential for influencing the growth and development of college students: (1) spontaneous, natural groups that occur when individuals come together, often by chance, in a new environment and are faced with the task of functioning and surviving in a loosely organized, initially unfamiliar milieu; and (2) groups that represent the institution's attempts to structure environments in systematic ways.

Spontaneous, Natural Groups. Considerable research suggests that one's peer group is the single most potent environmental influence on student development in college (Brown, 1972; Feldman and Newcomb, 1969a, 1969b; Newcomb and Wilson, 1966). Because the learning environment is made up largely of students, students are enormously influenced by each other, even though many others, such as faculty members, residence staff members, student-activities coordinators, and administrators, can influence students as well. Pace (1979) found that social development, appreciation of individuality, tolerance, and development of lasting friendships were highly correlated with a friendly, cohesive, group-oriented campus environment.

The natural, spontaneous groups with which students associate and identify are extremely important parts of the educational environment. Those concerned with the growth and development of college students need to be aware continually of the presence of primary and associational groups and of their potential influence on the students with whom they work. This powerful force in students' lives can be used constructively through ISGs.

Institutional Organizations and Groups. Historically, institutions of higher learning have exhibited a rather consistent pattern of integrating what often begins as spontaneous student groups and activities into the institutions' organizational structures. That is to say, institutions have sought to obtain and maintain some degree of control over student activities and groups and have, therefore, institutionalized many spontaneously developed student activities such as literary societies, Greek-letter societies, student government, student athletics, and student unions (Rudolph, 1962; Brubacher and Rudy, 1976; Miller, Winston, and Mendenhall, 1983). The natural groups from which many, if not most, of these activities and organizations derived were the result of students' needs for orientation to the college, intellectual stimulation and support, social identity, leadership opportunities, physical and recreational outlets, and nonacademic activities centers.

Realistically, there will always be room for natural, spontaneous groups on the college campus, for there is a need on the part of students to find and maintain informal educational, social, and physical outlets, activities, and identity groups. Likewise, there is organizational wisdom in college leaders' desires to find ways to institutionalize student groups and organizations so as to maintain reasonable control over them and integrate student groups and activities into the institution's mainstream in order to promote student growth and development. It behooves institutions of higher learning to capitalize on what they know about the growth and development that occurs in students as a direct result of being involved in various types of student groups and organizations.

Using ISGs as a strategy to enhance development is a constructive use of the power of peers. ISGs utilize the power and attraction of natural groups and the benefits that accrue from organization and planning.

Organizing
and Implementing
Successful Groups

All parts of an ISG deserve special consideration—from the needs assessment to inception of the idea through the planning process and implementation to the final evaluation report. Although the theoretical foundations are essential, the construction and conduct of the ISG are the true determinants of success or failure. Applying the theoretical principles and background knowledge requires insight and skills developed through extensive practice, in addition to conceptual comprehension.

We have divided Part Two into five chapters, following a basically chronological sequence from conceptualizing and planning through to closing the group. This organization may be somewhat misleading, however, because all components affect all others and cannot be considered in total isolation. We must obviously begin with a plan, but the plan must include what we know about the skills of the available leaders, the probable composition of the group, reasonable evaluation procedures, information about the content or subject of the ISG, and many other factors. Planning and leading ISGs is a complex process that requires extensive integration of knowledge and skills and personal flexibility.

Chapter Four identifies the important components and potential pitfalls in the planning of ISGs. A formulation for a comprehensive needs assessment of the college population, from which goals can be derived, is presented. A sequential model details the steps to follow in developing a functional ISG plan, which should ultimately be codified in a manual.

Chapter Five explains the meaning of, purposes of, and practical strategies for conducting evaluations. Commonly employed evaluation designs are discussed and related to ISGs. Salient features of and differences between formative and summative evaluation procedures are delineated and illustrated.

Chapter Six begins by briefly outlining prominent theories of group leadership. Leadership styles most appropriate for ISGs are discussed in detail, and a leadership model directly related to ISGs is proposed. The advantages and disadvantages of coleadership are investigated, as well as different leadership styles.

Chapter Seven considers common problems and issues that arise during the conduct of an ISG. Considerable attention is given to the preparations that are necessary prior to the first group meeting in order to anticipate and prevent problems during the course of the ISG. The model of ISG stage development presented in Chapter Two is employed as a diagnostic tool to identify possible difficulties that may occur at each stage of the group experience. Particular attention is paid to the crucial importance of the initial session and the closing session.

Chapter Eight concludes the book with examples of identifiable student groups appropriate for ISG interventions. The versatility of ISGs is illustrated through their application to a variety of nonstudent populations, such as staff. Finally, the societal implications of the uses of ISGs are briefly discussed.

The Planning Process: Establishing Needs, Resources, Strategies, and Objectives

For leaders of ISGs there may be some truth to the old adage "Those who fail to plan, plan to fail." As with most truisms, a too literal application may be problematical; an excessive devotion by the group leader to carefully constructed plans can lead to rigidity and loss of spontaneity, which in turn destroy member participation and the ultimate value of the group process. But when kept in proper perspective, the maxim succinctly highlights the importance of planning. Preparation cannot ensure success, but a lack of planning invites failure.

This chapter begins with a brief description of preliminary considerations that help determine whether an ISG is the most appropriate vehicle for achieving the desired student-development outcomes. Then, the chapter provides a detailed perspective of the most critical steps in planning effective ISGs. It ends with an outline for constructing an ISG manual.

Preliminary Considerations

A number of concerns need to be addressed prior to making a final decision about whether to make plans to develop an ISG. These initial steps are determining need, assessing and cultivating support, analyzing goals and processes, and appraising costs and benefits.

Determination of Need. Leaders need to begin by developing a quick capsule view of the need for an intervention by assembling all the evidence that a problem, need, or important concern requires attention. These data should be summarized in writing. The process of organizing the information into a short summary can help planners objectively evaluate the need. A written summary is also important in case higher-level staff should question why a program was developed or why time and resources were committed to the planning process.

ISGs should be developed and offered based on a determination of the needs or wants of students and not on staff interests or current professional fads. All student affairs divisions, ideally, should periodically collect systematic, theory-based data on needs from their students. This being a far from perfect world, however, such is not often the case. In the absence of periodic, comprehensive needs assessments, potential ISG planners can seek information from a wide variety of other sources (Hanson and Yancey, 1985), including:

- Published research on students at similar institutions
- Previous research studies conducted on the campus
- Existing data bases, usually maintained by the office of institutional research
- Utilization data — individual offices' or departments' records of requests for and use of services, and attendance records at programs, which may be available from annual reports
- Data from research and survey studies conducted by the planners to determine needs

Informal sources can also be used. These include faculty and staff, newspaper articles, colleagues, and student paraprofessionals who have extensive contact with students and often have a good feel for what is going on in students' lives. (See a later section of this chapter for a detailed treatment of the comprehensive needs-assessment procedures required once preliminary questions have been answered.)

Assessment and Cultivation of Support. Baldridge (1971) comments that the most realistic and profitable way to view higher education is as a political system. If this view is true, or even only partially true, then an ISG planner needs to be informed about the political dynamics operating on the campus and be prepared to incorporate that information into the ISG planning process. Barr (1985) offers several suggestions for assessing the political situation accurately and garnering support for one's plans: (1) Develop clear and concise goals for the proposed ISG, with supporting needs-assessment evidence and convincing arguments for why the proposed ISG can accomplish the goals. (2) Use strategic timing—that is, present ideas when decision makers will most likely have time to listen and when other events on campus do not overwhelm them in seeming importance; proposing an ISG on improving interpersonal communication is not appropriate during a period of violent demonstrations. (3) Build alliances with others on campus who are sympathetic to the set of student needs addressed; if possible involve them in the planning, or at least ask them to critique or comment on the proposal. (4) Make sure immediate supervisors are aware of the plan being developed from the beginning; they can often give valuable advice and keep planners from making political mistakes—for example, in determining how to slant the proposal. (5) Never surprise the boss; as Barr (1985, p. 77) says: "No one likes to be surprised, least of all the person who must protect you, your agency, and your resources in the political arena."

Analysis of Goals and Processes. Although ISGs are extremely versatile and flexible, they are not always the best or most appropriate type of intervention. For example, if the needs identified are widespread among the student population and students perceive a press to meet those needs, an ISG would not be the most appropriate intervention simply because there would not be sufficient staff and time to meet the student demands within a small-group format. Other types of interventions, such as environmental or milieu management, would most likely be a more effective approach than ISGs. Likewise, if an individual's problem is basically remedial in nature and has a long history, ISGs probably are not the best intervention; either individual counseling or group psychotherapy would probably be more appropriate than ISGs. ISGs are not the solutions to all student problems.

Appraisal of Costs and Benefits. Just as ISGs are not always the most effective means for addressing student needs, the benefits of ISGs may not be commensurate with the costs. In higher education most decisions require selecting among desirable alternatives, not selecting between desirable and undesirable ones. ISG planners need to ask themselves, "Where does this proposed intervention fit within the overall goals of the student affairs division and ultimately the institution?" In other words, staff need to keep their attention focused on the overall educational mission and the current set of institutional priorities. The decision about whether to develop and offer a given ISG should be made within this context. Because we know how to do something does not mean that we should do it.

Deciding on the Most Appropriate Intervention. As noted, ISGs are not always the most appropriate medium or kind of intervention for addressing students' concerns. Table 3 compares three types of interventions: ISGs, counseling (therapy) groups, and individual counseling (therapy). The reader should keep in mind that many factors must be considered when determining the most appropriate kind of intervention and that the data in Table 3 are primarily for heuristic purposes and should not be taken literally.

Overview of the Planning Process

Planning is not born *ex nihilo*, nor does it take place in a vacuum. Rather, the process emerges from an initial assessment of needs in the areas of student development considered important in higher education. Specifically, the areas to be assessed are the physical, social, emotional, academic, career, intellectual, esthetic, and moral (as described in Chapters One and Three). Effective planning thus requires an understanding of both the nature of an ISG and the nature of student development. Because the ISG is neither a panacea nor even the pre-

Table 3. Most Appropriate Interventions for Addressing
Different Types of Student Concerns.

		Intervention Medium	
Consideration	ISG	Group Counseling	Individual Counseling
Limited time (one academic term or less)	1	3	2
Nature of problem or concern			
Social adjustment	1	2	3
Academic adjustment	1	2	3
Academic skill	1	X	X
Developmental task	1	2	2
Future-focused issue	1	2	2
Severe emotional problem	X	1	1
Character disorder	X	1	2
Deviant behavior	X	1	2
Lack of information	1	X	2
Anticipated primary outcome			
Increased knowledge or information	1	3	2
Attitude change	3	1	2
Skill acquisition	1	2	2
Perceptual change	1	1	1
Symptom removal	X	1	1
Personality realignment	X	2	1
Concern shared by			
Relatively few in the population	X	2	1
Significant proportion of the population	1	2	3
Most individuals in the population	X	X	X

Note: 1 = preferred intervention medium; 2 = second best intervention medium; 3 = third best intervention medium; X = generally not an appropriate medium.

ferred intervention for all student-development needs, it is important to determine the fit between the identified need and the ISG process. Key questions to ask concerning the quality of the fit are: Will this developmental need best be met in a group format? Do the students need an opportunity to solicit feedback from others, model others' behavior, provide feedback to others, provide modeling for others, or practice new behaviors in a supportive atmosphere? The dynamic nature of group interaction can greatly influence behavior and attitude change in

Figure 3. A Model for Planning ISGs.

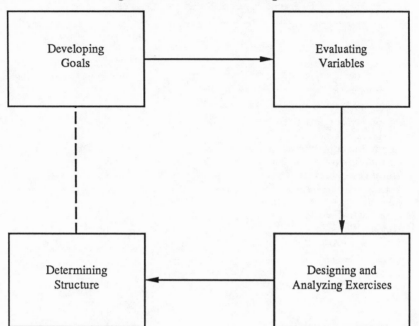

individuals. ISGs provide students with special opportunities to experience these changes as well as other unique opportunities for growth.

Planning is the process that prospective group leaders use to make decisions about the developmental needs of the target population, translate those assessed needs into goals, rank order the desired goals, identify effective learning experiences, design preferred exercises and put them in sequence, and establish evaluation procedures. A model for planning ISGs is depicted in Figure 3.

Although student affairs professionals should consider planning a continuous activity, the model described here is not a continuous cycle because an ISG is only one part of a much larger program of student-development functions and activities. Thus, the model's four phases are applicable only to the implementation of individual ISGs. The model is not a cybernetic loop that feeds input back into itself on a continuing basis, as is true of many planning models. Information regarding the relative effectiveness of a particular ISG is used only indirectly in developing future ISG plans (as indicated by the dotted line in Figure 3).

As outlined in Figure 4, the planning process consists of four basic steps, with each step including a natural progression of distinct but interdependent phases. Achievement of a step or phase in the process is naturally preceded by the successful completion of previous steps and phases. Thus, the planning process resembles a staircase of sequential actions designed to culminate in a functional plan for the ISG.

Developing Goals

Set Philosophical Guidelines. The first phase in planning ISGs (as noted in Figure 4) is to establish the philosophical guidelines. An institution's student affairs philosophy is usually contained in a mission statement. It is important that this statement be congruent with the institution's overall mission (Council for the Advancement of Standards for Student Services/ Development Programs, 1986). A philosophical position is the basis for all organizational, personnel, and programming decisions. (Planners, however, should be aware that there may be considerable difference between an espoused philosophy and daily practice. It is with actual practice that ISG planners should be most concerned.)

A philosophical position that incorporates a student-development approach will contain certain human-development principles and theoretical foundations (Miller and Prince, 1976). The decision to utilize ISGs as an intervention strategy will, to a greater or lesser extent, depend on the philosophical foundations on which the student affairs program is based. It is imperative, therefore, that campus administrators, faculty members, and prospective ISG leaders have a clear understanding of the assumptions that guide the institution's educational mission and its student-development intervention plans and activities.

Figure 4. A Staircase Approach to Planning ISGs.

Determining the Final Structure

16. Evaluate and Revise the Plan
15. Identify Referral Resources
14. Prepare Materials and
    Alternative Activities
13. Establish Formative and Summative
    Evaluation Procedures

Designing and Analyzing Exercises

12. Specify Performance and
    Process Objectives
11. Determine Sequence of Exercises
10. Develop Preferred Exercises

Evaluating Variables

9. Analyze Group Composition
8. Analyze Leader Competencies
7. Review Types of Learning Experiences
6. Adopt a Learning Model
5. Consider Design Parameters

Developing Goals

4. Write Goal Statements
3. Determine Priorities
2. Conduct Needs Assessment
1. Set Philosophical Guidelines

The model for conceptualizing ISGs described in Chapter One and the related professional literature (including Hurst and Jacobsen, 1985) summarized in Chapter Three, when added to the overall mission statement, provide the needed theoretical structure and empirical support for setting the specific guidelines that will direct the planning of the ISG. In fact, the developmental domains can serve as a conceptual framework for the identification and assessment of student needs.

Conduct Needs Assessment. The second step in the ISG planning process, assessing student needs, is not as simple as novice ISG planners are inclined to believe. It is, however, an essential action that, if bypassed or given short shrift, will lessen the capacity of leaders to accomplish their educational purposes through ISGs. A properly designed and implemented needs assessment answers these questions: What are the desired outcomes? And is an ISG an appropriate and desirable approach to use to achieve these outcomes?

The term *need* has been assigned several meanings as program leaders have struggled to come to grips with desired improvements in program development. Most commonly in education a need is the discrepancy between what is and what is desired. For our purposes, *need* refers to the discrepancy between a desired level of student performance (knowledge, attitude, skill) and a perceived or measured level of current performance.

Roger Kaufman (cited in Witkin, 1984) defines a needs assessment as a formal analysis that documents the gaps between current results and desired results (the gaps in outcomes), arranges the gaps (needs) in order of priority, and selects the needs to be fulfilled. The process is basically one of collecting data and converting them into decisions. Witkin (1984) holds that a needs assessment should be an essential part of a continuous cycle of program planning, implementation, and evaluation for the purpose of making decisions about priorities. Further, she points to the importance of keeping the needs assessment within context. The design of a comprehensive needs assessment should take into consideration the nature of the institution, its special characteristics, and its resources. More than anything else, a needs assessment should be considered a decision-making tool, enabling prospective ISG leaders to identify appropriate topics, set priorities, and allocate resources. According to Witkin (1984), there are two basic types of needs assessments: primary, which focus on the needs of service receivers, and secondary, which focus on the needs of the organization or the service providers.

Unfortunately, in higher education secondary needs assessments are predominantly employed, with general institutional needs rather than specific learner or program needs being assessed. Too often the purpose for undertaking a needs assessment is to assist in broad planning for the institution, particularly to obtain consensus on goals or on the allocation of resources, rather than to identify and analyze the specific needs of students. For example, a campus administration and faculty may be faced with deciding whether to retain a quarter system or to switch to a semester system. To gain information important to the decision, it is common to initiate a needs assessment focused on the system, on the needs of the institution: Will the quarter or semester system be the more economical? Which system will match more closely the resources of the institution? Which system will enable the institution to manage its residence halls more efficiently? Which system is preferred by the administrators, by the faculty, by the students? A primary needs assessment would instead focus on the degree to which desired learning and growth outcomes are currently being met, and on the relative merits of each system in promoting desired outcomes. The type of needs assessment advocated here is a variation of the primary type normally employed in education to plan curriculum because an ISG is, in effect, an educational program; it can be considered an extracurricular activity offered to complement traditional curricular offerings.

Beane, Toepfer, and Alessi (1986) characterize curriculum planning as being ultimately concerned with the experiences of learners. Planning is a process of making decisions about the purposes of learning, the teaching/learning situations through which these purposes can be achieved, and whether the means and purposes selected are both preferred and effective. Essentially, the same decisions confront prospective ISG leaders. What student outcomes do the leaders want to achieve? How might they facilitate learning?

Unfortunately, an all-too-common approach to program planning begins with a well-intentioned student affairs practitioner's personal, subjective impression of student needs. Although sometimes accurate, this intuitive approach to needs assessment is limited by the acumen of the individual's perspective. Too often, programming built on assumed student needs results in an inefficient use of available resources; personnel and time are reserved for poorly attended functions.

Similar limitations apply to other approaches such as the great-white-knight approach, where programming decisions are made on the basis of untested fads and new directions that tend to appear with some regularity in student affairs work in the saddlebags of would-be saviors on charging white horses (for example, encounter groups and sensitivity training were fads of the 1960s and early 1970s).

Other approaches employ a modified needs-assessment technique that is more of a wants survey than a true needs assessment. Programming emanating from periodic reviews of students' expressed wants and wishes tends to be a helter-skelter smorgasbord of unrelated interventions. Although it is important to stay attuned to students' wants, they are an insufficient data base for effective decision making about programs.

Yet another ill-advised (quasi–needs-assessment) system of program development is the crisis-intervention approach, where leaders react to student problems after they occur. At times some form of crisis intervention is necessary; after all even the best prevention programs cannot be 100 percent effective. Although crises do reflect manifest needs, to wait for them to occur before responding is a remedial approach that is costly in terms of both resources and students' development.

There are both positive and negative aspects to developing programming on the basis of staff interests, the what-do-we-want-to-do-this-year approach to needs assessment. This effort has the attractive advantage of making effective use of current staff talents and competencies but is not advantageous when those competencies are unrelated or only indirectly related to the needs of students. For example, a staff member may have recently attended a series of workshops on hypnosis or on the latest marriage-and-family-therapy techniques and strategies, but unless these newly acquired or refined competencies are relevant to student needs, ISGs related to these particular topics should be given low priority.

Another approach to needs assessment, which often receives an enthusiastic reception from staffs that are stretched routinely in a myriad of directions, is the clearinghouse approach. Decisions about programs are based on the availability of attractive intervention or testing packages from the various educational publishing houses, sometimes presented in the guise of intervention panaceas. Current examples include the many computer programs offered for comprehensive career development and for learning-style and study-skills improvement. The point here is not to disparage available support materials or packages, but rather to note that the proper use of the latest materials and resources is important. The acquisition of resources should never precede the systematic and objective identification of needs.

A final needs-assessment strategy that deserves an extended review is the empirical approach, which incorporates the advantages of the previously mentioned approaches and discards or controls for the disadvantages. Presented in Table 4, the empirical approach to needs assessment is somewhat complex and comprehensive. To a professional thinking about conducting an ISG, the approach may at first seem overwhelming; but it should be remembered that the model is an ideal—it describes the total assessment experience. Obviously, time and resources may limit a single staff member's ability to complete the entire needs-assessment procedure. However, each part of the process should be heeded in order to ensure quality control. In many instances, especially on smaller campuses, the practitioner desirous of providing ISGs will wish to collaborate with campus colleagues and allow considerable time for implementing the comprehensive needs-assessment procedures. The prob-

Table 4. Empirical Approach to Needs Assessment.

Sources	Information	Strategies
Students	Academic performance Involvement in extracurricular activities and events Special concerns Interests/values/needs self-reports Disciplinary actions	Grade records Activities records Survey and appraisal inventories Periodic interviews Discipline records
Faculty members	Observations of behavior Perceptions of student performance	Consultation Interviews and anecdotes
Employers	Performance assessment Perceived institutional needs	Surveys Interviews
Parents	Student achievement of developmental tasks	Surveys and interviews
Student affairs administrators	Student demographic data Institutional goals	Institutional records Reports and interviews
Profession	Process and outcome data Developmental tasks and stages	Professional literature Research reports
Alumni	Placement data Retrospective perceptions	Questionnaires and surveys Interviews

ability that programming based on an empirical approach to needs assessment will achieve success is sufficient cause to warrant such a commitment of time and resources.

Although there is no single correct method for conducting a needs assessment, several general principles apply to the process. First, a comprehensive needs assessment requires an institutional commitment to invest time, personnel, and financial resources. Because no single individual can be expected to conduct a bias-free needs assessment of sufficient magnitude and quality to produce useful results, a small committee or task force can be charged with the responsibility of developing a needs-assessment report that could then be used campuswide to guide planning efforts. When an institutional commitment is not forthcoming, a prospective ISG leader need not abandon the task. Rather, the leader may simply need to limit the breadth and depth of the assessment, and remain especially alert to the tendency to restrict the focus of the assessment to one's own perspective.

Second, because the questions asked in a needs assessment tend to determine the answers (Dagley and Hartley, 1976), a needs assessment should begin with a comprehensive conception of the desired outcomes. A model of student development provides the conceptual breadth and depth necessary to prevent the establishment of narrow parameters based on the personal biases or special interests of those representing a particular program area.

A third general rule is that it is important to select and develop appropriate instruments to elicit the desired responses. It is not enough to jot down a few questions, call them a questionnaire, and insert it in student mailboxes. Once desired outcomes have been specified, it is important to study the available appraisal instruments that may have special utility for assessing each identified outcome area. A comprehensive needs assessment consists of a variety of instruments, including some well-validated tests and inventories as well as other instruments of lesser validity. General surveys of students, faculty, parents, or alumni, if used, should complement measures that have more validity and reliability than surveys. Such surveys should demonstrate a sensitivity to the relative knowledge and status of those being assessed, and be free of jargon and esoteric items. It is also important to allow respondents some freedom to express thoughts about unanticipated areas of need. Examples of commercially available intruments that are appropriate for needs assessments designed to enhance student development include the Student Developmental Task and Lifestyle Inventory (Winston, Miller, and Prince, 1987), the Career Development Inventory (Super and others, 1981), the Defining Issues Test (Rest, 1974), and the Learning Styles Inventory (Kolb, 1976).

Developmental-assessment interviews with students also

have special utility in needs assessments, particularly if such interviews are conducted as a regular part of the student affairs program. The data can be translated into needs information somewhat routinely. Similar interviews with a sample of faculty on a regular basis can also provide important perspectives on the needs of students.

Fourth, effective needs assessments are characterized by inclusion in the sample of all appropriate subgroups on campus. Witkin (1984) refers to such groups as service providers (faculty, administrators, student affairs personnel), service receivers (students), and stakeholders (parents, alumni, employers, community members, professionals). A special effort should be made to include students of nontraditional ages, commuters, minorities, honors students, international students, transfers, athletes, and graduate and professional school students.

Fifth, a system for weighting responses should be established in order to ensure that all data receive fair attention. Some data, by their nature, may carry special significance even if few tallied responses are forthcoming. For example, if a small number of students indicate that they need help in dealing with alcoholism, drug or alcohol abuse, or loneliness and alienation, or in obtaining information regarding sexually transmitted diseases, then special weight may be appropriately applied to such responses. The assumption is that some need areas will be responded to differently by students because of their degree of readiness, the perceived personal threat or specificity of the items in question, or community considerations. For example, students are less likely to admit needs in such personal areas as sexual experience or personal feelings of inadequacy, loneliness, or alienation, because of the perceived personal threat of the items. Similarly, the specificity of an item affects the response rate: Concisely worded items elicit higher response rates than abstract or more general items. The norms of a campus or a community can also have an impact on response rates. Environmental pressure can be identified through a needs assessment. On some campuses, needs of a religious nature are perceived as more important than academic or leisure needs. Therefore, the number of responses should carry weighted significance. Likewise, some groups of students are larger than others, thereby creating a need to weight the response of the smaller subgroups accordingly.

To summarize, needs assessments require (1) an institutional commitment of time, personnel, and financial resources; (2) a guiding conceptual framework; (3) a well-considered selection of valid instruments; (4) a representative sampling procedure; and (5) a weighted analysis system for summarizing the data.

Determine Priorities. A student-development program should not make all outcomes priorities for any given year. Consensus decisions need to be reached regarding specific target areas. A comprehensive needs assessment will yield a working set of data from which priorities can be identified. The conceptual framework that guided the design of the needs assessment can also be used to place responses to the instruments into categories. Some instruments are directly related to identified areas of need. For example, Rest's Defining Issues Test (1974) measures students' moral and ethical development. Other surveys and questionnaires provide less definitive information about a wide variety of issues and concerns. The task is to bring together into meaningful order information from disparate sources.

A prospective ISG leader will likely find the most onerous task to be the weighting of responses from various subgroups of students. As previously noted, this step is necessary to ensure that the needs assessment is both representative and comprehensive. It is often helpful to set criterion levels for certain areas. Prior to the actual assessment, for example, a leader may wish to specify a certain percentage response, such as 20 percent of the sample, that will satisfactorily demonstrate a significant need in a selected area such as intimacy, loneliness, or drug abuse, where students' responses might be restricted because of a reluctance to admit to that type of need. Similarly, a readiness factor is associated with certain areas of need. For instance, one would normally expect college seniors to express greater concern about their employability and immediate career plans and to demonstrate higher levels of cognitive development than would freshmen.

Write Goal Statements. Once priorities have been determined for the year, appropriate goals can be identified. The translation of outcomes into goal statements is a relatively straightforward step. Consistency in language is important; therefore, it is desirable to adopt a single style for wording goal statements. Goals should define student behaviors, attitudes, or characteristics but not the processes designed to facilitate goal achievement. For example, assume these three needs-based outcomes: self-validation and interpersonal effectiveness; cognitive, ethical, and moral development; and career development and autonomy. A goal statement for the first area might read: "Students will improve their communication skills." A goal for the second area might read: "Students will use an assessment of their ethical and moral reasoning to make them aware of their critical-thinking skills and to increase their capacity to make effective decisions regarding ethical and moral dilemmas." And, for the last area a goal statement might read: "Students will assume personal responsibility for their own career planning." It will be relatively simple, at a later point, to convert a set of these goal statements to measurable performance objectives. It is not necessary to have a direct one-to-one relationship between needs statements and goal statements. Goal statements are viewed as being general in form and developmental in nature and tend to be more inclusive than either needs statements or performance objectives.

The first phase of planning is complete once goal statements are written for each of the needs-based outcome areas. The set of statements becomes not only a principal component of the needs-assessment report but also a blueprint to guide the identification and development of strategies. An ISG may be designed to facilitate goal achievement in a single area or in overlapping areas. At this point, the attention of planners shifts to an in-depth exploration of process considerations.

Evaluating Variables

The second phase of the planning model, evaluating variables, is an intermediate stage comprising actions that enable planners to determine important design parameters and to decide on a general approach that is appropriate for the specific types of learning experiences to be included in the ISG.

Consider Design Parameters. Important decisions are required before a prospective ISG leader can begin to select or develop structured experiences and activities for the group. Several variables determine natural design parameters for the ISG. Cooper and Harrison (1976) identify learning objectives and the learning environment as a set of initial variables that must be considered when designing experiential group activities. The three principal components of the environment are the participants, group structure, and training staff, all of which need to be considered in relation to the learning objectives prior to the preparation of the group design. Pfeiffer and Jones (1973, p. 177) describe the following major design parameters: (1) the contract (mutual expectations of sponsors, leaders, and participants), (2) the length and timing of the event, (3) the location and physical facilities, (4) the familiarity of participants with each other, (5) the previous experiences of members in training groups, (6) the availability of qualified staff, (7) the number of participants, (8) the accessibility of materials and other aids, and (9) the opportunity for follow-through. For example, some types of learning experiences may be too lengthy or may be too poorly suited to the available physical facilities. Some activities may not work because of the number of individuals expected to participate, because prospective group members are not familiar with each other or with ISGs in general, or because the prospective group is homogeneous.

Adopt a Learning Model. Once the relevant parameters are identified, ISG planners must select and adopt a learning model to serve as a conceptual framework for the group's design. *Learning by doing* is a common phrase in today's educational circles, reminiscent of the teachings of Dewey (1916), the great American educator and philosopher. His pragmatic philosophy viewed education as life itself; we learn best by doing, by living, and by reflecting on the consequences of our actions. The object of this approach to education was and is to enable and to encourage individuals to learn from experience. There is a similar valuing of experience in ISGs. "A small group can be an informal laboratory to supplement learning-through-experience in everyday life" (Luft, 1984, p. 41). Use of the experiential approach to learning in small groups evolved from the early work of Lewin (1951), the exceptional social psychologist, and of his students and colleagues. Lewin's basic assumption was that one could learn a great deal by observing and reflecting on one's own experience in small-group situations.

The nature of experience-based learning in small groups has changed and matured since the time of the mid 1940s when Lewin and his colleagues at the National Training Laboratories (in Bethel, Maine) nourished the movement through their pioneering innovations and scholarly research studies of small-group behavior. The basic premise remains that learning moves from perceptions of experiences through conceptualizations developed out of the experiences to generalizations about the learnings to be integrated into daily behavior (Wellman, 1967). The experiential-learning process is described succinctly by Johnson and Johnson (1975, p. 7) as consisting of a four-stage cycle in which "(1) concrete, personal experiences are followed by (2) observation of, reflection upon, and examination of one's experiences, which leads to (3) the formulation of abstract concepts and generalizations, which leads to (4) hypotheses to be tested in future action in future experiences."

Pfeiffer and Jones (1973) add a middle step; they postulate the stages as (1) experiencing, (2) publishing, (3) processing, (4) generalizing, and (5) applying. The second and third stages, publishing and processing, are referred to as sharing and interpreting by Gaw (1979), in an attempt to further clarify and characterize their main objectives. Sharing thoughts and feelings about an experience with others in a supportive atmosphere is one of the key contributions of the small group to the experiential-learning process.

Two characteristics distinguish the experiential model and make it a preferred model for ISGs. First, the experiential model is an active approach to learning. It is built on the assumption that the responsibility for learning is the learner's. Second, because experience is not necessarily an effective or consistent teacher by itself, the experiential model emphasizes both the internalization and the processing of the experience. The small-group format enables the members to generalize insights to new actions and challenges because it encourages open reflections and the sharing of insights and feelings about experiences. Self-disclosure and feedback are essential components of the experiential-learning model. Although it is not a requirement, experiential learning usually occurs in a group setting, such as an ISG. In such a setting, learning is retained for a greater length of time than in a more traditional and passive teaching-centered learning format. Major growth processes at work in the experiential group include self-assessment, self-disclosure, feedback, risk taking, and consensual validation (Jones, 1982). These processes are potent forces for shaping and influencing learning and behavior change.

The phenomenal growth of the small-group approach to helping leveled off in the early 1970s. The dramatic increase in the number of experience-based learning groups "generated a variety of excesses and absurdities. Instant insight and overnight changes, joy and fulfillment, panaceas of all kinds were offered" Luft (1984, p. 48). Today, experiential-learning approaches are quite common and the games, novel techniques, and strategies no longer create the same enchanting aura or produce the same results. "The bandwagon days are over, and with them the grab bag of gimmicks that represented effective 'training design' in an earlier era" (Napier and Gershenfeld, 1983, p. 10). Today, prospective group members are sophisticated in their knowledge of groups and experiential training. Consequently, they want to know how a group fits their objectives and how they will learn what they need to know directly from the group experience (Napier and Gershenfeld, 1983, p. 9).

Review Types of Learning Experiences. Once information regarding major design parameters and the nature of experience-based learning is obtained, the next step in planning ISGs is to review the professional literature on learning experiences. This review is essential to determine which alternative processes have relevance and a good possibility of achieving the goals of the particular ISG under consideration.

ISG planners have available several types of proven learning experiences. Some have broad utility and applicability, while others are specific and limited. Pfeiffer and Jones (1975b) identify and describe several kinds of structured learning exercises. These exercises include:

- Icebreakers and group formation activities
- Interpersonal and intergroup communication
- Leadership development
- Group problem solving
- Competition and cooperation
- Organizational development
- Dyadic and similar subgroupings
- Group process and functioning
- Personal awareness and feedback

Selection of the specific types of experiential exercises to be used in an ISG is based on the ISG's goals as well as on the developmental level and characteristics of the participants. Other critical variables are the three components of the model for conceptualizing ISGs: intervention focus, process focus, and developmental domains (see Chapter One for a comprehensive description of the model). Activity selection should be preceded by an analysis of the nature of the intervention—whether it is remediation, prevention, or enhancement. Similarly, it is imperative to base selections on the primary process focus: intrapersonal development, interpersonal development, information, or skill development. Finally, it is critical to make learning experiences available that are most appropriate for the specific developmental domains: physical, social, emotional, academic, career, intellectual, esthetic, and moral.

Typically, ISGs are initially introduced through the use of icebreakers or get-acquainted activities. The term *icebreaker* suggests the general anxiety that usually exists at the beginning of most small groups, anxiety that is often characterized by coolness or aloofness. Icebreakers are designed to relieve that anxiety through relatively safe, nonthreatening, and enjoyable exchanges. Unfortunately, icebreakers are more often abused than used properly. The tendency for group leaders, from classroom teachers to Boy Scout troop leaders to other leaders in a multitude of settings, is to use opening exercises solely for entertainment purposes. The professional challenge is for the leader to set the stage for goal accomplishment while introducing the participants to the group with a fun activity. No single type of exercise works best as an icebreaker, but a general rule is to select or adopt an activity that has either direct relevance to the announced goals of the ISG or significance for the types of interactions that will be required of the participants during the ISG. Also, the activity ought to initiate introductions and contribute to group formation. If the group is relatively large, twelve members or more, the activity may best start in dyads, triads, or other small subgroups. The complexity of the activity selected should depend on the sophistication and maturity of the participants. The opening activity ought not to mislead the participants about either the group's processes or desired outcomes. For example, it is not uncommon for a traditional lecture class to open with self-disclosing and interactive activities, leading students to expect opportunities for open interchange in forthcoming sessions, when, in fact, the instructor has no desire for student/teacher give-and-take during the remainder of the course and actively discourages it.

Structured learning exercises other than the icebreaking kind may contain interchangeable components. Although they often differ more in process than in content, there are a number of identifiable differences in the specific content of activities. For example, an ISG to help residence directors develop specific communication skills will contain exercises that differ from those used in a career-exploration group for freshmen. But many exercises may be equally effective in stimulating goal achievement in seemingly disparate areas, depending on the degree to which the leader helps the participants process their experiences.

Napier and Gershenfeld (1983, p. 100) describe several types of learning activities that can be used in small groups: fantasy, creative physical activity and exercise, games, simulations, role playing, competition, microactivities (modified life experiences), lectures, taping (using video and audio recorders to provide rich opportunities for supervisory review and feedback), and fish-bowling (modeling and demonstration activities in which the leader or a small group does role play while a larger group observes). The dimensions of structured experiences offered by Pfeiffer and Jones (1976, p. 4) are in some instances similar to Napier and Gershenfeld's: constructions (exercises involving the building or creating of structures or models), data collection, discussions, experiments, fantasy, games, graphics (depictions of ideas and models in graphs or symbolic displays as stimuli), instruments (tests, inventories, questionnaires, or surveys used to collect data), media (print, video, audio, and so forth), models (presentations of thoughts and data), movement and nonverbal communication, role plays, simulations, subgroups, and tasks (dilemmas, problems to be solved). Most processes selected or developed for ISGs are variations of the basic types of learning experiences included in these two lists.

The content and structure of experiential-learning exercises are critical components of any ISG plan and deserve a great deal of attention during the designing phase. The natural progression in planning is to proceed from the general to the specific. Once the general content and structures have been identified, then decisions can be made about a specific design for the ISG. Again, it is important to note that ISG planners need to select learning experiences on the basis of a knowledge of the participants as well as of the ISG's intervention focus, process focus, and targeted developmental domains.

Analyze Leader Competencies. Designing and leading ISGs requires considerable skill and knowledge. To begin, a planner needs to be skilled in identifying clear and distinct learning goals, not only for an ISG as a whole but also for each structured experience within the ISG. The clarity of the learning goals sets the tone for the ISG. Experiential learning is most effective when the learning goals are distinct and understood and valued by the group members. An equally important skill is helping group members clarify their own learning goals. These goals should be easy to relate to life outside the group. Transfer of learning from the group experience to real situations ought to be direct and clear. This transfer process depends to a large extent on the original establishment of specific goals. Without clear goals and opportunities for transfer of learning, the worth of the experiential learning is limited.

A second set of designing competencies, often referred to as strategic planning competencies, requires a conceptual understanding of experiential learning and a sensitivity to the possible responses of group members. Planners need knowledge about participants and learning activities that is sufficient to enable them to imagine the likely response of group members to specific ISG activities. It is helpful during the planning process to be able to predict the type of impact a structured experience may have on group members. To do so effectively, one needs considerable direct or vicarious experience with the student populations from which group members will be drawn in addition to a comprehensive understanding of structured group activities.

In addition to being sensitive to the probable types of participant response, effective design anticipates the possible cumulative effects of the combined ISG components. A planner needs to be able to conceptualize how the effects of one structured activity may influence the next. Thus, a third set of required competencies involves sequencing and the ability to design and organize alternative learning activities. Sequencing is discussed in detail later in this chapter.

In sum, competencies required in the design of ISGs include the ability to establish and clarify goals, to plan strategically, and to incorporate appropriate sequencing and pacing. These competencies have similarities to the kinds of qualities and abilities one would expect in a leader of ISGs; however, one could conceivably be a competent planner but a not-so-competent leader.

A critical concern at this point in the planning process is to analyze the competencies required to conduct each experiential activity under consideration for inclusion in the ISG. Thus, another step in this stage of developing an ISG design is to review in depth the kind of leadership competencies associated with the various activities. The learning experiences selected should require competencies of the ISG leader that are present or can be developed prior to the conduct of the group. Some activities inherently require more ability on the part of the leader than others. Examples might be such activities as role reversals, where an experienced leader may be more able than a nonexperienced leader to take participants through the important stages of warming up, empathizing, and acting out the imagined experiences of others. Naive leaders may assume that role reversal is easy, but it requires an advanced level of leadership and interpersonal skill. So too do exercises that may elicit defensive responses because of perceived personal threat, for participants are likely to consciously or unconsciously attempt to block the successful completion of the activity.

This discussion underscores the importance of conceptualizing the ways in which leadership skills need to be incorporated in the ISG design. For example, if a planner were to make effective use of Pearson's (1981) two-cluster (teaching and group management) model of basic leadership skills, then both direct and indirect opportunities for such leader behaviors to occur would be included in the design. This particular model follows the traditional descriptions of task and maintenance roles in groups (Benne and Sheats, 1948). (Leadership skills and strategies are discussed in detail in Chapter Six.)

Analyze Group Composition. Composition of the group is an important criterion in the design of a small-group experience. In fact, the makeup of the group is one of the two most influential contributors to group effectiveness, the other being the leader. In ISG planning, it is helpful to know the extent to which individual group members are likely to be familiar with one another and with the principles of the experiential-learning approach. Some learning activities depend heavily on the novelty of the experience, while others require that group members be unfamiliar with each other. If the group is relatively intact, such as a fraternity or a resident-assistant staff, then the design will need to account for prior acquaintanceship and previously established power and status relationships. For example, if an ISG on leadership development is being conducted with an interfraternity council on a small campus, then the ISG design will need to account for the already-existing subdivisions. Another important factor to know about when designing small-group activities is the general psychological maturity of the group involved. As described in detail in Chapter Six, the level of group maturity influences not only the selection of learning experiences but also the structure and style of group leadership.

One of the greatest risks ISG planners can take when designing groups is to plan learning experiences on the basis of untested assumptions about the group members (Napier and Gershenfeld, 1983). To lower that risk, the planner's task is to learn as much as possible about prospective group members prior to the start of the group in order to design the structured experiences around the needs and goals of that particular group. A comprehensive needs assessment and a clear public statement of the group's purpose and planned procedure will provide some perspective on volunteer group members' goals. Pregroup interviews or questionnaires administered to prospective members can also clarify goals and expectations. However, when such practices are possible, the ISG leader should build a brief interchange into the introduction that will test assumptions about members.

Key questions to ask during the screening interview or during the initial sessions (or both) include these (adapted from Napier and Gershenfeld, 1983, p. 89):

- What are the group goals, as understood by both the leader and the members?
- What activities and processes do the participants expect?

- What do participants want to happen during the group, and what do they fear may happen?
- How familiar are group members with each other? Do subgroups exist? Is there any unfinished business that may affect the group?
- What is the small-group experience of the group (the individual and collective sophistication as to group interaction)?
- What are the known facilitators and inhibitors that may influence group interaction and goal achievement?

Designing and Analyzing Exercises

Develop Preferred Exercises. Group leaders develop preferences over the years for particular types of activities or leadership behaviors and often fail to ascertain whether those preferences fit the needs and goals of a particular group. For example, popular myths that have negatively influenced the design of groups for some time include the myth of going with the flow, the mythical leader role referred to as the charismatic guru, and the myth of nondirection (Napier and Gershenfeld, 1983). Although there may be some virtue in going with the flow of the group as it continually changes needs and patterns, allowing a group to change direction on whim to deal with every problem or encounter risks the group's running amok. Such an approach may cause a group to lose sight of its long-term goal under the guise of leader flexibility. Likewise, if the leader's personal needs include appearing omniscient or magical, then the leader may consciously or unconsciously design exercises that reinforce an aura of mystery or superior insight. A better design, one which would more likely foster independent rather than dependent behavior, would be to include learning experiences with explicitly described purposes and rationales so that participants have the opportunity to understand clearly the potential contributions of all group members to growth and change.

The myth that has possibly had more impact on groups than any other is the one calling for a nondirective leadership style in which the leader is expected to allow the group to evolve. The myth of nondirection, in actuality a misnomer because this approach is essentially quite directive and manipulative, limits the value of the leader to the ISG participants because of the narrowly defined set of acceptable leader behaviors—typically reflection, clarification, support, and an avoidance of (even a disdain for) overt leadership or task achievement. This position of power, unshared by other group members, is based on an unnatural style of interaction. Just as a group cannot exist without structure, a leader cannot not be a leader; a leaderless group leader acts under the guise of superior psychological insight as well as the protection of narrowly defined roles. The challenge is to assiduously and creatively plan for a group on the basis of diagnosed needs and clearly identified goals and yet hold the design of the group tentative enough to alter it on the spot if changing needs so require.

The process of developing ISG activities is usually a combination of efforts to adopt, adapt, and create appropriate exercises. A leader should start by identifying appropriate types of activities available in the literature or in clinical practice and analyzing the fit between these known activities and the goals of the ISG. If the match is good, then the leader needs to review the appropriateness of the planned activity for the specific stage of the group's development and ascertain whether the proposed activity fits the pace and sequence needs of the ISG. If for some reason the activity does not fulfill these criteria, then the leader may need to specifically adapt it so that it fits the process or goals more precisely. If additional activities are required, the leader will need to conceive an exercise that will meet the unique characteristics of the planned ISG. The development process should start and end with a consideration of the ISG goals, for in the planning process, goals remain the energizers and the natural limitations. The activities the leader creates, like those adopted or adapted, should not only fit the ISG goals, but also be appropriate for the group's stage of development. Finally, the pace and sequence of the activity developed will again need to be analyzed to ensure that it will be effective.

The creation of a plan for an ISG ultimately requires

decisions regarding specific design variables. The decision-making process is both a science and an art, requiring planners to lay out sequential steps uniquely appropriate to the needs and goals of a particular ISG. It is doubtful, after all, whether a single design can be equally appropriate or effective for more than one group. Therefore, it is important to avoid the tendency to return to a favorite exercise, a comfortable group activity, or a packaged selection of gimmicks and games. The uniqueness of each group warrants an individual design. "The issues surrounding goals are at the heart of any effective design. The more specific the goal, the more explicit can be the design, with a better chance of meeting the needs of the population" (Napier and Gershenfeld, 1983, p. 97). Clear, distinct goals provide the planner with the initial impetus to make effective choices regarding preferred activities.

Determine Sequence of Exercises. Once preferred exercises have been identified, it is important to consider their sequence. The significance of sequencing for planning purposes is evident from an examination of the stages of small-group life as described by many theorists and practitioners (Bennis and Shepard, 1956; Bonney, 1974; Tuckman, 1965; Tuckman and Jensen, 1977; Yalom, 1985). To be effective, both the nature and sequence of planned structured experiences need to reflect the evolution and maturation of the small group.

Zimpfer (1986) points to the importance of knowing about group developmental stages when planning the sequence of activities. Certain types of activities are appropriate for inclusion during the early stages of group development, while others are appropriate later in the life of the group. Factors in the development of a group that must be considered when deciding on the sequence of structured activities include the amount of familiarity among members, the degree of group cohesion, and the amount of self-disclosure, risk taking, and openness required of group members in a particular activity. A group will reach a plateau at an early stage if all the structured experiences are icebreakers or if the exercises are randomly ordered. Likewise, the intensity of the group experience should build naturally and not be forced. For example, a self-disclosure exercise that requires a high degree of trust would not be appropriate in the beginning session. Too much self-disclosure at too deep a level in the beginning session of a group creates a level of intensity that many students perceive as excessive and frightening. The intensity of the experience must be appropriate for the stage of group development. (See Chapter Two.)

The general pace of the group's movement is an important variable to consider in planning the sequence of activities. Often, a group needs a change of pace after a deep and intense interchange, or possibly even a short break, because fatigue can become a negative factor in small-group work. At other times, a stimulating group-involvement exercise may be needed to provide balance for a detailed lecture or subgroup activities. The challenge in planning is to avoid a pattern that results in the extremes of boredom/hyperactivity, chaos/compulsive order, or dependent/independent action. Balancing the cognitive and affective content and style of interaction is yet another important factor in the sequencing of small-group structured experiences.

Napier and Gershenfeld (1983) suggest several ways of changing the pace of the group to maintain a creative tension in the learning environment:

- Vary the time allocated or required for specific activities; a shorter time period than is comfortably required to complete the activity can serve as a stimulus to increase the concentration of the members.
- Vary the physical setting; periodic rearrangement can add to the vitality of the physical space.
- Vary the presentation format; short lectures, information charts, and films can increase or hold the group's attention.
- Vary the amount of risk taking required of participants (keeping the intensity level parallel with the group's level of development).
- Vary the type and style of interaction; activities can be ordered so that dyads, task forces, or large groups can be used for team building, problem solving, or group processing in productive ways.

Variety is critical to successful sequencing of experiential-learning activities. The types of learning experiences described previously need to be varied to enhance member involvement and group development. For example, a learning experience involving competition between two subgroups might best be followed by a full-group activity in order not to run the risk of creating subgroup loyalties. For similar reasons, a cooperation activity may be arranged to follow a competition exercise.

Pfeiffer and Jones (1973) exemplify the principle of sequencing activities on the basis of the flow of participants' learning needs in their design for a personal-growth group: (1) getting acquainted, (2) closing expectation gaps, (3) legitimizing risk taking, (4) learning about feedback, (5) developing an awareness of process, (6) integrating conceptual models, (7) experimenting with self-expression, (8) planning back-home application, and (9) assisting reentry. "This general sequence does not imply a rigid structure. It is simply an attempt to highlight the needs of participants to develop an ability to talk with each other, to learn how to make sense out of the interaction which is occurring, and to heighten the development of ways that participants can use the experience in their everyday existence" (p. 190).

Sequencing is important because it helps leaders decide on techniques and strategies. Effective leaders consistently demonstrate situational responsiveness—that is, their responses are appropriate to the group's stage of development; they stay with the group and assist it to the next level. To respond appropriately, small-group leaders need to possess and be able to use alternative skills depending on the particular stage of the group's development. Of these skills, one of the most essential is the facilitation of processing—the participants' collective exploration, examination, and evaluation of group experiences. Such facilitation usually takes the form of effective questioning. The following stage-dependent questions are typical of the kinds of inquiries used by leaders in experiential-learning groups to help participants process their experiences (adapted from Gaw, 1979, pp. 150–151):

Experiencing stage

  What's going on now?

  How do you feel about that?

  Would you like to try?

Sharing stage

  What are your thoughts about what just happened?

  Did anyone else have a similar experience?

  Who might like to share their thoughts?

Interpreting stage

  What might that say to you?

  What special meaning might that have for you?

  How do you make sense out of that?

Generalizing stage

  Do you notice any patterns with other experiences?

  What does that say about us?

  Can you generalize from that?

Applying stage

  How might you build on your new self-awareness?

  How might you sabotage that plan?

Gill and Barry (1982) identify a similar set of stage-based responses, using a three-stage model (formation, awareness, and action). In their model, questions eliciting disclosures and observations are appropriate during the group's formation, whereas the awareness stage requires identification of conflict, the labeling of group behavior, and the encouragement of mutual feedback. The action stage, according to Gill and Barry, primarily involves identification of needs and exploration of alternatives and consequences.

Regardless of the specific nature of a structured experience, effective leaders use their processing skills to help group members explore what they learned from that particular experience. Therefore, it is important for planners of ISGs to bear in mind the time required for processing. Some activities require extensive time to experience and process, thereby eliminating them from consideration for use in a brief one- or two-hour session. The importance of allowing sufficient time for processing experiences cannot be overemphasized; processing empowers experiential learning. Similarly, sequencing helps leaders understand the value of transition discussions, which are possibly more vital to achieving the group's goals than are the design and implementation of group activities.

In sum, sequence is an important factor in ISG planning and design. Not only is sequence important in planning the structured experience, it is also important in planning the use of stage-based process-facilitation and transitional skills.

Specify Performance and Process Objectives. Once preferred learning exercises have been identified, tentatively placed in proper sequence, and conceptually integrated with stage-based processing techniques and strategies, specific objectives can be developed for each exercise or activity. The main task is to analyze the potential contributions of planned exercises to the attainment of previously established goals.

The ISG leader should have a comprehensive set of performance and process objectives when this phase of the planning process is complete. Performance objectives specify the behaviors expected of participants as a result of their small-group experiences, whereas process objectives specify how the group leader is expected to guide participants during each exercise. Performance objectives identify the specific attitudes, characteristics, abilities, and knowledge desired of group members. The process objectives include the name of the activity, any special instructions for conducting it, and suggestions to the leader for facilitating the processing of the experience.

The following performance and process objectives are provided as examples. The previously identified goal was: "Participants will assume personal responsibility for their own career planning." The performance objectives are:

1. Students will be able to describe personal reactions to formal and informal work experiences.
2. Students will be able to identify decisions they have made in the past that have influenced present educational and career plans.

3. Students will be able to describe a strategy for exploring employment possibilities in a field of interest.

The process objectives are:

1. Best/worst work experiences: Conduct an icebreaker activity in which each participant is asked to share with another person a favorite and least favorite formal or informal job (Daane, 1972). Processing should focus on the individual's own contributions to the work experiences, particularly what was learned about personal interests and abilities.
2. Worker interview: Ask participants to share results of an interview with a worker in a field of general interest; the interview was to be conducted between ISG sessions (Bolles, 1985). Processing should focus on what was learned about the field, the worker, and the interview process.
3. Family occupational tree: Participants are asked to record a family tree of occupational roles and then share with the group the family's vocational heritage. Processing should focus on the solicitation of feelings and thoughts relative to the expectations, myths, and decision-making approaches apparent in the family tree.
4. Commitment to personal plan: Participants share their next step(s) in career exploration or preparation. The processing of this exercise should concentrate on soliciting feedback from other group members concerning possible facilitators and inhibitors involved in the planned step(s). Attention should be given to helping participants discuss ways in which they might apply what they have learned in the small group to their personal career-exploration activities.

Determining the Final Structure

Establish Formative and Summative Evaluation Procedures. Systematic plans for both formative and summative evaluation need to be developed for use during the life of the group. Comprehensive attention is paid to evaluation in Chapter Five, so little detail is presented here. Nonetheless, it is important to note the special and unique value of formative evaluation for ISG planning purposes.

Formative evaluation can be implemented in both informal and formal ways. For example, informal observations of the quality and quantity of participation can provide the leader with subjective evidence about the impact of the various structured experiences on individual members. Such data can then be used to assess whether any design changes need to be made. Unanticipated events or reactions might cause a leader to avoid one type of activity or expand another. For example, if a particular small group seems to fare best in activities that call for interaction in dyads or triads, then the leader may wish to alter the design to accommodate the participants. Other groups may seem to want to remain as a whole in all activities, so similar modifications in the design could be made. Formative evaluation used in this way may modify the ISG structure. Likewise, informal observations can give the leader an understanding of the group's current stage of development.

Formative evaluation should incorporate a formal assessment of the leader's conduct while presenting exercises and processing group members' experiences. When coleaders are involved, this evaluative process can be handled fairly easily. When only one leader is involved, then objectively evaluating how well one has done in presenting, processing, or leading is difficult. Questionnaires that participants complete have minimal value, primarily because of distortions caused by the halo effect. Consultation with colleagues can add some useful data, but a videotape or audiotape of a session has the greatest usefulness. (The inhibitory effects of the taping on the group members or the leaders can be offset with careful directions and assurances.)

Formative evaluation is usually focused more on the leader's behavior than on that of the group members; however, the focus is certainly not exclusive. Any data that can shed light on how well the group is progressing are useful as long as their collection does not disrupt or negatively influence the experience for the participants. A common strategy is to ask each member, in a go-round fashion, for reactions to a particular exercise or to the session as a whole. This kind of processing gives the participants an opportunity to be heard and also provides the leader with important evaluative data. At this point, with the formulative evaluation plans set, the ISG begins to take its final shape.

Summative measures can be designed to assess the specific performance objectives. Effective outcome evaluation begins with measurable objectives. The wording of each performance objective should be specific enough to enable accurate measurement. Specificity comes from the distinctness with which attitude, skill, and knowledge objectives are identified. For instance, as a summative measure in the previous career-development example, the students could be asked to write down their future career-exploration plans, including possible internal and external facilitators and inhibitors. The degree of outcome achievement could be determined from an analysis of the written plans. Several other strategies could add to the reliability of this summative data. For example, informal interviews with randomly selected group members at the end of a session or at the end of the group could be used to obtain additional evaluative data. In fact, the leader might schedule exit interviews with each group member to obtain formal ratings. Additionally, it is becoming increasingly common for group leaders to use follow-up interviews or questionnaires or both several months after the conclusion of the group to assess long-term effects.

Prepare Materials and Alternative Activities. At this stage in the planning process, the ISG leader needs to prepare the materials and resources required to conduct the structured learning experiences that are to be included in the ISG. For example, exercises may require handouts, props, instructional aids, or special physical space. The importance of attending to such details is most noticeable when such attention is absent. Although it is impossible to predict everything, an effective planner considers as many details and contingencies as possible. Design "includes a laborious process of identifying where the crisis might lie, where the unanticipated might occur, and where the errors await, all of which demand the development of instant contingencies" (Napier and Gershenfeld, 1983, p. 79). An effective leader considers logical eventualities and makes general plans for pursuing alternate strategies or options. The best strategy is to have several backup structured exercises or alternate ways of processing experiences.

Identify Referral Resources. An ISG plan must include details regarding backup contingencies that may be required in emergencies or in response to unanticipated events and reactions. On occasion, group members who seemed to be appropriate prospects for the ISG prove to be unable to benefit psychologically from the group. Also, members sometimes become unduly upset by a structured experience during the group and require special attention. A leader should always have referral resources identified and available before initiating the group, for some structured learning experiences may cause unexpected harm (Cooper, 1977). A leader should also be prepared to personally provide one-to-one counseling should it become necessary or refer group members to another professional helper for such counseling.

Evaluate and Revise the Plan. The final step in the planning process is to conduct a systematic review of the complete ISG plan. The task here is to retrace each step of the plan and carefully examine the content and process from a systems perspective. It is especially important to view the finished plan as a comprehensive whole in which the various activities are intricately intertwined. Every proposed activity should be assessed on the basis of its capacity to enhance the ISG's goals. If an activity is included that does not meet this test, then it should be altered or eliminated.

In addition to making this kind of thorough review, a prospective ISG leader should ask a colleague familiar with group work to review the plan and to make recommendations. Yet another review strategy is to study published group designs and attempt to evaluate the particular design by comparison,

Table 5. Guidelines for Reviewing the ISG Design.

Things to do	Things to avoid
1. Check clarity and specificity of goals	1. Unclear instructions
2. Check timing and sequence of learning experiences	2. Untested assumptions about group
3. Check variety and pacing of learning experiences	3. Excessive reliance on a single type of structured experience
4. Anticipate points in design where changes are most likely to be necessary	4. Inadequate diagnosis of group's needs and development
5. Include contingency structured experiences (extra activities)	5. Lack of attention to processing and application of experiences
6. Include instructions and short lectures	6. Neglect of time parameters
7. Check facilitation of applications (transfer of learning)	7. Overwhelming participants with intensity and pace
8. Allow time for processing of structured experiences	8. Absence of evaluative review (formative and summative)
9. Review design with colleague	9. Plans that do not give closure opportunities
10. Consider ethical guidelines for group leaders	10. Unclear and nonspecific goals

being careful to maintain a clear focus on the proposed ISG's goals and purposes.

Table 5 highlights some of the do's and don't's for reviewing the ISG plan. The list of suggestions is also a concise synthesis of key steps of the planning process. Successful planning requires knowledge and skill. Experience in conducting ISGs will enhance the ability to plan future groups if the leader evaluates and reflects on the results.

Summary

A staircase approach to planning ISGs includes four critical steps: developing goals, evaluating variables, designing and analyzing exercises, and determining final structure. Each step can contribute significantly to the design of an effective ISG. Climbers, like ISG planners, make slow progress if their eyes are glued on only the next step, yet may fall if they do not attend to the task at hand. A key to success is to know both the proposed destination, which emphasizes the critical importance of clear, needs-based goals, and effective strategies for getting there. Leaders acknowledge the importance of planning through a commitment of sufficient time and resources.

Outline of an ISG Manual

In this chapter we briefly discussed how to determine whether an ISG is the most appropriate vehicle for producing the desired student-development outcomes. Then, we provided a detailed description of the critical steps in planning an ISG. In closing, we present an outline that can be used as a guide to construct an ISG leader's manual. Completion of all the steps suggested in the comprehensive planning process will provide the data required for the development of such a manual.

An effective plan for an ISG must be well thought out before beginning the group and should be written in some detail. Each session (and activity within each session) should be described in sufficient detail that an outside observer could replicate it without needing to ask questions of the planner. The significance of the manual is not so much in its content as in its development. To a certain extent, the process is more important than the product. The development of such a comprehensive document requires the leaders to put considerable time and thought into the conceptualization and organization of the ISG, thereby contributing significantly to the eventual success of the experience.

Each ISG should have such an accompanying manual. Readers are cautioned, however, that manuals do not travel well. It is generally not a good idea to attempt to conduct an ISG based on a manual developed by others — especially at other campuses. A knowledge of the institution and the intended clientele for the ISG is critical. A planner may get valuable ideas for exercises or approaches from others' work, but seldom can a complete ISG be transported from campus to campus. We also suggest that readers not attempt to develop manuals until they have read the entire book. A sample manual for an ISG intended for freshmen who want to become involved in the college experience is provided at the end of this book.

Although manuals need to be complete, it is not practical to record every consideration that led to adoption of various activities or exercise sequences. The sections of an ISG manual should include:

I. Title page
    Traditional elements to be included on a title page are a simple, descriptive yet appealing title for the ISG; the name of the sponsoring institution or sponsoring unit or program; the name(s) of the leader(s); the dates of the group; and possibly the location.

II. Table of contents
    A table of contents assists the leaders in locating materials or exercises quickly.

III. General overview
    This section contains the heart of the materials. It includes the following integral elements of the ISG:
    A. Evidence of the need for the group
       Why is the ISG needed on this campus at this time? This section should provide evidence from a variety of campus sources that there is a need for the group. The information ideally should be documented or backed up by research or needs-assessment data, but in any case a summary of available supporting information, from whatever sources available, should be presented. Specific points should be enumerated and briefly explained. The need for the ISG might be supported by observations, anecdotes, informal impressions, or general surveys, as long as the data emerge from the local campus.
    B. Professional literature support: theory and research
       A brief review of relevant theoretical and empirical support for the ISG should be presented in a narrative form. Although the literature search does not have to be exhaustive, the evidence supporting the need for the ISG should be clear and substantial. Particular attention

should be paid to providing a theoretical rationale for the group from the student-development literature. References ought to be included near the back of the manual.

C. Statement of goals

A list of goals for the ISG should identify performance outcomes: desired changes in awareness, understanding, observable behavior, or attitude. The list need not be exhaustive, merely representative of the major desired outcomes.

D. Group composition

This section of the manual should describe the desirable nature and composition of the group on several dimensions. Important questions to be answered, possibly during the selection or screening interviews, include: Who are the projected members? How familiar are the participants with each other, the leaders, and the topic? Is the group intact? Do members have a line-staff relationship? Is the group homogeneous or heterogeneous? What are the projected minimum and maximum sizes for the group? Will the group be open or closed to new members? This section should also include the kinds of questions to be asked in screening interviews, as well as information regarding other important variables in the selection and screening process. For example, it is appropriate to include comments about expectations, commitments required, fees, and other requirements that may affect voluntary membership. Criteria for screening potential members also need to be described.

E. Staffing and support

The intended leaders of the group should be identified, and brief summaries of their qualifications for leading the group should be presented. In this section, backup personnel and agencies should be identified. Who has been contacted to provide consultation should something go awry during a session? Who is prepared to help students who become overly emotional or disturbed as a result of participating in the ISG or who need additional assistance after completion of the ISG?

F. Advertising and promotion plan

How is the group to be promoted? How are students going to find out about it? The ISG manual should contain a detailed plan for promoting the group. If costs are involved, they should be estimated, and deadlines for submission of announcements, for example in the student newspaper, should be listed. One of the most common mistakes made in advertising student programs and services is failure to allow enough time between the initial announcement and the beginning date. Another frequent error is to use only one vehicle for advertising. The more avenues utilized in promoting the ISG the more likely a cross-section of students can be attracted.

G. Evaluation plans

Both formative and summative evaluation plans should be clearly described. Generally, it will be necessary to collect some preintervention data in order to determine whether any change took place over the course of the ISG. Formative evaluation plans should be spelled out in the plans for each individual session. (See Chapter Five for details about evaluations.)

IV. Outlines for individual sessions

A. Goals for the session

B. Step-by-step description of what is to take place during the session, with estimated time to allow for each activity. Each exercise to be used should be described in a consistent format, and lists of all needed materials and equipment should be included. The following format is suggested for describing exercises:

1. Goal(s)
2. Time required (minimum and maximum)
3. Physical facilities and arrangements required
4. Equipment and materials required
5. Step-by-step instructions
6. Suggestions, cautions, helpful hints
7. Processing guidelines

8. Variations (if any)
9. Suggested reading for background
10. Handouts or other materials required for the exercise

C. Formative evaluation guidelines for session
D. Homework

Deciding How to Evaluate the Group's Effectiveness

Evaluation is typically assumed to be a professional obligation for all those who design programs to encourage or enhance the education or personal development of college students (for example, see Council for the Advancement of Standards for Student Services/Development Programs, 1986, or American College Personnel Association, 1981). Often an evaluation is not done, or not done well, however, because it is an afterthought and is added on at the end of the workshop or program.

To be effective and useful evaluation must be carefully thought out; it is an essential part of the conceptualization and planning of successful ISGs. A leader should never go into a session without a plan and should always include in that plan an evaluation strategy. To do otherwise verges on lack of professionalism. For this reason we have chosen to include the chapter on evaluation here rather than at the end of the book, where such chapters traditionally reside.

What Is Evaluation?

After stating that evaluation is a professional responsibility in all student affairs programs, why is it necessary to talk about definitions? There is a general confusion in education about (1) what constitutes evaluation, (2) its relationship to research, (3) the conditions under which research and evaluation are generally conducted, (4) who should conduct evaluations, and (5) for what and for whom the results are intended.

Definitions. A number of definitions of evaluation have been proposed. For example, *evaluation* is (1) the collection and use of information to make decisions about an educational program (Cronbach, 1963); (2) the comparison of performance against standards (Provus, 1969); (3) the process for determining the degree to which objectives are realized or behaviors are changed (Tyler, 1949); (4) a process that produces information that important "audiences" want and need (Stake, 1975); (5) a process for delineating, obtaining, and providing useful information for judging among alternatives (Stufflebeam and others, 1971); (6) purposeful activities that have the objective of rendering judgments about the merit, or worth, of a program (Kuh, 1979). Each of these definitions points to important aspects or features of the evaluation process or product (or both) and suggests different foci or methodologies.

Evaluation Versus Research. Many practitioners eschew sound evaluation practices and procedures with the argument that evaluation is research and they do not have time to do research and still provide services and programs for students. Research is often equated with any procedure that produces data analyses more sophisticated than percentages. In reality evaluation and research share some features and have some differences. The primary distinction between the two is the purpose for which the activity is conducted. Evaluation's primary purpose is to judge the effect of the activity, often from many different perspectives and for a variety of audiences; research's primary purpose is to test hypotheses grounded in theory or to collect data that can shape the development of a theory. Some would say that researchers seek "truth," whereas evaluators seek to determine worth or practical benefits (Oetting, 1976; Worthen and Sanders, 1973). (Table 6 presents some of the major distinctions between research and evaluation and examples of activities often passed off as research or evaluation.)

Conducting Evaluations Under Less Than Ideal Conditions. As can be noted in Table 6, evaluation is generally less rigorous than research. In other words, evaluators cannot and must not allow the collection of data and maintenance of experimental conditions to interfere with the potential benefits of a program

Table 6. Research, Evaluation, and Pseudoevaluation/Research.

	Evaluation	Research	Pseudoevaluation/research
Purposes	Assess effects of intervention (Did it work?) Is this program more effective/ efficient than another approach? What is the cost/benefit ratio?	Test theory (Did result conform to the theory's prediction?) What mechanism is operating in Method A that can account for the difference between it and Method B? What explains the result?	No clear purpose. May confuse staff activity with goals. Makes no comparisons. Usually provides self-reported satisfaction data. Confuses participant satisfaction or lack of it with accomplishment or nonaccomplishment of goals.
Audience	Multiple (institutional decision makers, professional colleagues, students, ISG implementers)	Professional colleagues, researchers, and theoreticians	No one. Report is just filed away. ("We did an evaluation. It's here somewhere.")
Methods	Generally naturalistic and less rigorously controlled than in research	Controls are critical (sampling, assignment to groups, protection from outside influences).	No controls are attempted.
Setting	Relatively uncontrolled natural setting, but conditions are described thoroughly	Relatively controlled natural setting or laboratory with specific information about conditions to allow for replication	No controls and not enough information provided to allow others to attempt replication
Focus	Multiple variables and combinations of conditions	Limited number of variables under controlled or limited conditions	Shotgun approach. Reports anything that is "statistically significant" or any difference of at least 10 percent between groups or sessions.
Instrumentation	Best available given budget and time constraints	Best available	"Homemade," with no known reliability or validity

Sources: Based on Brown (1979), Guba and Lincoln (1981), Oetting (1976).

to participants or with the number of students served. For instance, credible research experiments in the social sciences usually require at least one control group. To obtain a comparison group, therefore, a researcher might divide volunteers for a structured group into two small groups. However, a practitioner who offered a structured group to students would generally accept into the group all who could be accommodated even though there remained no equivalent group for comparison purposes. Evaluators would be willing to compromise scientific rigor for practical benefits to the clientele. However, the practitioner, even though accommodating the larger group, still has an obligation to evaluate the ISG outcomes; the evaluation design must be one that does not require a separate control group, such as an interrupted-time-series design.

Who Conducts the Evaluation? Evaluations can be conducted by either internal or external evaluators. As Brown (1979) notes, there are advantages and disadvantages to both approaches. External evaluators—personnel who are not directly involved in the planning and implementation of the program—are more likely to be unbiased, and their evaluations are generally more credible to outside constituencies. The disadvantage of outside evaluators is that they generally have limited knowledge of the program; they need start-up time to learn about the program and can also miss important features and subtleties. Internal evaluators are generally more attuned to the salient features of the program and are less expensive to utilize than external evaluators—that is, there are usually no direct costs associated with an internal evaluator's services. Disadvantages of using an internal evaluator include less credibility to outside groups, less knowledge and experience in conducting evaluations, and greater potential for unintentional or unconscious biases to influence findings.

Often there is no choice of whether to use internal or external evaluators. On many campuses no student affairs unit is designed to conduct evaluations and no funds are available to contract for services. Thus, most professionals who conduct ISGs must also assume the responsibility to evaluate them. The remainder of this chapter assumes that the evaluation is conducted by those also responsible for planning and leading the ISG.

Audience. As noted in Table 6, evaluations are generally conducted for multiple audiences or stakeholders. For example, the effects of an ISG to teach resident assistants (RAs) interpersonal helping skills would be of interest to (1) the director of housing and those professional staff members who were involved in planning and leading the training, (2) the vice-president for student affairs, to whom the director of housing reports and who is involved in making decisions about allocations of resources within the student affairs division, and (3) the RAs themselves. Each of these stakeholders have different interests and needs that should be addressed in the evaluation.

The planners and leaders need information while the training is in progress to help them assess whether the processes and materials being used are producing the desired effects. They also need to know, once the ISG has been completed, whether the RAs have developed interpersonal helping skills that are better or more effective than those they had before.

The vice-president also will be interested in whether RAs developed communications skills but will likewise want to know the approximate costs of the program and whether new students are more satisfied with the residence-hall program as a whole or are better prepared to begin classes than they were when there was no helping-skills training program (or when a different approach to training was used).

The RAs will be interested in receiving feedback about their individual performances. Reporting the results of the ISG evaluation to the RAs can have the added benefit of emphasizing the importance placed on their acquiring and using the skills and of demonstrating that the data they provided for the evaluation were actually used. (If it was worth spending time to evaluate systematically, it must be important!)

Formative and Summative Evaluation

These different audiences obviously need different kinds of information and make different uses of it. Scriven (1967) proposes a fundamental distinction between formative and summative evaluations to assist in conceptualizing some of these differences.

Formative evaluation takes place during the time that the ISG is taking place. It is concerned with refining the implementation process in order to allow corrections or changes to be made when problems are identified. In other words, it provides data for making mid-course corrections when obstacles are spotted or when unforeseen or unplanned events occur. The audience for formative evaluation is those who have responsibility for leading the ISG and perhaps the ISG participants in an indirect way. Data collection is generally informal and utilizes methods such as informal observation, oral or written feedback from participants at the conclusion of exercises or sessions, participants' journals, or evaluations of homework assignments.

Summative evaluation concentrates on outcomes or changes in participant behaviors. Its purposes are to (1) judge the effects of the ISG; (2) determine its usefulness, merit, or worth; (3) conclude whether the ISG should be repeated or discontinued; and (4) ascertain the cost-effectiveness, the ratio of resources expended to results produced. Generally, data are collected at the conclusion of the ISG and are compared either to earlier data from the same people or to data from a comparable group or to previously determined norms. The standards for evaluation design and controls and for the reliability and validity of data-collection instruments or techniques are much higher for summative than for formative evaluation. Evaluation generally attempts to assess change over the period of the ISG using psychometrically valid and reliable instruments and methods. Other data may include structured or semistructured interviews or unobtrusive measures such as records and reports of incidents, costs or budget information, and systematic observation.

Stake (1976) proffers an analogy that makes the distinction between formative and summative evaluation clear: "When the cook tastes the soup it is formative evaluation, and when the guest tastes the soup it is summative" (p. 19). Many of the differences are illustrated in Table 7. It is important to use both kinds of evaluation. Quite often, as Brown (1979) notes, program

Table 7. Comparisons of Formative and Summative Evaluation of an ISG.

Concern	Formative	Summative
1. What decisions need to be made?	How to improve ISG or correct previous mistakes	Choosing between different ISGs or other interventions
2. What is the primary focus?	Monitoring ISG process (especially as compared to plan)	Outcomes: changes in behaviors, attitudes, or knowledge
3. What are the principal sources of data?	Informal observations, interviews, anecdotal information, informally observed group dynamics	Tests and inventories, records and reports, questionnaires, systematic observations, expert evaluators using standard rating scales (for example, with videotapes)
4. What is the evaluation design?	Naturalistic inquiry	Experimental or quasi-experimental
5. What types of analyses are used?	Qualitative methods	Quantitative methods
6. What type of report is made?	Informal, oral reports	Formal, written, and documented reports
7. What is the audience for the results?	ISG planners and leaders	Institutional decision makers and professional colleagues
8. What are the primary advantages?	Utility and practicality	Objectivity
9. What are the primary disadvantages?	Weak credibility for external reviewers	Less utility for helping improve ISG while it is in progress

Note: The distinctions between formative and summative evaluation in this table are in emphasis and should not be taken as sharply defined differences.
Source: Based on and adapted from Brown and Sanstead (1982, p. 60).

evaluation has been summative only, designed to demonstrate the usefulness of programs to outside agencies—often to the holder of the purse strings. Summative evaluation, however, seldom provides timely, useful information to the professionals responsible for making the program successful because its results are known only after the ISG has been completed.

Planning Formative Evaluations

Good evaluations do not happen by chance. Unless they are carefully planned and integrated into the ISG plan, it is unlikely that the results will be meaningful or in some cases that any data will even be collected. Professionals who intend to use ISGs should develop formative evaluation plans as they plan the ISG.

Once an ISG session is planned, exercises are created or selected, and the necessary materials are prepared, the designers should ask themselves a series of questions.

1. How will we know whether an exercise worked or accomplished its intended purpose?
2. What cues or clues will give us this evidence?
3. What indicators should be present to signal that the session is progressing as planned, or is in trouble?
4. Who is to assume responsibility for collecting and recording the needed data?

It is important to formulate specific areas or behaviors that will be evaluated in order not to allow the leaders' subjective evaluations (whether negative or positive) to unduly influence the appraisal. It is not uncommon for a leader to obtain a misconception about the effects of a session based on interaction with only one or two participants, thereby deflecting attention from the group as a whole.

For example, for Session 3 (outlined in Table 8) of an ISG for teaching orientation leaders helping skills, a formative evaluation plan may be as shown in Table 9. The ISG leaders (Joanne and Roger) would meet in the interval between Sessions 3 and 4 to share their formative evaluation data and to prepare for the next session. Any problems identified in the evaluation can be discussed; modifications in the plan for Session 4 can also be made if the formative evaluation data suggest that the previously planned activities need revision.

A systematic formative evaluation plan is most feasible when ISGs have coleaders. Generally, a single leader finds it

Table 8. Sample Session 3 of an ISG to Train Orientation Leaders
to Use Interpersonal Helping Skills.

Goals: Students will

1. Practice active listening and giving interchangeable responses
2. Observe the effect of appropriate and inappropriate responses

Activities

1. Ask trainees to report their experiences using interchangeable responses with fellow students. Discuss what seems to work best and why,
   what did not seem to work and why. Discuss problems with written
   homework assignment. Discuss each item in group. (twenty-five minutes)
2. Continue "You feel. . . because. . ." exercise from Session 2. Do the
   exercise at least twice. (twenty minutes)
3. Practice exercise in responding. (thirty minutes)
4. In total group discuss practice exercise in responding. Trainers answer
   questions about what to do when. . . (fifteen minutes)
5. Brief lecture on determining what the helpee is seeking and whether a
   peer can appropriately provide what is desired. Explain the differences
   between developmental and remedial concerns (Handout 5). Identify
   when referrals are appropriate (Handout 6). (thirty minutes)
6. Homework assignment: Instruct students to practice using interchangeable responses with fellow students. Record experiences in journal.
   Complete interchangeable responses worksheet (Handout 7).

---

difficult or impossible to focus on leading and facilitating activities while also attending to the group dynamics and the
nonverbal behaviors of all the individuals. Formative evaluation
with a single leader is possible in a systematic way only if the
sessions are recorded, preferably on videotape. The formative
evaluation can then be accomplished by viewing the tape. Although this procedure has the advantage of allowing for repeated observation, logistics and time constraints generally do
not make it practical on an on-going basis outside of counseling
centers and similarly equipped facilities.

Planning Summative Evaluations

Six steps should be taken in constructing an adequate
summative evaluation of an ISG. As proposed by Fink and
Kosecoff (1978), they are (1) formulating credible evaluation
questions, (2) constructing evaluation designs, (3) planning data

Table 9. Sample Formative Evaluation Worksheet for Session 3, Orientation Leaders' ISG.

Activity or goal	Cues of success	Observations	Who is responsible for data
1. Students practice using interchangeable responses	Each student can accurately use the formula response ("You feel... because...")	Students appear sincere and make honest effort	Roger attend to: Mike Larry Mary Sally Juan Jacqueline Joanne attend to: Hank Joan Mary Beth Bubba Sue John (Make notes immediately after session.)
2. Students observe the effect of appropriate and inappropriate responses	Students express an interest in learning the differences between what worked and what did not Disagreements are aired and attended to	How many students make contributions to discussion?	Joanne: keep record of who made contributions Joanne: keep count of how many contributions were made
3. Overall nonverbals	Attending to activity	Voluntary contributions	Roger: make notes immediately after session

collections, (4) collecting data, (5) planning and performing analyses of the data, and (6) reporting the results of the evaluation.

Formulating Credible Questions. Before beginning to formulate evaluation questions, ISG planners and leaders must first ask for whom the evaluation is being conducted. In other words, who is the audience? This is a political question that is only indirectly related to the purpose for which the ISG is conceived, but it cannot be ignored. Once the intended audiences have been identified, then evaluators must ask: What will each audience accept as evidence or value as an indicator of outcomes?

For instance, student affairs practitioners might value highly evidence that students were able to form more meaningful relationships with their peers as a result of having participated in an ISG. Although forming meaningful relationships is rather difficult to measure accurately and describe objectively, it fits within the value system and philosophical orientation of many student affairs professionals. However, a college president may not be impressed by the fact that a small number of students formed meaningful relationships as measured by an obscure psychological instrument. That president, however, may pay serious attention to data indicating that students who participated in the ISG expressed greater satisfaction with their college experience as a result or became more involved in classroom discussions or caused less damage in residence halls than if they had not participated.

For illustrative purposes an ISG for training orientation leaders in helping skills will be used. Session 3 of a hypothetical four-session ISG (total of eight hours of training) is outlined in Table 8. After considerable analysis and discussion the ISG evaluators decide that there are three important audiences for their summative evaluation—the staff of the Department of New Student Programs, the vice-president for student affairs, and the orientation leaders (OLs). Each of these audiences has somewhat different interests in the outcomes of the ISG. The staff would be most interested in whether OLs were able to use the skills and techniques taught with new students during orientation. The vice-president would be most interested in the overall performance of OLs, how well the orientation program functioned, and the approximate costs. The OLs would be most interested in learning whether they were effectively using the skills they were being taught and how well they were performing as OLs.

The evaluation questions for each of these audiences might be as follows.

For the *staff:* Are OLs able to demonstrate use of the helping-skills communication model taught in the ISG? Specifically, (1) can the OLs state why advice giving is usually an ineffective helping strategy? (2) Can the OLs describe the concept of the "sounding board" and give reasons why it is a useful technique for helping? (3) Can OLs accurately identify the affective and content components of communication? (4) Can OLs accurately paraphrase the content of messages? (5) Can OLs identify common nonverbal messages often encountered in helping relationships? (6) Can OLs demonstrate effective helping through implementation of the model taught in the ISG? In other words, were the goals specified by the ISG planners reached?

For the *administrators:* Were the helping skills of OLs evaluated differently this year than last by new students? Was the overall evaluation of OLs more positive than last year's? Were there fewer orientation dropouts — that is, new students who left before completion of the orientation session — than last year? Were the costs of training kept within reasonable limits?

For the *OLs:* How much did I change in using the helping skills I was taught over the course of the ISG? How effective were OLs in using the "new" communication skills?

The next step after identifying possible evaluation questions is to identify what activities in the ISG relate to each question and what evidence, both for and against, might be presented. Table 10 provides an example of two evaluation questions and possible activities and evidence for answering the questions.

After identifying the questions various audiences would

Table 10. Sample Evaluation Questions.

Evaluation question	Activities related to question	Possible evidence for answering the question
1. Do OLs understand the concept of being a "sounding board"?	a. Lecture by trainers b. Handout materials c. Demonstrations by trainers of application of the concept	a. Responses on a test about the concept b. Observations of OLs during exercises c. Performance on videotape demonstrating use of the model
2. Can OLs apply the helping-skills model?	a. Exercises b. Assigned homework c. Feedback from trainers about performance	a. Performance in group exercises b. Performance on videotape demonstration

like answered, the evaluators must carefully determine whether the questions can be logically and practically addressed. In other words, are the questions legitimate and are there resources and time available to answer them? The questions for the staff, which relate directly to the stated goals of the ISG, are obviously legitimate and should be addressed. The questions for administrators largely go well beyond the scope of the ISG. One would be quite naive to think that eight hours of training in the use of a helping-skills model could dramatically change or affect the whole orientation program. Although the vice-president's concerns are appropriate, the ISG leaders should resist the temptation of suggesting that this intervention alone would produce such effects. Because many factors, besides the performance of OLs, influence the relative success of the orientation program, one must be careful to specify clearly what the ISG's goals are and what effects it can reasonably produce. Only the question concerning new students' perceptions of the OLs' helping skills could logically be expected to be affected by this ISG alone.

The OLs' concerns are legitimate. They should receive individual (private) feedback about their performance during the ISG and some general information about the performance of the group. The attention to evaluation can itself emphasize the importance placed on use of the skills taught. An indication that data related to their use of the skills will be collected during the orientation program could also encourage OLs to be aware of how they interact with new students.

Constructing Designs. A number of important issues must be addressed when constructing a summative evaluation design: (1) sampling, (2) blocking, (3) randomization, (4) pretesting, (5) establishment of comparison or control groups, and (6) follow-up (Oetting and Cole, 1978).

The purpose of *sampling* is to help account for characteristics in the population that might have an effect on the outcomes of participation in an ISG so that the findings can be generalized to a group larger than the one that actually participated. Sampling can be contrasted with a census, which involves gathering data from or about all elements of the population (Anderson, Ball, Murphy, and Associates, 1975). To obtain a sample, the evaluator must determine who composes the intended population—that is, to whom would one expect the results to generalize? Because participants in ISGs are generally volunteers who have identified the ISG as addressing a personal need or concern, the population to whom ISG outcomes might generalize would be students with similarly identified needs or concerns, not necessarily all students within a college.

Two approaches are commonly taken to sampling. Most commonly, evaluators divide volunteers who expressed an interest in participating in an ISG into two groups. One group participates in the ISG immediately; the other is placed on a waiting list to participate at a later date. The waiting-list students then become the comparison group for those who are participating in the ISG. The other approach is to identify variables thought to be related significantly to the needs and concerns of students who volunteered to participate. The evaluator collects data related to the variables of interest from a large number of students and then selects the comparison group from those students who are similar to those participating in the ISG. For example, students who indicate they are undecided about their intended academic major and feel anxious about making the decision might be similar to students who decide to participate in an ISG designed to assist in the decision-making process.

When ISG participants have characteristics (such as age, class standing, gender, ethnicity, expressed needs or concerns, socioeconomic background, or place of residence — commuter or on-campus resident) that potentially could affect how they respond to or deal with the ISG as a whole or any given exercise or activity, it is important to assure through *blocking* that both the ISG participants and the comparison group are similar in regard to these characteristics. The evaluator is attempting to eliminate or minimize potential interaction effects — that is, those that could occur if students with different characteristics responded or reacted to ISG activities in different ways.

An approach often taken to blocking comparison and treatment groups is the use of matched pairs. Matching involves pairing individuals on the salient characteristic(s) and then randomly assigning one in the pair to the ISG and the other to the comparison group. Suppose that one wished to evaluate the effect of an ISG on assertiveness training. Experience conducting such ISGs might suggest several characteristics of participants that could affect how they respond to the planned activities — for example, gender and socioeconomic background. Data about each potential participant's gender and socioeconomic background would be collected. Then participants would be paired on those two characteristics, with one person in the pair assigned to the ISG and the other assigned to the waiting list or to some other kind of treatment activity — a counseling group, for example. The summative evaluation would then be able to attribute any observed differences between the two groups to the treatment. If an alternative treatment were employed, such as a counseling group or another ISG with different approach or content, then it would be possible to compare alternative approaches to dealing with a particular set of student needs and concerns. It is generally preferable that, in addition to blocking, adjustments to account for differences in the groups be made statistically (see Anderson, Ball, Murphy, and Associates, 1975, p. 240; and Rubin, 1972).

Using some technique for randomly assigning participants is highly desirable in creating summative evaluations. (See Law and Fowle, 1979, for descriptions of a number of relatively simple random-sampling procedures.) *Randomization*, which simply means that each individual in a population has an equal chance of being selected, helps the evaluator protect against the unconscious biases of those making selections and also disrupts any relationship between naturally existing factors and treatment effects, even if those involved do not know what these factors are (Oetting and Cole, 1978). For example, if selections are made on the basis of interviews, the leaders may unconsciously choose students for participation in the ISG whom they already know or with whom they are able to establish rapport. This bias, however, would prevent evaluators from determining whether it was the personal affinity between students and leaders that accounted for changes in student attitudes or behaviors or whether it was the content and process of the ISG.

One of the questions that often haunts evaluators is whether the comparison group and the treatment group were already different from each other before treatment began. One means of dealing with this question is to *pretest* both groups before beginning the ISG. This approach is not without its problems however. As Campbell and Stanley (1966) point out, pretesting may affect how students respond to the ISG, making it difficult to ascertain what effects, if any, the ISG produced. Given the restrictions that exist in most settings in which ISGs are likely to be used however, it is seldom possible to exercise sufficient controls to justify using a design that does not employ pretesting. Oetting and Cole (1978, p. 39) note that "the additional information and the increase in statistical power make pretesting a potent tool when the reliability and validity of the outcome measures are likely to be limited and when random assignment to groups may be difficult," which is usually the case with ISGs.

To make decisions about continuation, termination, or expansion of programs, data from *comparison groups* are needed. Three kinds of control groups are (1) pseudo-treatment (placebo) groups, (2) alternative treatment groups, or (3) waiting-list (control) groups (Oetting and Cole, 1978).

In a pseudo-treatment group students participate in activities that have high face validity (that is, they appear to participants to be related to the announced subject of the group) but which previous experience has shown to be ineffective or not to affect the outcomes being measured. This approach is highly recommended in evaluating ISGs because it is important to assess the effects of the ISG content and process apart from effects that accrue from simply being a part of a congenial group experience.

Using an alternative treatment group is appropriate when the decisions to be made are not whether students will receive a treatment—for example, in a classroom setting or a mandatory training program—but which approach produces the most desirable results. By randomly assigning students to different ISGs, it is possible to compare different approaches.

A waiting-list group is appropriate when the question is Does the ISG produce the specified outcomes any better than providing no attention? Such a group is not, however, the same as a no-treatment control group because students assigned to such a group are under an implicit injunction not to change until the ISG has had its chance to influence them. The use of waiting-list or pseudo-treatment groups raises an important ethical consideration. The American College Personnel Association (1981, p. 187) states: "When control groups are used, care is exercised to assure that they are not deprived of services to which they are entitled." As important as evaluation is to professional practice, the welfare of students should be paramount. Great care must be taken to assure that students receive help and assistance as quickly and expeditiously as possible by assigning evaluation a lower priority when the two conflict.

Follow-up is important in evaluation designs in order to determine whether changes observed at the conclusion of an ISG persist. Considerable research, as well as personal experience, suggests that many people tend to return to old behavior patterns or attitudes after initial changes in behavior—witness the typical cycle of weight loss and gain experienced by many people. Probably the most significant evidence of the success of an ISG is behavior change that persists weeks and months after the ISG is over.

There are many books about evaluation designs; consequently, we will only briefly describe five common designs and identify some of the major advantages and disadvantages of each. For detailed information the following sources are recommended: Campbell and Stanley (1966), Law and Fowle (1979), Fink and Kosecoff (1978), and Isaac and Michael (1971). (The designs are described in Table 11.)

Design 1 provides the maximum amount of controls, which in turn allows for the greatest amount of generalizability about the results. Its power as a design comes from taking into consideration individual differences at the beginning of the ISG through blocking and from the elimination of complications of treatment effects through random assignment. The comparison group may be either a waiting-list group or a pseudo-treatment group. A variation of this design is to assign students randomly to the two groups without blocking. The major limitation of this alternative is that individual characteristics of participants (such as gender or ethnicity) are unaccounted for, and therefore the evaluator will not know whether the characteristics of the students produced some unique interaction effect.

Design 2 is weaker than Design 1 or its variation but is still an acceptable design, especially if there is little reason to believe that individual characteristics are likely to interact with the treatment. The acceptability of this design, however, rests heavily on random assignment. Because it is not possible to ascertain whether the two groups were different from each other in the beginning, scrupulous attention to unbiased selection procedures is critical. This design is particularly appropriate when it is thought that pretesting could sensitize participants or interact with the treatment effects.

Design 3 covers occasions when there is no population from which to draw a comparison group. For example, an ISG might be used to teach leadership skills to a group of students selected to serve as student union board chairpersons for the following year. There are no similar students from whom to

Table 11. Evaluation Designs.

Design 1
**Two groups (with blocking and random assignment):
Pretest and posttest data collections**

Conditions	Pretest	Treatment	Posttest
Blocking and random assignment	C_1	T	C_2
Blocking and random assignment	C_3	T_o or T_x	C_4

Design 2
**Two groups (with random assignment):
Posttest only data collection**

Conditions	Pretest	Treatment	Posttest
Random assignment	None	T	C_1
Random assignment	None	T_o or T_x	C_2

Design 3
Interrupted time series

Conditions	Pretest	Treatment	Posttest
None	C_1, C_2	T	C_3, C_4

Design 4
**Two preexisting groups:
Pretest and posttest data collections**

Conditions	Pretest	Treatment	Posttest
Already established group	C_1	T	C_2
Already established group	C_3	T_o or T_x	C_4

Design 5
**Two preexisting groups:
Posttest only data collection**

Conditions	Pretest	Treatment	Posttest
Already established group	None	T	C_1
Already established group	None	T_o or T_x	C_2

Note: C = data collection (with subscript numbers identifying data collection events), T = ISG (treatment), T_o = pseudo-treatment, T_x = waiting-list group (or no treatment).

draw a comparison group because the chairpersons were already selected prior to the training, and at least theoretically they possessed desired characteristics not possessed by the unselected applicants. This design uses students as their own controls. Repeated data collections allow evaluators to establish a baseline measurement and then to observe the effect the treatment produces. For example, suppose an evaluator wants to determine the effect on students of a four-week ISG taking place in the middle of the term. Data would be collected at the beginning of the term, at the beginning of the ISG, on completion of the ISG, and at the end of the term. This procedure would allow the evaluator to estimate where the students began in regard to the variables measured, how they changed immediately after completion of the ISG, and whether the behavior or attitude changes persisted a few weeks after completion of the ISG. No fixed number of data collections is specified for this design, but usually at least three are required. (See Campbell and Stanley, 1966, and Anderson, Ball, Murphy, and Associates, 1975, for detailed discussions of time-series designs.)

Design 4 is similar to Design 1. It, however, lacks the power of that design because it has no mechanism for taking into account potential differences between the groups at the beginning, such as self-selection, level of motivation, acquiescence, and demographic variables (Hanson and Lenning, 1979). This design would be useful if one wanted to compare two different ways of teaching a particular skill during in-service education for resident assistants. The ISG would be offered to the paraprofessional staff in one residence area, and the comparison group would be the staff in another living area. As much as possible, the evaluator would attempt to assure that the groups were comparable on obvious variables; for example, one staff would not be all women while the other were all men, or one staff would not be all seniors while the other were all sophomores.

Design 5 is similar to Design 2 in that it lacks both random assignment and blocking. Therefore, initial differences in the groups will not be detected, weakening the conclusions an evaluator can draw about the effects of the ISG. Because of the likelihood that any two preexisting groups will differ from each other in important ways, it is difficult, if not impossible, to detect behavior changes of the limited magnitude likely to result from an ISG using this design. Because of these limitations, this design is the least desirable of those described, but it is preferable to not using any comparison group in the evaluation. When it is necessary to use a preexisting group, it is highly recommended that Design 4 be used in preference to Design 5.

Planning Data Collections. The most frequent problem encountered in evaluating ISGs and similar programs has been identifying measurement instruments or techniques that can accurately reflect changes in the behaviors or attitudes that the ISG is designed to affect. In regard to measurement, four common mistakes plague ISG evaluations:

1. Evaluators often do not measure the relevant variables. Oetting (1976) relates an example of a graduate student who was designing an evaluation of a training program for the paraprofessional staff of a crisis center. The goal of the training program was to help participants develop skills for interviewing highly emotional people. The student proposed measuring changes in self/ideal-self discrepancy and locus of control. Possibly a training program could affect these variables, and they are also of some theoretical interest; however, the proposed measures would not provide the data needed to determine whether participants improved their interviewing skills and would, therefore, not provide the information needed for an adequate summative evaluation. The evaluator must keep the purposes of the ISG in mind at all times when constructing the evaluation plan. If the data collected do not relate directly to the ISG's goals, then the data do not contribute to evaluation (although they may produce interesting and useful information for research projects).

2. ISG evaluators often equate satisfaction with behavior change or success of the ISG. Asking participants how satisfied they were with the experience — "Would you recommend it to your friends?" — is a relevant question about the process used in the ISG but seldom is directly related to whether the goals of the ISG were accomplished unless entertainment was a goal. It is generally important that students appreciate what the ISG lead-

ers are attempting to do and that they perceive the activities in a favorable, receptive manner in order for the ISG to affect them. It is possible, however, for everyone to have a good time, especially if there are fun group exercises, without affecting students' attitudes or behaviors in any significant ways.

3. Evaluators often assume that participants in an ISG can accurately assess their own behavior and will (can) honestly report reactions or changes through unsophisticated questionnaires. Many hastily constructed questionnaires are subject to a variety of biases, especially social desirability and demand characteristics. It is difficult to write objective items that do not have an obvious "right" or "preferred" response. Students who have been participants in an ISG know its intended purpose and are likely to report changes in behavior or attitudes because such change has been expected and was even advertised before the group began. On many occasions students may be unable to compare objectively their current behavior with that at the beginning of the ISG; frequently, only after a period of time can students reflect back and recognize what changes occurred.

4. The tendency is either to use commercially available instruments simply because they are available and possess known psychometric properties or to create "homemade" questionnaires that are of dubious, or at best unknown, quality and precision. Many well-known instruments for measuring personality, career-development, or other developmental dimensions are valid, reliable instruments for assessing a student's status or level but are not sensitive enough to detect the relatively slight behavior or attitude changes that can reasonably be expected to result from participation in an ISG that is only several sessions long.

Another measure frequently used because it is convenient and easily understood is grade point average (GPA). It is well documented that GPA is influenced by a multitude of factors, such as aptitude, prior academic preparation, motivation to achieve, course difficulty, and instructor attitudes and teaching style. Even an ISG of exceptional power designed to improve study skills and habits is unlikely to influence GPA more than about 10 percent in the short run. Although in relative terms that may reflect major, even radical, changes in individual students' behaviors, it is not likely to be reflected as a significant change in the group's overall GPA.

Mines (1985) suggests that evaluators focus on "microdevelopmental changes," which he defines as "skills or behaviors that represent varying degrees of mastery of a given stage or task. Microdevelopmental changes are assumed to occur in smaller time periods than global stage changes" (p. 101). For example, if an evaluator wants to assess changes in the intellectual development of students over the period of an ISG, the evaluator should identify specific skills needed for more complex reasoning (for example, devising better alternatives than "right" and "wrong" for solving a specific personal problem or dilemma). Mines also cautions the evaluator to use for assessment purposes the same content that was used in the intervention both to maintain face validity and to recognize the fact that skills learned may not be generalizable but are limited to the content area of the ISG.

Three basic approaches can be used to collect data for assessing behaviors, attitudes, perceptions, and cognitive processes: a production format, a preference format, and a comprehension format (Mines, 1985).

The *production format* requires the student to produce a product that illustrates the level of skill or development under investigation. This product is typically elicited through interviews, written essays, systematic observations, or role-playing. The Reflective Judgment Interview (Kitchener and King, 1981) is an example of the use of a semistructured interview to measure intellectual development. The students are asked through a series of probes to explain their reasoning in response to a series of standardized dilemmas. For Knefelkamp (1974) and Widick's (1975) Measurement of Intellectual Development, students write short essays explaining their reasoning in solving a series of dilemmas. A somewhat similar approach is taken by the Measure of Epistemological Reflection (Taylor, 1983; Baxter Magolda and Porterfield, 1985), in which students respond to six open-ended questions about their classroom experiences and preferred ways of learning. All these approaches require extensive training of judges in order to evaluate the responses; in addition the Reflective Judgment Interview requires that the interviews be tape-recorded and then transcribed before being judged. Because these approaches measure not radical or rapid change but intellectual development in stages, they are not generally appropriate for evaluating short-term interventions such as most ISGs. A product approach that is both feasible and effective for many ISGs that are designed to teach a skill, however, is role-playing, in which the student is expected to demonstrate mastery of the skills taught. For example, an ISG devoted to teaching interpersonal helping skills or social skills could easily include videotaping the participants in role-playing situations; the participants' performance could then later be judged.

The *preference and comprehension formats* are usually objectively scored and are done with pencil and paper. Students are required to select from among alternatives—for example, Rest's (1979) Defining Issues Test—or to indicate a preference through use of a Likert-type, yes/no, or true/false response—for example, Winston, Miller, and Prince's (1987) Student Developmental Task and Lifestyle Inventory, Super and others' (1981) Career Development Inventory, or Jackson and Hood's (1986) Iowa Developing Autonomy Inventory. With these approaches the evaluator cannot ascertain why students responded as they did but must infer the underlying condition or process. In addition, there is the traditional difficulty of relying on self-reports, the accuracy of which depends on the level of the student's self-awareness and self-understanding, accuracy of recall, candor, and honesty. These approaches have the advantage, however, of being much less time-consuming and easier to administer and score than production approaches.

Collecting Data. ISG planners need to build time for collecting data into the ISG plan. When evaluation is added after the ISG is planned, there is seldom sufficient time for participants to complete questionnaires or to provide data in other ways. As a consequence, the data that are collected are unreliable, even if the instruments have high reliability and validity, because the students were too rushed to provide thoughtful information or they saw the process as unimportant and not worthy of careful attention.

Those collecting data need to make sure that ISG participants understand why the data are being collected, how they are to be used, and what protection is provided the participants and the data they produce. (It is preferable that students complete a formal statement of informed consent in most cases.) Most institutions have a committee to review proposals for research on human subjects. To assure adequate protection of participants, ISG leaders should submit their evaluation plans for review before executing them.

Planning and Performing Statistical Analyses. As they are constructing the evaluation plan, evaluators should have a clear picture of which statistical procedures they intend to use. The level of measurement of the instruments determines which statistical tests are appropriate or even possible. It is important to plan the statistical analyses in advance to ensure that all the information needed is collected in a form that will allow the desired analyses. If the ISG planners are inexperienced in statistical design and analysis, they should consult experts on their campus during the planning phase of the ISG. It should always be kept in mind that no statistical test can compensate for data of poor quality. Remember the slogan of the computer operators: GIGO — garbage in, garbage out.

Reports. Previously in this chapter we recommended a careful analysis of the audiences for whom evaluations are conducted. Different report formats should be utilized to match the needs or interests of different audiences. If we assume that the ISG leaders are also the evaluators, then at least two evaluation reports should be prepared. One should be prepared for their own use and for the use of future ISG planners and leaders. This report should clearly describe the evaluation questions, the instruments or techniques used to collect data, and a summary of the results. *Do not assume that a computer printout of statistical analyses is sufficient.* The evaluation data and analyses in computer printouts can be unintelligible six months or a year later.

Whoever performed the analyses will likely have forgotten what the symbols meant, what criteria were used to classify subgroups, and why one statistical test was used rather than another. The leaders should prepare a formal report about the outcomes of the ISG, including a literature review and references. It should resemble a journal article manuscript in format and style, except that professionals' or departments' contributions should be clearly identified.

Other shorter, less formal, reports should be prepared for the other audiences. For these reports, Brown (1978) suggests several guidelines:

1. Be brief. Institutional decision makers probably will be less interested in the details of the evaluation and more interested in the final results or conclusions (such evaluation reports should always have a full, detailed, formal report to back up this less formal report).

2. Avoid technical language and jargon as much as possible. Often it is easier to present data in graphs and charts than in tables with means and probability levels and other technical data.

3. Focus the report on issues that require decisions, and provide the report before decisions must be made. In some cases it may be necessary to present preliminary, incomplete reports to decision makers in order to meet their needs for timely information.

Returning to the example of the ISG to train orientation leaders described previously in this chapter, the formal, complete report would be of interest to and needed by both the director of orientation and the other staff member who led the ISG. The vice-president for student affairs would be most interested in a short, concise report that presented the conclusions, perhaps illustrated through charts and graphs. The OLs would be interested in a brief, purely descriptive report that described the conclusions only, presented in nontechnical language. Each of these audiences has a valid interest in the evaluation results but at different levels of detail.

❂ SIX ❂

Strategies and Skills for Effective Group Leadership

This chapter addresses some of the many issues associated with leading ISGs. It begins by considering several of the major theories of group leadership and then presents a model of leadership specific to ISGs. Also considered in this chapter are the skills and competencies needed for successful leadership of ISGs and the issues associated with coleadership.

Theories of Leadership

Theories of group leadership that have potential for application to ISGs can be divided into three general categories: leader traits, leadership behavior, and contingency theories.

Leader Traits or "Great Man" Theories. From the 1920s through the early 1940s the basic approach to studying and attempting to understand the phenomenon of "good" leadership focused on a search for personality traits and other personal characteristics that distinguished leaders from followers. Stogdill (1948) summarized the previous research and concluded that the "average" group leader exceeded that group's members' abilities, such as intelligence, scholarship, verbal facility, and adaptability. Leaders were found to be more dependable, socially active, cooperative, and popular than members. Leaders were also found to have more initiative and persistence. Equating leader traits with good leadership has two drawbacks. First, although the findings on leader traits have been relatively consistent over time, they have been able to explain or predict only a small amount of the variance in "successful" and "unsuc-

Figure 5. Blake and Mouton's Managerial Grid.®

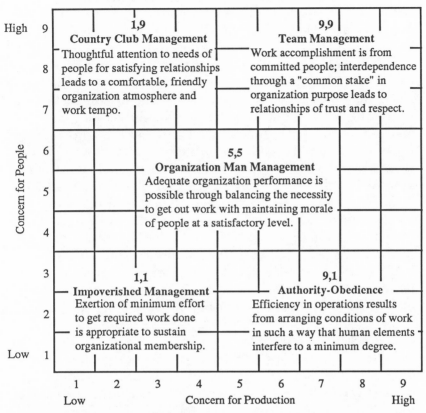

cessful" groups. Second, adopting such an approach to leadership means that educationally there is little that can be done to teach leadership. We simply must wait for or seek out the "right" person.

Leader Behavior. This approach to understanding leadership has sought to identify specific behaviors or categories of behaviors that explain differences in group productivity and member satisfaction. This family of theories has tended to explain leadership by reference to continua of from one (Katz, Maccoby, and Morse, 1950) to four dimensions (Bowers and Seashore, 1966).

One of the better known of these theories is Blake and Mouton's (1964) two-dimensional paradigm called the managerial grid, which they also adapted for higher education and called the academic administrator grid (Blake, Mouton, and Williams, 1981). Their dimensions are (1) concern for people or relationships and (2) concern for task or performance. Using these as vertical and horizontal axes — each numbered from 1 (low) to 9 (high) — they created a grid that allowed for a range of leader behaviors. In the four corners of the grid leadership styles range from low relationship and low task (1, 1: "caretaker") to low relationship and high task (9, 1: "authoritarian") and from high relationship and low task (1, 9: "comfortable and pleasant") to high relationship and high task (9, 9: "team approach"). The center of the grid (5, 5) is called "middle of the road," with emphasis on both production and people but with less than total commitment or concern for either. (See Figure 5.) The dimensions basically describe leadership styles, or characteristic ways of behaving. Blake and Mouton (1975) assert that most people have a dominant style, which they prefer to use and use most frequently, but they can use another of the grid styles (as a backup) when the normal or typical approach does not seem to be working.

Contingency Theories. The fact that neither the theory based on leader traits nor the theory based on leader behavior explains why some leadership styles work quite effectively in one setting or circumstance but are total failures in others has been argued to be a fatal flaw of these theories (Fiedler, 1967; Hersey and Blanchard, 1977).

Fiedler (1967) proposes a contingency theory of leadership, which maintains that the context or situation determines which style of leadership (relationship-oriented or task-oriented) is more appropriate. These situational variables fall into three major categories: member/leader relationships, which can range from good to poor; task structure, which can

Figure 6. Fiedler's Contingency Variables and Situations.

Type of Situation	I	II	III	IV	V	VI	VII	VIII
Favorableness	High ←						→ Low	
Leader-Members Relations	Good				Poor			
Task Structure	High		Low		High		Low	
Leader Position Power	Strong	Weak	Strong	Weak	Strong	Weak	Strong	Weak

Source: Sashkin and Lassey, 1983, p. 98. Reprinted by permission of the authors.

vary from high to low; and leader position power (power derived from the position itself rather than from leader characteristics) or perceived legitimacy, which can range from strong to weak. These variables can be combined to produce eight types of situations along a continuum of "favorableness for exercise of leadership" (see Figure 6). The exercise of leadership is easiest in Situations I, II, and III and most difficult in VI, VII, and VIII. Research by Fiedler and his associates has suggested that task-oriented leadership styles are generally the most effective in Situations I, II, and III; relationship-oriented leadership styles are most effective in moderately difficult (IV and V), and task-oriented leadership styles are again most effective in the most negative or unfavorable situations (VI, VII, and VIII).

To use ISGs as an example, most ISG situations are likely to be favorable (I or II) or moderately difficult (V). Leader/member relationships are likely to be good because participation is usually voluntary and leaders are interested in helping participants. (Somewhat less favorable situations may be encountered when ISGs are used with intact groups for training purposes. If the members do not value the content or if they perceive participation as additional work, then there may be considerable resistance and a negative situation may exist.) The task structure is basically high because the ISG is planned and advertised to address a given topic and to be time limited. The leader's position power is usually high in ISGs because the leader role is built into the ISG structure.

Research (Fiedler, Chemers, and Mahar, 1976; Fiedler and Mahar, 1979) suggests that leaders can be trained to recognize the nature of the situation and to change the situational variables (for example, modifying the task structure, sharing power with members or assuming authority, and creating positive interpersonal relationships) in order to maximize the effectiveness of their leadership.

Hersey and Blanchard (1977) built on the constructions of Blake and Mouton (1964) and Fiedler (1967) to develop their situational leadership model. They maintain that leaders can change their leadership styles to fit the situation (rather than, as Fiedler proposes, changing the situational variables) and that the members' level of task maturity is the primary situational factor to which the leader must respond. They argue that there is no best leadership style, only effective and ineffective ones, and that style should be determined by the maturity of the group and its members in regard to a given task or situation. Task maturity should not be confused with general psychosocial or intellectual maturity. For Hersey and Blanchard a group's maturity is based on the members' ability to perform the task (that is, their knowledge, skills, and experience) and their willingness or confidence to perform it (that is, their motivation and commitment). Maturity is specific to a given task and is not generic or generalizable across different tasks.

As can be seen in Figure 7, there are four basic leadership styles in this model: telling, selling, participating, and delegating. Each of these styles puts relatively different emphases on the leader's relationship and task behaviors. The leader selects the appropriate style based on a diagnosis of the maturity level of the group. As the group becomes increasingly mature, the leader changes style.

The telling style of leadership (S1) is appropriate for

Figure 7. Situational-Leadership Model.

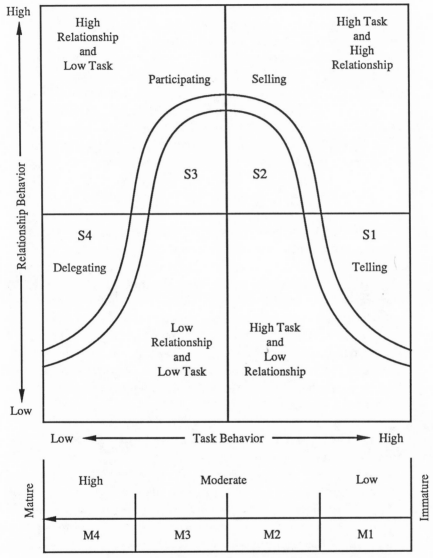

Source: Paul Hersey/Ken Blanchard, *Management of Organizational Behavior: Utilizing Human Resources*, 4th edition, © 1982, p. 153. Adapted by permission of Prentice-Hall, Inc., Englewood Cliffs, New Jersey.

groups with low maturity (M1)—that is, members are unable to perform the assigned tasks without detailed instructions. Members need roles defined and to be told what, when, where, and how. Leaders should minimize (but not omit) supportive behavior and emphasize task behavior.

The selling style (S2) is most appropriate for groups whose members are willing but unprepared to take responsibility for the task (M2 level of maturity). This style involves both high relationship and high task behaviors. The leader is directive and also reinforces members' enthusiasm and desire to perform.

The S3 quadrant (participating style) is high on the relationship dimension and low on the task dimension and is appropriate for groups with a moderately high level of maturity (M3). The group has the requisite knowledge and skills to accomplish the task but lacks the confidence or enthusiasm to carry it through. The leader provides high levels of support and encouragement, sharing in the decision-making process, but provides little direction.

The delegating style (S4) is for groups with a high level of maturity—groups (M4) with both the technical competence and knowledge and the enthusiasm, motivation, and commitment needed to carry the task through to accomplishment. This style is low in task and relationship behaviors. The leader's role is primarily as a consultant and interested supporter of the group's efforts; the leader gives the group a large degree of autonomy to solve problems and make decisions.

Leaders can facilitate progression through the cycle by first providing the directions, training, and instructions that members need to accomplish the tasks successfully, then slowly withdrawing the directive behavior to encourage members to assume responsibility. Leaders can increase supportive or relationship-oriented behaviors by giving praise and rewards for good performance. As group members gain competence and confidence in their ability to perform without outside support or direction, leaders slowly withdraw both relationship and task-oriented behaviors and allow the group to assume full responsibility for and direction of itself.

Applications of Leadership Theories to ISGs

These theories of leadership are intended for application primarily to intact, on-going, task-oriented work groups. There are some important differences between these kinds of groups and ISGs. The most obvious one is the difference in purpose: ISGs' purposes are primarily educational and generally are not intended to produce a tangible product. Also, because of the temporary nature of the ISG and its relatively short duration, there is neither sufficient time nor adequate reward structures to fully apply either the leader-behavior or contingency theories. These models, with slight modifications, however, do have utility in helping to understand the nature of leadership in successful ISGs.

Figure 8 illustrates a model of leadership appropriate for application to ISGs; it is based on the work of Fiedler (1967) and Hersey and Blanchard (1977). There are two axes of the model: structure and facilitation. The *structure* axis ranges from high to low and refers to the leader's introduction of content parameters and forms for dealing with them, such as structured group exercises or homework assignments. Structure also relates to the process of helping the group make meaning from the group experience or from exercises. High structure is evident when the leader introduces preplanned activities in specified ways. Low structure is evident when the leader exerts little direct influence on the group's activities, allowing (even encouraging) the group to make decisions, to assume responsibility for devising activities, and to fulfill leadership functions with minimal involvement of the leader as a leader.

The *facilitation* axis also ranges from high to low; it refers to the leader's attention to and attempts to influence group process as well as to how the leader relates to individual members and the coleader if there is one. High facilitation includes activities such as encouraging member participation and contributions, focusing the group's attention on its dynamics, and making observations about the group's functioning. Facilitation also includes the attitudes the leader models in interactions —

Figure 8. Leadership Model for ISGs.

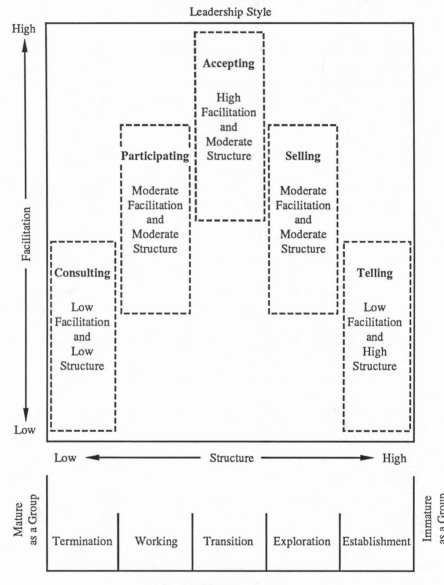

Stages of ISG Development

Source: Paul Hersey/Ken Blanchard, *Management of Organizational Behavior: Utilizing Human Resources*, 4th edition, © 1982, p. 153. Adapted by permission of Prentice-Hall, Inc., Englewood Cliffs, New Jersey.

showing understanding and empathy for members, communicating warmth and acceptance, and demonstrating a willingness to self-disclose. Low facilitation involves allowing the group to manage its own activities, diagnose and shape the dynamics, and make decisions about how they want the group to function. Basically, low facilitation requires the leader to delegate or abdicate the leadership functions to the group and to assume a member role, giving up most of the authority as a leader.

The maturity of the group or its stage of development is most important in determining an appropriate leadership style. The leader needs to be a good diagnostician and to alter leadership style as the group matures or moves through the stages of development.

As Fiedler and as Hersey and Blanchard have clearly demonstrated, there is no single best leadership style, nor one that will be effective in all situations. The context and the purpose of the ISG dictate the most appropriate style.

ISG Leadership Styles

Our adaptation of the Hersey and Blanchard leadership model to ISGs also incorporates our theory of group development for ISGs, presented in Chapter Two. Our model identifies five leadership styles (telling, selling, accepting, participating, and consulting), which correspond to the five stages of ISG development (establishment, exploration, transition, working, and termination).

Telling. In the beginning, at the establishment stage, the leader should assume responsibility for providing a high level of structure (high structure and low facilitation). This style of leadership can be characterized as telling. The leader needs to instruct the participants about the purposes for which the group is being formed, clearly specify the leader's expectations of members, and announce the general ground rules (such as attendance, confidentiality, and behavioral expectations). ISGs are formed for a particular purpose and with predetermined goals; participants need to have a clear understanding of these features in order to determine whether they want to commit the time and energy expected from group members. The emphasis on structure helps students overcome the natural uncertainty and stress associated with joining a new group of people and undertaking new activities. The leader accepts a relatively high level of responsibility for the effects of participation in activities and exercises when using this style: "Give it a try; I am telling you that I think it will turn out OK. Do it because I asked you to." (The basic ground rules still apply however; students may elect not to participate in any activity without providing an explanation [see Chapter 1].)

Selling. As the group moves through the establishment stage, members become familiar with each others' names and backgrounds and more socially comfortable with each other; the group then moves into the exploration stage, and the leader needs to shift to a style that increases the level of facilitation while maintaining a high to moderate level of structure. This leadership style is called selling because the leader is attempting to establish the conditions that will convince members to buy into the group, or make a psychological commitment to the people in the group, and to invest the time and energy required to make the group a successful learning experience. The focus is on helping the group to become aware of itself as a group and to develop a stake in the group's successfully accomplishing its goals. The leader maintains the focus of the group on its goals but also begins to encourage members to interact with each other without the leader's direct involvement.

Accepting. As group cohesiveness develops, usually the group feels the need to challenge the leader's authority and to exercise greater control over its activities. This is the transition stage of group development, and it requires a leadership style called accepting. This style is high on facilitation with a moderate level of structure—that is, the leader needs to keep the purposes of the ISG before the group but must be willing to listen seriously to and consider carefully the group's desire to make modifications. In some sense this process may be viewed as the leader's initiation into the group as a member—a closing of, but not elimination of, the "we/they" gap. It may also be viewed as the group's attempt to establish ownership of the experience by making its imprint on it in some way. The group needs to move through this stage of development in order to become optimally productive as a unit, even though this stage may last only a few minutes. The leader should respond non-defensively to the group's challenge, focusing its attention away from the leader and on the dynamics of the group and the stated purposes for which the ISG was formed while encouraging the members to propose solutions or strategies for dealing with their concerns. The leader needs to act something like a sponge, absorbing the group's criticisms without debate or self-defense. The leader can, and usually should, accept the criticism at face value as the members' honest reaction without having to acknowledge its validity or accuracy if the leader does not agree with the evaluation. As Corey and others (1982) correctly point out, the substance of the challenge to the leader generally is not without a basis in reality even though there may be a significant symbolic component as well.

The challenge to the leader, however, may not be a highly emotionally charged event; it may be focused on a seemingly trivial procedural point, such as changing the meeting time or place or changing expectations that members do work outside the group. Only in rare instances will a group reach the working stage without first passing through the transition stage. The transition stage is likely to be less evident or dramatic, however, if (1) the group members are already acquainted with each other before beginning the ISG, (2) they have experience working together cooperatively as a group (for example, an intact staff group), and (3) there is a high level of commitment to or interest in accomplishing the goals of the ISG from the beginning.

In some groups there may be a reluctance to move through this stage (with the group seemingly content with the leader assuming most of the responsibilities and the members playing basically passive roles). The leader may need to prod the group gently into assuming ownership and into a confrontation. One tactic that often helps the group move into the transition stage is for the leader to focus attention on the group experience itself by asking members to talk about their reactions. The purpose is to stimulate the members to give the leader honest reactions about the group to this point and to encourage members to give direct and honest feedback to each other. At this point any member who is bothered by something or someone's behavior can bring it into the open. Leaders, however, must be cautious in their diagnosis of the level of group development. If their diagnosis is mistaken and the group is not yet ready to move to the working stage, it may regress back through the establishment stage or even break up rather than move through the transition stage.

Participating. Once the group and the leader have negotiated the transition stage successfully, the group is ready (even eager) to move into the working stage, which presents optimal conditions for successful ISGs. An ISG that successfully moves into the working stage will have developed a high level of cohesiveness and relatively high level of *esprit de corps* and will therefore be committed to achievement of the ISG goals and to supporting and assisting each other. The most appropriate leadership style for this stage of group development can be characterized as participating, which requires the leader to maintain a moderate level of facilitation but to decrease the focus on structuring or directing the group's activities. Leadership functions and authority become widely shared by members of the group. Although the leader maintains a certain authority status because of knowledge of and experience dealing with the subject matter, the leader does not relinquish responsibility for planning and implementing activities; members, however, assume responsibility for making activities meaningful and are increasingly willing to complete assignments diligently, wholeheartedly participate in group exercises, take personal risks in the group, and assume responsibility for assisting and supporting others.

Consulting. In the final stage of ISG development, the termination stage, the group needs to attain psychological closure and devise strategies for applying what has been learned in the ISG. The leadership style most appropriate at this stage may be called consulting, which is low on both structure and facilitation, allowing the group to assume most of the leadership functions and structuring of activities. Individuals must make their own decisions and must begin to find their own internal structure for changing their behavior or maintaining changes made during the ISG. The experience must be evaluated from each individual's unique perspective, and personal decisions must be made about how, or if, the information and skills acquired in the ISG will (can) be integrated into daily life without the frequent support, reinforcement, and encouragement of the other group members and the leader.

Psychological closure is most likely to be achieved satisfactorily if members of the group feel that others respond to them honestly and in a caring and sensitive fashion and are allowed to share verbally their honest evaluations of the experience and their personal plans following termination of the ISG. Achieving closure is also important for the leaders; they need to evaluate their work to let go of the group experience if it has been successful or to cope with the sense of failure if the group did not produce the results planned or anticipated.

Leadership Skills and Competencies

It is one thing to present a leadership model for ISGs and quite another to implement it. Models are intended to be simple; but the reader should not confuse simplicity with ease of application. In order to lead ISGs successfully leaders need a good understanding of the content and process of human development, extensive knowledge about the content or subject matter of the ISG, an extensive repertoire of leadership skills and competencies, and experience as members of ISGs.

Many of the skills needed to lead ISGs are presented in Table 12, which is adapted from a list of group counseling skills proposed by Moreland and Krimsky (1982). No particular theoretical orientation or type of ISG is assumed; these skills are generalizable to most kinds of groups. Skills have been assigned

Table 12. Taxonomy of Skills Needed for Successful Leadership of ISGs.

Facilitating	*Structuring*
Coordinating	*Managing*
1. Pacing	1. Introducing exercises and giving clear instructions
2. Maintaining group focus	2. Starting and ending sessions
3. Making observations about group dynamics and group norms	3. Gatekeeping
4. Reflecting group feeling tone	4. Topic tracking
5. Responding to confrontations	5. Keeping time
6. Inviting participation	6. Protecting vulnerable members
7. Checking perceptions	7. Introducing ISG goals and ground rules
8. Dealing with conflict or crisis	8. Enforcing ISG ground rules and ethical parameters
9. Encouraging member-to-member interaction	9. Sequencing
10. Being flexible	10. Making physical arrangements and securing use of facilities and equipment
Empowering	
1. Self-disclosing	*Making meaning*
2. Showing empathy	1. Helping the group remain focused on the present
3. Demonstrating respect for individuals and individual differences	2. Asking open-ended questions
4. Being genuine and honest	3. Summarizing content
5. Being understanding and accepting	4. Processing exercises and homework assignments
6. Showing warmth and concern	5. Challenging the group
7. Delegating leadership functions and authority	6. Encouraging member self-disclosure
	7. Reflecting content
	8. Reflecting feelings
	9. Focusing—for example, individual to group, group to individual, group experience to outside experience
	10. Giving feedback

Source: Adapted from Moreland and Krimsky (1982).

to two broad categories—facilitating and structuring—which correspond to the axes of the ISG leadership model. (These categories overlap somewhat and the assignment of skills to a given category was somewhat arbitrary. Many of the skills can be used in several of the categories. There is also no claim that the list is exhaustive.)

Following are brief descriptions of the identified skills and competencies for leading ISGs. No attempt is made, however, to explain each in great detail; many of them are quite obvious.

Facilitating Skills. This category includes two subcategories: coordinating and empowering. Coordinating skills are needed by a leader to assist the group members in their interactions with each other and to educate members about or make members aware of the dynamics occurring in the group. As members become adept at recognizing the dynamics that affect the group's functioning, they will be better able to understand and exert control or influence over their own experiences in the group.

It is important that the group perceive that there is movement, that important things are being dealt with and that what is occurring in the group is related to the ISG goals. The leader helps create this sense of movement through pacing. As Pfeiffer and Jones (1973) note, "When things begin to drag [due to fatigue or boredom], it is probably time to make a change. Sometimes the most effective change is simply to point up the process that is emerging" (p. 186) and to allow the members to determine what is "bringing them down." Frequently, sessions begin to drag because of design errors — that is, the leaders did not sequence activities to maintain variety, or the leaders attempted to include too much in a single session, or they underestimated the amount of psychic energy required by a particular activity. Leaders, however, should not feel compelled to intervene when things get slow because there is a danger that members will come to depend on the leader to always intervene when the group begins to lose its excitement.

Many of the skills in the coordinating category relate to the leader's ability to comprehend the dynamics of the group and to communicate that understanding to the group in a nonauthoritarian manner. When conflicts arise between group members or when a member becomes highly emotional, the leader must assist both the individual(s) involved and the group to deal with these unsettling events. Napier and Gershenfeld (1983) point out that a major advantage to ISG-type experiences is that they can encourage participants to reevaluate their ideas, long-held assumptions, stereotypes, and customary behavior patterns. An important method of experiential learning involves stimulation, challenge, and confrontation. The authors note, however, that "confrontation by itself does not encourage taking risks or trying new behaviors. Only when it is imbedded in an atmosphere of support will a person explore or reexamine or rethink" (p. 31). When thinking about confrontation, the leader should always ask, "What is the potential benefit or purpose of this confrontation?" If the leader cannot provide a relatively clear answer to the question, then the likelihood is great that confrontation will produce minimal positive results and probably should be avoided if possible.

Empowering is another major category of skills group leaders need to exercise. Empowering refers primarily to the leaders' attitudes toward group members and how they interact with them. If leaders are respectful, open, honest, and accepting in their dealings with group members, they will empower them to take chances and to risk appearing "dumb," "ridiculous," or "inept." These characteristics and attitudes are most closely associated with the Rogerian "person-centered approach." As Rogers (1962, p. 33) noted, "If I can provide a certain type of relationship, the other person will discover within himself the capacity to use that relationship for growth and change and personal development." Even if we do not accept all the philosophical assumptions and techniques of this approach, research has shown that display of these kinds of behaviors and attitudes often produces positive, growth-engendering outcomes (Carkhuff, 1972; Kasdorf and Gustafson, 1978; Strupp and Hadley, 1979; Lambert, 1982).

Perry (1970) notes that learning by its nature is an ego-threatening experience. By the leaders' affirmation of each individual's worth and importance to the group, members are strengthened in their quest to explore new ideas or develop new skills. These conditions are activated almost exclusively through

modeling. Leaders must demonstrate these qualities throughout the ISG; talking about them alone will probably have little
impact.

Self-disclosure by leaders—providing information to
members about their own experiences, especially those related
to uncertainty and fear, which expose the leaders' vulnerability—can help members feel more comfortable with their own
sense of vulnerability and to risk trying new behaviors. Leaders
can also empower the group by abdicating certain leadership
functions (such as being the person to initiate discussion after
exercises or being the one to summarize discussion). By refusing
to assume some leadership functions and roles, the leader encourages members to invest in the ISG experience and the
group is encouraged to move to increasingly mature levels of
functioning.

Structuring Skills. This broad category of skills has to do
with establishing conditions designed to stimulate learning or
to provide a framework for activities, exercises, tasks, and assignments that promote achievement of the ISG's goals. Two subcategories define this group of skills: managing and making
meaning.

Managing involves setting up the conditions and framework of each ISG session and the activities or exercises within a
session. These kinds of skills range from assuring that the
physical setting and arrangements are suitable for the activities
planned to introducing exercises with clear instructions, to
keeping track of time, and to opening and closing sessions
promptly and appropriately. Two of the most frequently made
mistakes when using structured group exercises are failing to
provide an introduction that enables the members to understand the purpose of the exercise and how it relates to the ISG
goals and failing to give clear, concise instructions. To add
instructions (such as "I forgot to tell you that you cannot talk
during this exercise," for example, after the group is already five
minutes into it) greatly diminishes the power of the exercise and
often generates hostility and destroys the credibility of the
leader. Managing also includes presenting the ISG's goals and

purposes to the group and introducing and monitoring compliance with the fundamental ground rules and ethical parameters for the ISG. Other important management skills include gatekeeping, which is helping to direct interchanges so that everyone is not speaking at once, preventing one individual from dominating the discussion, and preventing the isolation or exclusion of less gregarious or less self-confident individuals.

A critically important part of managing the structure is protecting vulnerable members. When the leader senses that a member is unable to control emotions or is experiencing an unusually high (and unanticipated) level of stress, the leader should intervene to protect the individual. This intervention may take the form of cutting an activity short, directing attention away from an individual's reaction, temporarily suspending the exercise and assisting the affected member to talk about or work through the feelings, or stepping into a member/member confrontation. The leader should also follow-up with the vulnerable member after the session, either by offering assistance in dealing with the emotional difficulties or by making an effective referral to appropriate campus professionals. (See Winston [in press] for a discussion of effective approaches to making referrals.)

The other collection of structuring skills may be called "making meaning." An ISG by definition has an educational purpose: Its goal is to help its members learn about themselves or acquire new knowledge or skills. An important skill for leaders, therefore, is to assist members to understand the significance of activities, to apply concepts, and to practice skills or new behaviors. The leader can assist ISG members in making meaning through a number of techniques, such as leading discussions, asking open-ended questions, encouraging members to verbalize their affective reactions to experiences, summarizing comments, and reflecting feelings back to individual members. Another important skill is helping the group remain focused on what is happening in the group at the moment (immediacy) and discussing how what is happening reflects the ISG's goals or the group's typical ways of behaving. Leaders can also assist a member in making the connections between what has just happened within the group or in an interchange and that member's behavior patterns.

The single most frequently made mistake in employing structured group exercises is the failure of the leader to assist the group in processing the experience (that is, in examining the exercises' meaning and significance in relation to the learning goals). Sometimes the arrangements and materials are so complicated or the activity itself is so interesting that the members lose sight of the principal reason for using these types of exercises — to stimulate learning. As Pfeiffer and Jones (1973) describe it, "processing refers to the talking through of behavioral and feeling data that emerge in a particular structured activity. . . . It is both dangerous and unethical to leave large portions of data hanging that might be integrated in dysfunctional ways within the consciousness of a given individual participant" (p. 185). The same can be said for homework assignments. Members need time in the group to talk about what they learned as a result of completing the assignment, to find out about other participants' experiences and reactions, and to begin the generalization process.

Potential ISG leaders should carefully compare their skills with those in the list. If there are obvious deficiencies, then leaders should take steps to remedy the situation (perhaps through academic courses offered by a counseling or student personnel program or through professional-development workshops offered by colleges, professional associations, or individual entrepreneurs). There is truth to the maxim "It is not a sin not to know, but it is a sin not to try to find out."

Coleadership

A viable and often-recommended approach to ISG leadership is to use coleaders rather than a single leader. Coleadership, however, must be clearly thought through and the reasons for using coleaders need to be examined carefully because both advantages and pitfalls are associated with it.

Advantages. The advantages of coleadership compared with single leadership include (1) more opportunities for modeling, (2) more effective use of skills and knowledge, (3) better organization, (4) more accurate observation of group dynamics, (5) less fatigue and stress, and (6) greater opportunity for professional growth (Pfeiffer and Jones, 1975a; Yalom, 1975; Hansen, Warner, and Smith, 1980; Galinsky and Schopler, 1981).

1. One of the major advantages of coleadership is that leaders can model with each other the behaviors, skills, or attitudes being taught or promoted in the ISG. Often participants will better understand a behavior, skill, or attitude presented in an ISG if they can see others demonstrate it. Having two leaders present, who have different personalities and styles, often also helps members appreciate the diversity of means available for dealing with the same problem or for accomplishing a task. The presence of two leaders also enhances the probability that each participant will find at least one leader with whom to identify. Coleadership also allows members to observe how disagreements or different perspectives can be resolved or accommodated.

Leaders must keep in mind that they are models whether they intend to be or not. Group members meticulously observe leaders' behavior down to the smallest detail and assign credibility to the ideas presented in direct relation to the congruence between what is being said and what is being acted out. A lack of congruence, or a conflicting message, usually results in the members' doubting the leaders' competence, sincerity, integrity, or all three.

Byrum-Gaw and Carlock (1983) suggest that leaders can most effectively model interpersonal skills. The modeling can be affected by focusing on the self, on others, or on the relationship. When focusing on *self* leaders may disclose facts about themselves, their current feelings, desires, or expectations. If a group member seems to resist hearing or comprehending the message being sent by the leaders or the group as a whole, the leaders can use the "broken-record" technique developed in assertiveness-training programs; the leaders repeat the same message no matter what responses are given until the group member comprehends what is meant.

A leader can focus on *others* by (1) nondefensively accepting what a group member says who disagrees with the leader, (2) confronting a member about a behavior that adversely affects the leader (it is important to clearly specify what the leader finds offensive and to indicate unambiguously what the leader wants the member to do), (3) giving a member feedback about how the leader perceives the member, and (4) providing support by acknowledging a member's contribution and expressing appreciation.

Leaders can also concentrate on the *relationship*. In conflict situations the leader can identify areas of disagreement and then work with the member to generate alternatives en route to finding a mutually agreeable solution. Leaders can use immediacy by telling a member exactly how they are feeling about the member at the moment. By changing plans or accepting suggestions from group members, the leader can model flexibility and mutuality.

2. Coleadership allows for labor to be divided in ways that build on each leader's strengths or compensate for weaknesses. One leader may tend to focus primarily on maintenance or facilitating functions, while the other leader focuses principally on content or structuring functions. This approach can lead to problems on several fronts. The leader who focuses on the relationship aspects will most likely receive more positive evaluations from members and will be liked better. In addition, this approach may promote the idea that content and affect are separate and that participants need focus on only one aspect, which is usually a mistake. Generally, both leaders should have alternating primary responsibility for attending to content and process functions.

ISGs that have coleadership allow for a better use of skills and knowledge than do ISGs with a single leader. Because they are based on each leader's strength, the materials and exercises presented are likely to be more interesting and more personalized; each leader likely has a reservoir of personal experiences related to some aspects of the ISG that can be used to illustrate the concepts being taught.

3. Coleadership enhances the organization of the ISG. The careful planning and communication required prior to

sessions in order to prevent duplication encourage (require) more detailed planning on each leader's part than would generally occur if there were only one leader. Coleadership is seldom successful when one or both leaders attempt to "wing it."

4. Coleadership allows for more systematic and meticulous attention to group dynamics than does solo leadership. It is difficult to manage materials, conduct exercises, interact with individual participants, and also be aware of the entire group and its functioning and development. With coleaders, a good technique is for one leader to take primary responsibility for a session or part of the session, while the other leader takes a more passive leadership role but pays particular attention to the dynamics in the group. It is important that the observation of the dynamics be planned, although not necessarily written, with specific areas to receive attention predetermined as part of the formative evaluation plan (see Chapter Five). If possible, immediately after a session the leaders should discuss what happened. Pfeiffer and Jones (1975a, p. 229) call this procedure "clinicking." They suggest that the leaders (1) share perceptions of what happened, (2) identify any participant who is "hurting" or who seems to be having difficulty being accepted into the group or participating in group activities, (3) give feedback to each other about what worked and what did not, (4) react to the way they are functioning as coleaders, and (5) respond to each other on a personal level and as coleaders—renegotiating past agreements or altering plans for future sessions.

Napier and Gershenfeld (1983) caution that it may be best to wait several days before dealing with a particularly difficult or emotion-laden session because the leaders may be too invested in the events and personalities to deal objectively with leadership issues immediately after the session. We recommend that leaders meet immediately after such a session to discuss what happened and also meet a second time shortly before the next session to reevaluate their previous perceptions and diagnoses. This procedure has two advantages: The incident can be reviewed while it is still vivid in memory and before defensive reactions begin to form, and a reasoned examination can be made once the emotion has subsided somewhat. At the second session the leaders can formulate their plan for dealing with important issues during the next session.

5. Coleadership makes the leadership function less fatiguing than solo leadership is. Simply knowing that an informed ally is there to rescue the situation if things begin to go badly or to deal with the unexpected or unplanned relieves some of the stress associated with leading an ISG. It also means that two people share the tasks of preparing materials and making arrangements, which can often be time-consuming.

6. Coleadership can enhance professional growth. Working closely with another professional and seeing how that person responds to problems or situations provides a new perspective and an opportunity to acquire new skills. This relationship also allows each leader to receive direct feedback about her or his leadership skills and techniques, which many practitioners lack simply because there is no one available to observe their work closely.

Disadvantages. There are several potential disadvantages to coleadership: (1) economics, (2) overleading, (3) expenditure of extra energy, (4) transfer of outside relationships or problems to the group, (5) incompatible styles or theoretical orientations, and (6) threat and competition (Pfeiffer and Jones, 1975a; Galinsky and Schopler, 1981).

1. From a simple economic perspective it is more expensive to have coleaders than a single leader. Coleadership necessitates spending time not only at group meetings but also on debriefing sessions after each meeting and on planning before the next meeting. From an economic perspective one needs to show that coleadership produces a greater impact or better effect than can be produced by a single leader. One piece of evidence is that in many cases coleadership has a synergistic effect (Pfeiffer and Jones, 1975a) — that is, the effect of coleadership is greater than the individual leaders' contributions.

2. There is the danger of overleading with coleaders. Because there are two leaders present, they may feel the need to earn their keep, and thus they may intervene too frequently,

which has the effect of stifling member participation, group development, and ultimately learning.

3. Extra energy is required to colead a group. Each leader must be aware of what is happening with group members and also must be aware of what the other leader is doing. Contributions need to be made in a manner that complements the other leader's thrust or approach and must be timed appropriately so as not to interrupt the flow of the group's activities. Maintaining this degree of awareness requires a high level of concentration and energy.

4. It is extremely important that the coleaders not transfer problems from the work setting or interpersonal-relationship problems to the ISG. Unresolved tensions, hostility, or disagreements that exist between administrative units or individuals can easily find expression within the group, possibly even being projected onto individual participants. This situation can be destructive to group development and is unfair to the participants. Because these disagreements or tensions have their genesis outside the ISG and are probably unknown to the ISG participants, members are often bewildered by the nature of the leaders' interactions with each other and may model inappropriate behaviors that are not conducive to attaining the ISG's goals. The leaders can become so involved in dealing with their conflicts or extragroup concerns that the group's own development can be hampered or disrupted (Winter, 1976).

5. Successful coleadership requires individuals with compatible, though not necessarily the same, styles of interacting and theoretical orientations. For example, it would be difficult for a leader who holds rigorously to a person-centered approach to work effectively with a leader who is concerned primarily with content and skills development. The leader with the person-centered approach would expect most of the structure and stimulation to emerge from the group, while the other leader would be setting up conditions that promote a predetermined outcome. The two leaders would likely find themselves often working at cross-purposes and creating confusion for the group members.

Leaders may also have different intervention rhythms,

which can be somewhat independent of theoretical orientation (Pfeiffer and Jones, 1975a, p. 221). Some leaders intervene often, say on a three count, while others intervene less frequently, say on a ten count. The ten-count leader, who makes less frequent comments or other interventions, is likely to be thrown off stride by the other leader, while the three-count leader will find it uncomfortable waiting for the ten-count leader to do something. This contrast in style can disrupt the group unless the leaders make efforts to blend their usual intervention rhythms.

6. Coleadership can sometimes dissolve into one-upsmanship. If one leader does a good job and receives favorable comments from participants, the other leader may try to top the other's performance. Most ISG leaders have at least a moderately high need to be liked because of the types of personalities that are attracted to the field. When one leader seems to be more popular than the other, it may unconsciously create a sense of competition that satisfies the leaders' ego needs but that is not supportive of the ISG's goals and blocks group development.

Coleadership also can be perceived as a threat by some ISG participants, especially those who have difficulty dealing with authority figures. Leaders can sometimes unwittingly, in the spirit of supporting each other and presenting a united front, dominate the group, making it difficult for members to express their opinions or feelings honestly. The mere presence of two professionals in the group may inhibit some individuals from venturing input (Galinsky and Schopler, 1981).

Strategies for Effective Coleadership. Although coleadership is not necessarily easier, and certainly not less work, than solo leadership, in our opinion the potential advantages far outweigh disadvantages. Several steps can be taken prior to and during the ISG to make coleadership successful: (1) careful exploration of leadership and intervention styles, (2) development of the coleader relationship, (3) planning, and (4) use of formative evaluation data.

As the leaders develop the ISG, they should also begin exploring each other's ways of dealing with problems and working in groups. Pfeiffer and Jones (1975a) developed a structured questionnaire that coleaders can use to guide their exploration. They propose that the coleaders think about and then discuss: (1) their theories of how learning takes place and what motivates both participants and them as leaders; (2) what they expect to happen during the ISG—including both best- and worst-case scenarios; and (3) intervention styles and rhythms, by addressing questions such as "When someone talks too much, I usually. . . ," "When someone cries, I usually. . . ," and "When the group is silent, I usually. . ." A systematic survey of intervention styles and approaches to group leadership can be obtained by completing and discussing the results from instruments such as the Intervention Style Survey (Arbes, 1972), the Group Leadership Functions Scale (Conyne, 1975), and the Group Leadership Questionnaire (Wile, 1972). We recommend that coleaders spend some time systematically and openly discussing these kinds of issues before announcing the ISG, even when they are well acquainted with each other. Working through the Pfeiffer and Jones (1975a) Cofacilitating Inventory is a good way to begin the process.

The coleaders need to examine the nature and quality of their relationship prior to assuming the leadership roles. The leaders need to have established a personal relationship that allows them to share honest feedback and criticism with each other nondefensively. Unresolved issues or conflicts need to be dealt with openly. If coleaders cannot resolve controversies or at least truly hold them in abeyance for the duration of the ISG—which is a difficult task—then alternative arrangements should be made for leading the ISG. Disagreements that are smoothed over at this stage will generally reemerge during the ISG, often in unconscious and sometimes destructive ways.

Obvious differences in status between the leaders may cause problems. Apparent differences in age, administrative position or title, experience in leading groups, or expertise in the subject matter of the ISG can create a disparity in how the group members perceive the leaders; they will assign the one with more status greater credibility and power or give that person idiosyncratic credits (see Chapter Two). These issues need to be discussed thoroughly before beginning the group. If the leaders wish to operate as equals, then careful attention needs to be paid to establishing this equality early in the group. The more experienced leader must be aware of her or his behavior, especially nonverbal behavior, so as not to upstage the other leader.

An equal sharing of the leadership functions, however, is not necessary or always desirable. It may be appropriate to form a "limited partnership"; the person with more experience and the more extensive background may serve as the principal leader, with the understanding that the other leader will assist or serve as an apprentice. It is generally best to acknowledge the differences in roles and responsibilities openly to the group, especially when a graduate student is coleading with an experienced practitioner. Alley (1981) suggests that a student coleader may enhance the group's effectiveness. She argues that some ISG participants may feel more comfortable dealing with the student leader than with the principal leader on some issues, and may use that person as a sounding board for issues or concerns before presenting them in the total group.

Effective coleadership depends primarily on leaders' carefully thinking through the ISG plan, developing contingency plans to deal with foreseeable problems, and establishing a comfortable working relationship and understanding with each other.

The primary issue in most coleadership teams is control — who has it and how it will be exercised. The leaders need to have discussed and decided who is expected to intervene when things are not going well or seem to be getting out of hand. Otherwise, each leader may wait for the other to act with the result that neither acts in a timely or effective fashion. Or both leaders may attempt to act at the same time, employing incompatible strategies and making matters worse, or at least making them seem worse to the participants. Another issue that often develops in ISGs is related to time. It is not uncommon for an activity or exercise to take more time than was allotted to it during planning. One of the leaders needs to have been designated to make the on-the-spot decision about whether to cut the activity off and go on to another, or to eliminate something else that was planned for the session in order to carry an exercise to its logical conclusion. Because leaders seldom have an opportunity to confer privately in making that decision, one leader needs to have the authority to do so before the session begins. However, the designated leader does not have to be same for each session.

Careful and thoughtful use of formative evaluation data is also necessary for effective coleadership. The leaders need to make sure that systematic formative evaluations (see Chapter Five) are made and that they remain flexible enough to modify their plans and styles if the evaluations indicate that changes are necessary.

The Good Leader

In a landmark study of encounter groups, Lieberman, Yalom, and Miles (1973) identified four basic leadership functions: emotional stimulation, caring, meaning-attribution, and executive. A leader who provides emotional stimulation expresses feelings and publicizes values. Such a leader emphasizes the intentional release of emotions and often demonstrates this release to the group through self-disclosures and interactions with individual group members. The leader challenges members and is involved in dialogues with individual members, placing a high value on personal confrontation. This type of leader has a strong personality and might be described as charismatic.

Leaders who emphasize the caring function protect vulnerable members and offer friendship, affection, support, praise, and encouragement. This kind of leader downplays distinctions between members and the leader, invites member participation and feedback, and is warm and accepting.

A leader who concentrates on the meaning-attribution function provides members with a framework for understanding or interpreting what is happening in the group and seeks to make connections to behavior-change strategies. This kind of leader emphasizes cognitive processes, giving names to experiences or translating feelings and behaviors into conscious thought processes.

The executive function involves setting limits, laying down ground rules, managing time, and establishing structure or procedures for the group. Leaders who concentrate on the executive function are task oriented and see it to be their responsibility to manage the group as a social system with specific goals to be attained.

In their analysis of encounter groups, Lieberman, Yalom, and Miles (1973) concluded that the most effective leaders were those who employed moderate levels of emotional stimulation, showed a high degree of caring, made moderate use of the executive function, and frequently used meaning-attribution techniques. The least effective leaders were either very high or very low on emotional stimulation, low on caring, did not use (or infrequently used) meaning-attribution techniques, and were either very high or very low on executive function.

This research has several implications for leading ISGs. First, no formula or set of personality characteristics guarantees effective leadership. Second, good leaders are not gurus; when the leader is the primary focus of attention and the leader's ego needs become more important than the welfare of the group, little of value is likely to result. Leaders have ethical and professional responsibilities to place the welfare of the group members ahead of their personal satisfaction. ISGs should never be used as a vehicle for leaders to demonstrate their power in the institution, professional (therapist) prowess, or personal charisma. Third, as Luft (1984, p. 114) notes in his comments on the Lieberman, Yalom, and Miles findings, "dramatic interventions aimed at instant insight and radical personality change" are not helpful to members and in some cases are harmful.

Successful ISG leaders must (1) be sensitive to individual group members, (2) be aware of the dynamics operating within the group, (3) understand the process of group development, (4) be able to diagnose where a group is within the developmental framework at any given time, (5) understand the processes of human development, and (6) be knowledgeable about the specific content and outcome objectives of the ISG. The most successful ISGs are those that are carefully planned based on needs-assessment data, have modest but meaningful goals, and are led by persons who have a sincere interest in helping students. The best ISG leaders are well aware of the great responsibilities their position of leadership places on them, yet keep in mind the fact that the group, its stages and dynamic processes, as well as its composition and the opportunities for interaction available to group members will ultimately be the means by which group goals are achieved—not primarily the leader's personality or charisma. Likewise, good intentions and a sincere interest in helping students are important attitudes for successful leaders to have, but they are not adequate substitutes for a sound understanding of the ISG's content, a functional knowledge of group-dynamics principles, and effective planning and organization.

♡ SEVEN ♡

Starting, Conducting, and Concluding the Group

When implementing an ISG, readers should use the stages of ISG development (establishment, exploration, transition, working, and termination, described in Chapter Two) as an indicator of how well the ISG is progressing and as a diagnostic tool should difficulties be encountered. Because these stages are common to most ISGs, they are used in this chapter as a framework for discussing critical issues and implementation problems that are often encountered. This chapter is designed to help group leaders understand the important relationship between group development (and the associated group dynamics) and ISG implementation and to suggest strategies for dealing with problems as the group progresses.

In this chapter we discuss a number of tasks that need to be accomplished prior to the first session, issues as they will likely appear at each of the stages of group development, and strategies for dealing with common problems.

Preparation

Because ISGs by definition are of short duration (usually from four to thirty hours of meeting time), leaders need to maximize each session's effectiveness. The only way that success can be reasonably assured is through careful and thoughtful preparation (see Chapter Four). Many of these activities are mundane, but each is important to the efficient management of the group and, more importantly, to the group's effectiveness as a growth-producing and learning experience.

ISG Checklist. We recommend that leaders develop a checklist to assure that essential arrangements have been made

Form 1. Sample ISG Checklist.

1. Title: _____

2. Leaders: _____

3. Approval to offer ISG received from: _____

4. Support and referral resources:

Name	Office phone number	Home phone number
_____	_____	_____
_____	_____	_____
_____	_____	_____
_____	_____	_____

5. Meeting arrangements

   A. Dates confirmed: _____

   B. Time for facility use confirmed: _____

   C. Facilities reserved: _____

   D. Equipment reserved: _____

6. ISG manual completed: _____

7. Handouts completed and duplicated: _____

8. Promotional materials completed: _____

9. Screening interviews

   A. Dates and times established: _____

   B. Interview questions formulated: _____

   C. Deposit determined (approval received if necessary): _____

10. Participant demographic data obtained: _____

11. Participants reminded of initial session: _____

12. Scheduled dates and times for planning and preparation before each session:

and materials have been obtained. Form 1 is a sample ISG checklist; it identifies important considerations and may serve as a springboard for leaders in creating their own checklists. Important questions that deserve attention include: Have referral personnel been identified and contacted? Few problems are more painful to ISG leaders when something goes awry than to have one's superiors caught off guard and be unable to respond to questions because they were uninformed. Consequently, do appropriate persons in the administrative structure know about the planned ISG and its content? Should any faculty members, administrators, or other campus leaders be informed about the ISG or, even more importantly, be contacted to gain their blessing? Likewise, some institutions have policies and regulations concerning research with human subjects. Although ISGs are seldom designed for research purposes, their nature may make them subject to such policy concerns. Clearance through the institutional review board and with professional staff members is important. An adequate checklist should thus identify offices from which to seek clearance or individuals who should be informed.

Another extremely important consideration requiring prior attention is confirmation of the specific meeting arrangements. Although most of the arrangements will have been decided on during planning (see Chapter Four), confirmation just prior to the first scheduled meeting is important. Occasionally it is necessary to change meeting times, places, or settings between the time of original planning and the time the ISG is initiated. If such changes have occurred, participants need to be told well before the first session. (It is also a good idea to contact participants by telephone two or three days before the first session to remind them of the time and place and to build enthusiasm for participation.) Even if no changes have occurred, it is still important to assure that the meeting place is reserved and that the room is arranged appropriately for the first session. For instance, for an ISG design that requires a relaxed, informal setting for the first meeting, having the room set up in classroom fashion with rows of desks facing a lecturer's podium can make the leaders seem ineffective or even incompetent. Even if the leaders and the participants can quickly change the seating arrangement to a circle of chairs or to beanbag chairs and pillows that were stored in a nearby closet, the implication is that the leaders did not have the arrangements under control. In an even worse case, another group or class may be holding forth in the room at the time the ISG is scheduled to begin. On such simple factors can a leader's credibility be destroyed. (Negative first impressions are generally quite difficult to overcome.) Consequently, including arrangement confirmation on the ISG checklist is a must.

ISG Manual. The effective ISG leader carefully prepares for each group meeting. Problems with physical arrangements are relatively minor compared with not having a well-organized plan ready for each session. It is imperative that group leaders prepare a written manual (see Chapter Four and the Sample ISG Manual at the end of the book). Although no one can ever precisely predict how a given ISG will function or what alterations will be required as a result of formative evaluations, it is extremely important that a comprehensive manual be prepared and carefully reviewed immediately prior to each session. Planning to "wing it" on the basis of previous experience will invariably lead to problems. A comprehensive, carefully organized ISG manual will enhance implementation of an ISG. Failure of leaders to develop and use an ISG manual will likely result in an inferior group experience for the participants. The ISG manual should include a comprehensive outline for each session, as well as each exercise or activity within the session, because there will be no time to plan once the session has begun.

Materials. If workbooks or other published materials are needed by group participants, they must be prepared and available prior to the first meeting of the group. The group's purposes, goals, and objectives should be clearly written out. If a pregroup screening is done, each participant should receive a copy of the proposed ISG goals at that time, but it is also important that these goals and purposes be provided in written form during the initial group meeting.

Exercises. If the leaders have never led a particular exercise before, it is essential to rehearse the instructions and the way the exercise will be set up and to run through the entire activity mentally, including possible processing questions. What will the leader do if the participants do not understand the directions? What if they resist? What alternative exercise can be used in case of trouble? What if the plan calls for dyadic interaction, but there are an odd number of participants? These and other minor problems can become major inconveniences if leaders have not thought about them prior to the session. In most instances, what takes place during the initial session will influence the remainder of the ISG and may well actually determine whether participants return for the remaining sessions.

Anticipating Members' Needs. The group leader should be prepared to deal with participants' *initial expectations*. It is not uncommon for prospective group members to have exceedingly varied expectations for the ISG and to anticipate being exposed to rather divergent activities. ISG leaders can invite participants to share their expectations and desired outcomes with other group members. If it becomes obvious that some individuals' expectations and desired outcomes conflict with the purposes of the group, then it is important to deal with them early on. How leaders attend and respond to these different expectations in group discussions may make the difference between a quality ISG experience and a disaster. When expectations are clearly out of line with the group's purposes, it is the leaders' responsibility to clarify the discrepancies and to help the individuals understand the extent to which their expectations can and will be met within this particular group and the extent to which they cannot or will not be met. In some instances this clarification may result in some participants' deciding to withdraw. Leaders should not feel they have failed if they lose members. Rather, they should realize that they helped these individuals make a thoughtful decision about how to best use their time and energy for personal growth and development. Few things can be more detrimental to an ISG than the continued participation of members who hold unrealistic expectations for the group or who passively resist the group and its leaders' efforts. When a screening or selection process is implemented prior to beginning the group, many expectation discrepancies are resolved before the initial session. Nevertheless, even the best-planned screenings have limitations. It is important that everyone involved come to hold a relatively similar view of the intent and purpose of the ISG and "own" the group's goals.

Building the *commitment* of participants is an important consideration as well. The fact that students express an interest in participating in an ISG does not mean that they are committed to becoming actively involved in the group experience when it is offered. A written contract between the student and the ISG provider is useful here, for it is an agreement on the student's part to follow through on the original decision to participate. Sometimes a reasonable fee can be charged to symbolize this commitment. Better yet, if the fee is a deposit that will be returned to those who complete the ISG, the fee can help motivate students to follow through when the press of time and circumstances requires them to make choices. If a developmental-transcript program exists on campus, recording the student's completion of an ISG can be a motivational factor as well (see Brown and DeCoster, 1982; Fried, 1981).

A final area that requires planning prior to the first ISG session is the *demystification of the group process*. Although all college students have experienced many forms of instruction during their years of schooling, some may be unclear about the processes of the ISG. Leaders need to be prepared to help participants clarify their roles in the group, understand the roles of other group members, understand expected group interactions, comprehend their personal responsibility to the group, and develop a working relationship with other members. For a leader to assume that group participants understand the processes and potential power of the group is, in most instances, unrealistic.

Establishment Stage: Essential Elements

The initial session of an ISG is critical to eventual success or failure because it establishes the climate and nature of the group. As noted in Chapter Two, the establishment stage is an essential period in the life of any ISG. What occurs during the initial session will be especially important to the way this stage develops and whether the collection of people becomes a group.

Responsibilities of Leaders. The saying that "one never gets a second chance to make a first impression" underscores the critical nature of the opening group session. Just as children begin to form lasting impressions about themselves and others in the early stages of childhood, group members form impressions based on early perceptions of each other and the group leaders. Unfortunately, individuals tend to make such judgments on the basis of little data, often generalizing from biased perceptions and half-truths. Although impressions can change as a consequence of additional experience, it is important to provide new members with positive exposure to the group from the outset.

It is important for leaders to share a sense of optimism and encouragement by coming to the group prepared and alert, with a reasonable amount of energy. In order to be effective, leaders must communicate clearly and listen attentively to others without letting preconceived notions, personal biases, or outside business interfere. For this reason a coleader is recommended so that one of the leaders can focus on sensing the process while the other guides the activity.

Leadership is a singularly significant factor in an ISG throughout its life. Leader behavior during the establishment stage is of particular importance because leaders intentionally or unintentionally serve as role models for group members. Leaders can be positive models by encouraging member involvement and acceptance and by demonstrating respect for members and effective attending skills. Further, because premature in-depth self-disclosure by a group member can inhibit group interaction, group leaders should make a special effort to model appropriate levels of self-disclosure during introductory comments.

Initial comments and behaviors of the ISG leaders establish their credibility with the group members. A preferred method of sharing qualifications is for leaders to include casual comments about their credentials and previous group experiences. For instance, a leader may say, "I am excited about this opportunity to work on decision-making skills with you not only because of my interest in the topic but also because it gives me a chance to continue working with groups, something I've enjoyed for three years, ever since my graduate training program in college student affairs." In this fashion, the leader can focus the group's attention on the ISG's goals and the relevance of the leader's credentials to the goals rather than divert attention to the leader's personal and professional record of achievements.

Clarification of Purpose. For any ISG to succeed members must come to value the group and to identify with its purpose and goals. Group members deserve opportunities to both verbalize their personal goals and respond to the ISG's stated goals. It is important to clarify purpose early in the group. Leaders can explain in clear and unambiguous terms the initial reasons for offering the group and then invite member response. If modifications of purpose become necessary, then the group can collectively negotiate the changes. The more opportunities the members have to contribute to group goals, the more the ownership is shared and the greater is the resulting group cohesion. The central purpose of the ISG should remain clear throughout the group's existence but should not be used as a weapon to keep the group in lockstep. It is important to remember that purpose serves the group, and a group needs to have faith in its ability to achieve shared goals.

Establishment of Ground Rules. Group leaders must take responsibility for explaining basic ground rules to the members. Even though no prescribed set of rules applicable to all ISGs exists, at least three general principles apply when establishing a set of rules. First, it is important to keep the rules simple. Second, the rules need to include those of the sponsoring agency. For example, if smoking is not allowed on the premises, then group members need to be apprised of this fact. Third, ground rules should include explanations of relevant parameters such as time and duration of meetings, limitations on types of interaction, and ethical expectations such as confidentiality (see Chapter One for details and the Sample ISG Manual for an example).

Time limits are more important than may appear at first glance. Much time will be wasted if the group consistently waits for one or two members to begin its work. At the other end of the session, some members may wish to continue beyond the stopping point because of an unwillingness to bring closure to a task. A group needs a natural stopping point. Simply stated, time parameters add stability and predictability to a group.

The goal orientation of an ISG provides a natural guideline for members as they struggle, during the establishment stage, to develop limitations on group interaction. The specific focus of the group may preclude certain content or kinds of interaction. For example, if the primary process focus of the group is task skill development (see Chapter One), then it would be inappropriate and inefficient to focus the group's attention and use its time on helping one member resolve anxiety over separation from family (help by the leaders outside the group or referral to others would be appropriate).

Structured Exercises. The development and use of appropriate exercises can be important contributions to a group's establishment. To have the desired impact, the exercise needs to be both interesting to participants and directly related to the group's expressed goals. These features are equally important. A well-designed exercise during the initial session can be a positive influence on later group discussions (Elman and Rupple, 1978).

The general anxiety that often accompanies new social experiences commonly characterizes the early moments of an ISG as well. Early concerns of group members tend to be rather self-oriented. "Will I be accepted by these people?" "I'm afraid I'll say something stupid." "What am I going to do if I don't like other members of the group?" "What am I supposed to do in here?" An effective activity, usually gentle and relatively nonthreatening, will enable group members to reduce their initial anxiety and begin to focus positive energy on the group's task.

A popular ISG strategy for opening activity is to use a subgrouping approach where the first task is for two group members to share introductions or identify commonalities, then join with another dyad and share more of the same, and so on until the group is interacting as a whole. The gradual buildup often contributes to a trusting atmosphere without creating the unnecessary pressure associated with having to relate directly to the entire group immediately. Both trust and tension reduction can also be achieved through the specific focus of the activity. For example, an introductory exercise for a career-exploration group could be directed at some aspect of the individuals' work histories or future plans. A person may be asked to introduce a partner to another dyad by describing the partner's favorite work memories or unique occupational experiences. It is important that the structured exercises used during the initial group session include opportunities for participants to get to know each other, with the aim of eventually interacting on a first-name basis.

As mentioned, introductory exercises should be carefully selected for their relevance to the specific purposes of the group. Care must be taken to avoid using introductory activities that have no relationship to either the group goals or the desired mode of interaction among members. This caution applies particularly to the indiscriminate use of icebreakers. The less directly the initial exercises relate to the stated purpose of the ISG, the greater responsibility the leader assumes for the outcomes. In other words, if there is not high face validity to the exercise, then members must trust the leaders not to harm them or to place them in embarrassing situations because they have nothing else to guide them.

Establishment Stage: Group Dynamics

Norms. From the beginning groups develop and modify norms for behaviors that are appropriate in the group. Leaders and members alike contribute to this on-going process. Common norms are that members

- Arrive on time and attend all sessions
- Provide honest feedback (expressed in a caring fashion) to other group members
- Share feelings and thoughts openly and honestly
- Actively participate in group interaction
- Listen to what others have to say and allow them to complete a statement before speaking
- Do not discuss information obtained from or about other group members with people who are not members

Confidentiality should be a group norm that emerges from within rather than simply being established by the leader. Special note about confidentiality is made here because of its critical importance to the functioning of the group. Leaders need to explain the significance of members' holding in confidence the content and nature of the group's interactions not only early on but also at different stages throughout the group's life. Because of its subtle nature, confidentiality can be elusive for some group members to comprehend. Obviously, confidentiality holds special significance for young-adult college students, who are dealing with identity issues that are also closely intertwined with peer-group and family issues. Group members of all ages, however, gain a sense of psychological assurance and protection when the group commits clearly to holding its content and activities in confidence. Whether a simple ground rule or a group norm (ideally both), confidentiality is a highly volatile commodity that can enhance or limit group cohesiveness, depending on how group members adhere to it.

Sometimes groups have negative norms, or group-accepted conventions of behavior that are not conducive to goal achievement. In such situations, the leaders may decide to help the group attend to its collective behavior and evaluate the relationship of such norms to its goals.

Group Characteristics. Group theorists and experienced leaders tend to agree that one of the two most influential variables in group dynamics is the group members' characteristics (the other is group leadership) (Napier and Gershenfeld, 1983;

Zander, 1985; Corey and Corey, 1987). From the outset, it is therefore incumbent on ISG leaders to concentrate on understanding both the intrapersonal characteristics and interpersonal dynamics of the group members. The group may be heterogeneous or homogeneous in terms of the members' personal characteristics. Although both kinds can facilitate goal achievement, depending on the nature of the goals, heterogeneous groups tend to have more varied resources and may, therefore, provide greater stimulation, challenge, and diversity to the participants than do homogeneous groups.

Trust. An essential element of group work is trust. A group leader endeavors from the beginning to foster a trusting atmosphere in which members sense mutual acceptance and caring. Typically, initial resistance needs to be overcome. This resistance may be directed toward the leader or toward the group itself. Regardless of its exact nature or direction, the resistance will remain evident in the group until it is replaced by a growing spirit of mutual trust characterized by self-disclosure, feedback, and moderate risk taking. ISG leaders often include trust-building exercises in the beginning session. Such exercises may take the form of problem-solving tasks, which require immediate group interaction and cooperation, or team-building activities, which require joint planning and execution. These kinds of exercises are designed to enhance a sense of trust that is earned by working together.

Cohesiveness. One of the defining characteristics of a group is the reciprocal nature of the members' interactions because group membership requires a degree of interdependence. As a direct result of this dynamic relationship one member's behavior affects that of all others. It is largely the reciprocal nature of the group that differentiates it from an audience or other collection of individuals (see Chapter Two). The relative strength of the members' interrelatedness affects the group's goal-related behavior. Generally speaking, a minimum level of cohesiveness is required for a group to remain together and to function effectively. Group membership must be attractive, or the individuals involved will not care to maintain the group's existence. From this perspective, the development of a group identity is an important task in the establishment stage of the ISG. Cohesiveness is naturally enhanced as the group moves toward goal achievement. Likewise, it is strengthened by the leader's use of such techniques as linking and pairing, used primarily to help individual members recognize commonalities.

Establishment Stage: Desired Outcomes

Certain outcomes should result from the initial ISG session, outcomes that will determine to a considerable extent the group's chances of accomplishing its goals. Although Chapter Six dealt with basic leadership skills, they are emphasized here again because they are so essential to assuring that desired outcomes are achieved. These initial ISG outcomes are providing structure, clarifying goals, establishing ground rules, formalizing strategies, establishing leader credibility, and recognizing group members.

Structure Provided. Structure (the degree to which a group is focused on its goals or purpose and the degree to which leader and member roles are fulfilled and remain relatively stable) within the psychological entities known as groups can be a two-edged sword. It can promote learning and self-exploration or it can destroy the group and produce negative results for members. If an individual attempts to use the structure to satisfy ego needs for attention and power through manipulating other members, leaders, or the process, then the structure may become a weapon used against the group. This possibility is of particular concern during the initial session because the group has not yet formed and established its norms of acceptable conduct and thus has not developed effective means to oppose dominating or manipulative individuals. At the other extreme, leaders and members can hide behind structure or planned exercises and rapid-fire activities as a way of maintaining control of the situation or of avoiding personal and potentially ego-threatening interactions or confrontations. In either case the G (group) is lost from the ISG.

ISGs are optimally effective when structure is tight enough for members to feel secure in taking risks that have relatively predictable consequences but loose enough for participants to have a meaningful role in making decisions and influencing the group's direction. Members must be willing to trust the good intentions of other members; leaders must be willing to share authority and control with the group; and both leaders and members need to believe in the power of the group to produce significant learning opportunities. This balanced view of structure needs to be communicated, examined, and revised if necessary during the early ISG sessions.

Goals Clarified. Goals and objectives need to be restated and examined during the initial group session so that discrepancies of interpretation can be resolved. As noted previously, false expectations on the part of even a single participant can play havoc with the ISG experience for everyone. During the initial session it is important that false expectations be identified and altered and, if necessary, that those who hold them too dearly be encouraged to withdraw from the ISG.

Ground Rules Established. As previously noted, the establishment of ground rules is essential to a group's cohesion and task achievement. The basic parameters and normative expectations need to be clearly identified, examined, and stated in final form early in the life of the group if it is to prosper. Ground rules should be neither established by whim nor discovered by chance.

Activities Explained. ISG members need to be made cognizant of both the types of activities in which they will be expected to participate and their rights regarding these activities. For example, dyadic interactions or learning contracts may be activities that participants have seldom or never participated in. Such methods, strategies, and techniques should be discussed with participants during the initial session to assure that they understand both what is expected of them and why the activity is relevant and essential. Often, for instance, participants do not expect homework assignments. If such expectations exist but are not mentioned in the initial session, they may be rejected or seriously challenged later after informal group norms have been set. In addition, members should be informed that they can opt not to participate in a particular activity without fear of penalty or that they can resign from the group if its processes seriously conflict with their personal needs or values. (See Chapter One for suggested guidelines.)

Leader Credibility Established. Nearly all group leaders are assigned certain idiosyncratic credits by virtue of their position status (see Chapter Two for a discussion of these credits). Leaders cannot, however, rely on such credibility to carry them through the full ISG. Rather, they must earn their credibility repeatedly, and that process should be intentionally begun during the initial group session, largely by exhibiting appropriate and recognizable leadership skills (see Chapter Six for specifics). Napier and Gershenfeld (1983, pp. 104–105) refer to a grace period of about one hour that most group leaders can expect. During this time participant hostility and antagonism will be submerged and courtesy will prevail, no matter how outrageous the intervention or presentation might be. These authorities identify a number of techniques that leaders can use to good effect during this grace period to strengthen their credibility. These leader behaviors include:

- Presenting . . . credentials, an especially important consideration for members who tend to exhibit dependency needs.
- Exhibiting enthusiasm about what the group is intended to accomplish.
- Displaying self-confidence which makes others feel comfortable.
- Exhibiting an optimistic attitude about the potential for the group's chances for success.
- Displaying basic knowledge and leadership skills that sug-

gest the leader knows what he or she is doing and that he or she is "in control."

- Exhibiting that one is capable of handling group members who might be obstreperous or obnoxious, thereby preventing a group disaster.
- Displaying a high level of organization and thoughtful planning without evidence of overcontrolling or manipulating the group.
- Exhibiting a sense of humor and the ability not to take himself or herself overly seriously.
- Showing the group that she or he is a good listener, and that she or he does hear what individuals are saying. This might be manifested by altering the structure or time line of the ISG in some fashion to accommodate members' needs or wishes.
- Providing the group with an early success so that participants are more optimistic about the potential for the long-range value of the group [Napier and Gershenfeld, 1983, pp. 104–105].

Taking advantage of this grace period to lay a sound foundation of leader credibility will, in most instances, result in the ability of the leader to maintain the high levels of credibility essential to success.

Group Members Introduced. Finally, the initial session should provide group members with the opportunity to be introduced to each other and to establish at least a modest acquaintanceship. Because group interaction is such an important ingredient in any ISG, group leaders should make sure that members have sufficient opportunity to build a cohesive group with which to interact. Cohesiveness results from members' coming to know and recognize one another as unique individuals. The earlier this task can be accomplished, the better.

Exploration, Transition, and Working Stages: Frequently Encountered Problems

Numerous predictable issues, problems, and events occur and recur during the life of an ISG. These may or may not become manifest during any ISG stage. Rather than attempt to arbitrarily relate them to a particular ISG stage, we present and discuss them in the context of the group's three middle stages. (See Chapters Two and Six.)

To resolve these problems, well-prepared leaders will have a repertoire of strategies. If ISG leaders have not thought about response options for dealing with these potential problems prior to encountering them in a group, they are likely to be caught off guard, creating awkward or unnecessarily tense situations in the group. Although it is neither possible to foresee all problems nor desirable to have canned, or programmed, responses for all situations, leaders can respond in productive ways when they have thought through and discussed with coleaders the most commonly occurring problems. Before selecting a response strategy for a particular problem, leaders should always analyze and seek to understand the events that led to the situation, the frame of reference of each person involved (personalities, backgrounds, and group behaviors), and their own behavior as leaders. Although there are seldom any pat solutions for a given situation, there are invariably some responses that are more effective and appropriate than others. In fact, it is not uncommon for a group to evolve to an advanced stage as a result of dealing effectively with such problem situations. Following are some of the common situations with suggested approaches to dealing with them.

Transference and Countertransference. A psychoanalytic concept, transference is the projection of repressed experiences or feelings from the past onto a person or persons in the present. The person has a distorted or unrealistic view of the leader or others in the group and behaves toward them (1) as if they were actual persons from his or her past or (2) in the same manner as he or she related to significant others in the past. Even if one does not accept the basic tenets of psychoanalysis, most would agree that an individual's previous interpersonal experiences will affect how that person behaves in the present. In other words, past learning affects present behavior (Hansen, Warner, and Smith, 1980).

Transference is likely to become evident in an ISG in

several ways. Usually, transference will be expressed as an attitude toward the leader, such as making the leader an expert, authority figure, superperson, friend, or lover (Corey and Corey, 1977). The leader-expert is viewed as someone who has all the answers; if the member only listens carefully enough, the leader will make him or her better. If the leader does not do so, the transferring member may begin to feel resentful and may reject the leader as being incompetent. The leader-authority or, from the transferring member's perspective, parent figure is perceived as being intimidating, controlling, and the judge of the member's worth as a person. The member may previously have perceived parents as respected but feared authority figures. Members transferring in this way will exhibit approach/avoidance behaviors or vacillation in the relationship. The leader-superperson is viewed as being perfect, having no faults, fears, or inadequacies. When the member finds that the leader is not perfect, the member will continue to behave as if it were true or will reject the leader as being unworthy and as having betrayed him or her. The leader-friend is viewed as being someone with whom the member has a special relationship—a friendship—not shared by other group members. It is reasonable to expect that the leader will be friendly with all group members, but it is unprofessional on the leader's part—and likely to be detrimental to the ISG—to establish a private friendship with a group member (at least for the duration of the ISG). The leader-lover is viewed as being romantically attracted to the member, who as the leader's lover has attained special status in the group. The member will likely react to the leader as a betrayed or jilted lover would react when the member discovers that the leader has no reciprocal romantic interests. In order to understand a member's transference behavior we must always remember that it is based on a fantasy or a nonexistent history of a relationship.

Several different strategies may be used to deal with transference: (1) Humor: "You're not really coming on to me?" or "Do you really want me to be your father and pay you an allowance?" (2) Acceptance: Recognize what is happening, but be careful not to respond to the member in the ways expected and do not make an issue of it. Because ISGs are of relatively short duration, the best solution for the group and probably for the affected member may be to not deal with the transference directly. (3) Direct acknowledgment: The leader can note at the appropriate moment, "You seem to want me to be your mother (father, friend)." As a result, it may be unnecessary to explore the transference further. As a general rule, transference can be most effectively dealt with, causing the least disruption in the group or pain for the member, when the leader begins to make observations about apparent transference early in the life of the group.

Leaders also need to be aware of the phenomenon of countertransference — that is, when the leader responds to a transferring member in the way desired by the member — as parent, lover, or authority, for example. Countertransference has the potential for substantially impairing the effectiveness of the ISG, will almost surely impede the development of the group, and is likely to be resented by other group members and cause them to respond with hostility to the leader and possibly the transferring member. One of the advantages of coleadership is the availability of someone to point out what may be unconscious behavior relating to countertransference. Corey and Corey (1977) suggest three strategies for dealing with countertransference: (1) Do not be gullible and uncritically accept all the positive feedback received from group members. (2) Do not attribute everything that happens — positive or negative — to transference (coleadership and use of formative evaluation data can help keep events in the proper perspective). (3) Recognize that all feelings toward members are not the result of countertransference and that a leader generally will be more attracted to some members and like them better than others.

Sexual Feelings and Behaviors. Leaders should not be surprised when sexual behaviors become manifest in a group or when sexual feelings are evident — even in groups dealing with career exploration or leadership training. Sex is a normal part of life and can be expressed in relation to almost any topic. As a general rule talking about sexual feelings should not be discouraged as long as it is germane to the ISG's goals and appropriate in the current context. If it is not germane or appropriate, the leader can express an opinion to that effect, similar to an opinion about inappropriate talk related to any other topic.

Evidence of a sexual or romantic relationship between members is of greater concern than manifestations of sexual behavior or feelings. Members who fall in love (or lust) during the course of the ISG or who have established a relationship prior to beginning the ISG generally create problems. Because of their special relationship, in which others cannot share, they are viewed as being different by other group members. The leader can employ several strategies for dealing with these situations: (1) Acknowledge the relationship, which will probably have the effect of giving the group permission to deal with it. (2) Make humorous references to behavior that is disruptive or negatively affecting the group's functioning—for example, "We can get started as soon as Mary and John finish examining each other's eye color." (3) Make a point when dividing the group for activities to separate the "lovers." (4) Explain to the group in an abstract way how these kinds of behaviors can influence others in the group and its functioning. (5) Deal privately with the members and help them understand how their behavior is affecting the ISG. If the expression of sexual feelings is focused on the leader, it can be dealt with in ways suggested in the previous section on transference. Also, as noted in Chapter One, it is unethical for a group leader to be sexually involved with members of the group.

Clowning and Joking. Humor can serve an important function in groups. It is often a healthy means for releasing tension and providing breathing space between activities. Sometimes it will be used by a member as a way of providing "safe" feedback to another; the giver of the feedback may say "I didn't mean it, I was only joking!" if the receiver reacts defensively or negatively. The leader may or may not wish to deal with such "denied" feedback, depending on the circumstances and the group's current stage of development.

Joking and clowning can also disrupt the group, especially when engaged in by a minority of the members, and can have a number of complex and interrelated causes. The first step in selecting a strategy for dealing with this kind of disruptive behavior is to attempt to understand why it is occurring. Are some members acting as clowns because this is a role on which the group insisted? Does the group reinforce the behavior by laughing at everything the clowns do? Are the jokers so insecure in the group that they are afraid to expose themselves to serious attention from the group? Is this typical behavior for these people in all groups? Several strategies may be useful once a diagnosis has been made. The leader can (1) focus attention on the joking members by having them stay on the topic they found uncomfortable even after a joke, (2) make observations about the effect the clowning around has on group dynamics and on accomplishment of the ISG's goals, (3) give the clowns leadership responsibilities, and (4) make observations about when the clowning tends to occur—for example, that it occurs when a member seems about to deal with a heavy or emotionally laden topic.

Blocking. Blocking can take a variety of forms. Blocking behaviors prevent the group from accomplishing its goals or prevent members from participating fully. Members exhibit blocking behaviors when they:

- Are generally hostile or react negatively to whatever is proposed
- Continually play the devil's advocate, prolonging all discussions
- Overintellectualize every experience in the group, offering a theory for everything
- Gossip during group sessions
- Tell long stories to the group

The first step in dealing with these problems is to determine why the member is blocking. Is it a reaction to a special circumstance, or is this the individual's usual way of responding in groups? Is the member aware of the effect this behavior has on the group? Techniques a leader may use for dealing with blocking behaviors include: (1) Request question askers to make only declarative statements for one session. (2) If a member is talking about another person in the group, request that the member speak directly to that person. (3) Recognize the positive aspect of a statement (even if it was not intended) and fail to respond to the negative aspect; for example, respond to a member's criticism of the way an exercise was set up by saying, "I am pleased that you are concerned about getting the most possible from this exercise." (4) Confront the behavior directly and request the member to stop: "I appreciate your understanding of psychology, but your theorizing makes it hard for me to concentrate on our group goals. Would you please hold that for now?" (5) Reflect hostile feelings back to the giver: "It sounds to me like you are very angry because everyone didn't agree with your proposal." (6) Challenge the critic to propose an alternative way to do things. (7) Ask other members of the group to express their opinions about whatever it is the critic objects to. (8) Sidestep the issue: "You may be right about this exercise, but let's go with it anyway. OK?" (9) Acknowledge involvement without acknowledging content of statement; for example, respond to a member's objection to the leader's decision to move to another exercise by saying, "I appreciate the intensity of your involvement, and I think that you will get a lot from the next activity we have planned also."

Participation Issues. Problems often arise from behavior at either of the extremes of a participation continuum—that is, individuals who dominate the group and people who remain silent or are nonparticipatory. The most effective interventions for dealing with these issues will invariably come from the group rather than from the leader once the group has reached the working stage because the group can then give members direct feedback about how they are perceived. The leader, however, will usually need to make direct interventions in the earlier stages of group development. Several strategies can be used with dominators: (1) Make a period. That is, the leader can say (even cutting into a long speech if necessary), "Thank you for contributing that. . . . Our next topic is. . . ." (2) Make observations about the group process: "Thanks, John, but you have taken most of the time; let's give everyone a chance to have a say." (3) Approach the dominators outside the group, thank them for their involvement, and enlist their support in encouraging others in the group to take an active role. In other words, co-op them into a leadership role.

Several techniques are available for dealing with nonparticipant or silent members, including: (1) Note publicly in the group that some members do not seem to have much to say and that the leader has found that maximum benefit can usually be gained from an ISG when everyone takes an active part. Ask the group what can be done to encourage everyone to participate actively. (2) Design exercises involving dyads or triads. Many silent members will become actively involved when dealing with only one or two other people. (3) Assign silent members leadership responsibilities or tasks. If asked directly, these members may capably take on active roles. (4) Discuss the apparent lack of participation with the members privately outside the group. It may be that they are shy and do not usually voice their opinions in group situations, even though they are having a meaningful learning experience in the group.

Unexpected or Inappropriate Emotional Outbursts. Many leaders of ISGs experience considerable anxiety when a member unexpectedly becomes highly emotional in a group and begins crying or becomes extremely angry. These reactions can occur seemingly out of the blue. Because ISGs have limited time frames and predetermined goals, leaders are not usually free to go with whatever happens. A leader may want to consider dealing with these situations in several ways: (1) If the leader has the requisite counseling skills and experience, a good approach is to encourage emotionally distraught members to talk about what is disturbing them and to invite others in the group to help resolve the problem. (2) If the leader does not feel comfortable dealing with the emotional outburst directly at that time or if the dictates of time or structure prevent dealing with it then, the leader can acknowledge the emotion, but change the subject. "I know you are very upset right now, Mary, but we have only ten minutes left in this session and I think it is important that we talk about the homework for our next session. I would like to talk with you about this immediately after the session" (or at some specified time if it is not possible immediately after the session). (3) In coled groups the coleader can take the disturbed member aside and help the person deal with the situation. Whatever strategy is chosen, however, the leader should follow-up with the member after the session and either offer individual assistance or make a referral to an individual qualified to assist with the problem.

Exploration, Transition, and Working Stages: Useful Techniques

Feedback Strategies. One of the best ways to determine whether an ISG is effective and of value to group members is through the use of systematic individual and group feedback. Feedback should be sought throughout the ISG, not only when the group is terminating. Opportunities for group members to comment on and critique the ISG, its content, processes, and leadership should be provided in various forms. Leaders can ask open-ended questions that stimulate members' thinking in a particular direction: "What do you see as the primary strengths or shortcomings of this session?" "What can we do to make this a better learning experience for you?" "What group activities were most significant and helpful to you?" Questions that can be answered with a simple "yes" or "no" are of little value in most instances. Numerous other feedback approaches can be used. For instance, a process circle, where group members openly discuss their feelings and experiences in the group by responding to "I learned . . . ," "I feel . . . ," and "I think . . ." sentence stems, often generates valuable feedback. A short written feedback form designed to assure anonymity is also a useful tool. Probably the best way for a leader to stimulate honest, open, and objective feedback within the ISG is to model similar behavior by giving feedback to participants.

Valid and honest feedback is sometimes difficult to obtain if the leader seeks it directly and personally. Although group leaders usually possess positive personality characteristics, the most valuable feedback is not that which occurs in direct response to the leader's personality. Although a leader may be a "great person" with much charisma, or an "enigmatic shadow" who is difficult to get to know, or an "S.O.B." whom no one trusts, requests for direct feedback to the leader may produce uniformly positive responses. Because group members are often inclined to tell a leader what they think the leader wishes to hear rather than to give an objective report, it is usually better to seek feedback through less direct methods. Trust is the key element in obtaining valid feedback, and trust develops if the leader is open, honest, objective, trustworthy, and fair. Leaders and group members alike must remember that the most useful feedback includes both positive and negative aspects, both of which deserve close attention.

Encouraging the Application of New Learnings. ISGs are designed with particular goals and outcomes in mind. Those outcomes are typically concerned with the provision of a body of knowledge or a set of coping skills that, when learned, can enhance the quality of life of the individual members. Usually, the long-range effects of ISGs depend largely on whether individual group members have either assimilated the knowledge and skills to which they have been exposed into their current modes of thinking and behaving or, more desirably, have accommodated their thinking and behaving patterns to the new learnings (see Chapter Three concerning the cognitive developmental processes involved). Mastery of new learning implies the ability to apply that learning in everyday situations, which usually calls for regular daily practice until the new learning is imprinted on the way one thinks and functions. Because one of the ISG's primary purposes is to facilitate advanced levels of development in group members, continued use of the knowledge and skills acquired in the ISG is of the essence. Group members must be helped to understand this fact during the working stage, when they are practicing new behaviors and experimenting with new roles.

Most individuals have experienced an enjoyable learning situation in which some new skill was introduced, discussed, and even practiced only to have it slip away because of their failure to use it on a regular basis. The old adages "practice makes perfect" and "use it or lose it" apply here. It is one thing to learn something; it is another to integrate that learning into everyday living. Summarizing the learnings that were intended to occur during the ISG is an essential, although not sufficient, instructional strategy. Leaders must also assign participants homework to complete between sessions and encourage them to establish plans for practicing the skill or using the knowledge on a regular basis. It is a good idea to give the group members a practice schedule and recommend that they follow it even after the ISG has ended. Providing group members with tangible materials and schedules increases their awareness of the importance of such activity and reinforces its implementation. Another form of outcome reinforcement is the personal contract. If group members make a contract with the ISG leader or better yet with other group members to regularly practice the ISG learnings, they will probably continue to use the new learnings until they accommodate their thinking and behavior to them.

Interval Closure. Most ISGs, even though designed for a single purpose, include several components. These components are typically the equivalent of lesson units, which, when combined, make the ISG complete (for example, a leadership-training ISG might include separate units on democratic leadership style, delegation, leading a meeting, and parliamentary procedures). Similarly, many ISGs are presented in separate sessions over a specified time period (for example, weekly three-hour sessions for four weeks; two ninety-minute sessions a week for six weeks). Usually both the lesson units and the individual ISG sessions are relatively self-contained in that they focus on a particular content area or skill that participants are supposed to learn. As a result, there are a number of rather natural points during the ISG where a certain level of understanding or kind of learning should have occurred and when content, process, or activities should be shifted.

Interval closure is pausing at these natural points to help group members process the information to which they have been exposed, discuss the relevance of the skills they have been learning, and examine the extent to which these learnings relate to the purposes of the ISG. For group members, interval closure is an opportunity to reflect on a particular learning or to contemplate and assimilate what was covered during a particular session. Interval closure is the act of finding meaning in one or more parts of the ISG experience as well as assessing how effectively the ISG is progressing toward its goals. In this sense, it is a kind of formative assessment, which may call for structural or substantive changes to be made in the ISG.

It is thus of paramount importance for both ISG leaders and participants to stop the presentation or action from time to time to examine the meanings the content or skills have for group members. Often the materials covered are cumulative in nature; advanced understanding and behavior are based on previous exposure to simple concepts or procedures. If the early learnings are not complete or the individual group members have not assimilated them, then the desired learning and development will probably not occur. Participants should have an opportunity to complete the learning intended for a particular time period before moving on to new material. To assure that members have such opportunities, time should be built into each session for participants to (1) process and achieve closure on the new learnings and (2) review learnings from previous sessions that are the basis for new content to be covered or new skills to be learned in the present session. It is important for group members to understand the relationships between what was covered previously and what is to be covered in the future. It is also important for group members to obtain a reasonable degree of closure at the end of each session so that the new learnings will become firmly established. Effective interval closure increases the transfer of learning from one session to the next and beyond into real situations. This transfer of learning is an essential part of the ISG experience. Achieving interval closure helps members acquire a sense of accomplishment and allows them to see the value of investing their time and energy in the ISG.

Termination Stage

Termination is a natural part of any group's life. With ISGs the termination stage is planned from the beginning. In most instances it is a time for individual members to celebrate completion of a development experience, although in some instances extenuating circumstances may need attention. The well-qualified ISG leader understands the role and function of group termination and uses it to enhance group members' transitions to new and different experiences.

The unique nature of the ISG requires that the group come to an end at a predetermined point. The length of the group's life, in other words, is built into the original plan on the basis of the projected time it will take to accomplish the group's goals and objectives. Once processes and procedures for achieving outcomes have been determined, it should be possible to establish a reasonable time for the procedures to be accomplished. At termination the ISG has accomplished its goals and stops meeting. Decisions about when to implement these ISG terminal points should be made even before group members are recruited or identified. As noted in Chapter Two, termination calls for special attention during the planning phase (see Chapter Four).

Obtaining closure and terminating the group, however, are neither simple nor perfunctory procedures because both the participants and the leaders have invested much time and energy in the group and its activities. If the ISG has been successful, significant, meaningful relationships have also been established. Anyone who has become intimately involved with others has experienced the tension, stress, and sadness that occur when the relationship ends and the individuals go their separate ways. Because of this phenomenon, achieving closure within the ISG deserves careful attention.

Three types of termination are important for ISG leaders to consider: (1) premature termination, (2) group termination, and (3) psychological closure. Each is an important component of the ISG's termination stage. Premature termination is undesirable, will inevitably be detrimental to the ISG, is not typical for most participants, and can limit the overall value of the ISG. Group termination is the procedures used to bring the group to an effective and planned close. Psychological closure focuses on individual group members and the unique ways they may respond to termination issues.

Premature Termination. During the course of an ISG some members may contemplate leaving the group prematurely. The reason for this decision may be lack of satisfaction with the group's progress, determination that time and energy demands are too great, loss of interest in the content of the ISG, dissatisfaction with the leader, feelings of alienation from the group, or disillusionment about the group's value. Any of these considerations may result in the member's quitting the group outright or being late for or missing sessions. Often participants will not share these concerns with group leaders unless confronted directly about them. Premature termination may also mean that the individual withdraws psychologically from the group rather than ceasing to attend sessions. As a result of premature termination, the terminating member no longer benefits from the ISG experience and is denied a natural closure to it, and the continuing group members lose the input and involvement of the lost member, which will diminish the group's positive influence on everyone. For leaders, premature termination can evoke a negative response and may result in doubts about their competence and feelings that the ISG was not successful.

To date little research literature is available to help ISG leaders understand the nature of the phenomenon or the characteristics of those who terminate prematurely. Pekarik (1985), who studied premature termination in individual counseling, notes that the research has produced conflicting results and that there appear to be small observable differences between clients who persist in therapy and those who withdraw prematurely.

The fact that a group member decides to leave the group is not necessarily bad or undesirable. In some cases it may be the best decision that an individual can make under the circumstances. For instance, if the ISG demands more time and energy than a member is able to allot, there may be good reasons for withdrawing. Nevertheless, it is appropriate for the group leader to intervene, for it is the leader's responsibility to support and encourage all group members throughout the ISG experience. If a member fails to attend sessions or is late for sessions, it behooves the leader to ascertain, through some type of formative assessment, what is causing the member's lack of involvement. If the reasons for premature termination are judged to be beyond the ability of the group member or leader to alter, then termination may be a logical solution. However, if the group's processes and procedures or the leader's approach is at fault, factors that can be explained or altered in many instances, then the leader may help the group member understand the circumstances and rethink the decision to terminate. It is not uncommon for more than one member to be concerned about a similar factor. Often a discussion of one member's feelings or concerns by the full group will result in all members' obtaining an increased understanding of the situation and being able to use the ISG for personal growth and development.

Premature termination is sometimes based on the group member's sense that the ISG is not living up to its initial promise. If a group member becomes disillusioned with the group, it may be because there has been a breakdown in communications with the leader or other group members. Such breakdowns usually result in group conflict (if the group member is assertive and presents the issue to the group for consideration) or premature termination (if the group member does not bring the issue into the open).

Another relatively common reason for premature termination is that members conclude that because one part of the goal has been achieved, the complete goal has been achieved. This false assumption may be referred to as *pseudo–goal achievement*. If group members make the assumption that a small shift in behavior or viewpoint is equal to a major shift, then they may be led to believe that they have learned or accomplished all they need to and that they do not have to be further involved in the ISG. This phenomenon is not unlike false crystallization in vocational-development theory, where an individual concludes erroneously that a clear direction has been achieved and therefore stops examining or considering alternatives. In this instance, however, the result is that the individual terminates the ISG prematurely, thereby foreclosing further learning or understandings that may result from continued group involvement. Because instances of pseudo–goal achievement are somewhat common in ISGs, group leaders must be alert to the cues and clues of this phenomenon, including apparent lack of involvement in ISG activities, tardiness, and absenteeism.

Yet another cause of premature termination is group members' desire to avoid the pain and sadness associated with the foreseeable termination of the group. Although they continue to attend the ISG, their participation is at a relatively low, uninvolved level. This type of uninvolved behavior can be a defense mechanism to lessen the pain of termination by avoiding recognition that the group's end is inevitable. Such behavior is a serious concern for leaders who wish to provide a healthy, growth-enhancing group environment. Serious unfinished personal business of this nature needs to be dealt with in a direct and timely fashion.

Group Termination. Nearly every group will ultimately reach a point when it is time to stop functioning as a group and to have its members disperse into other activities and relationships. This is especially true for ISGs because they are designed to accomplish selected outcomes within predetermined time frames. Although it is possible that a given ISG may, through negotiations among leaders and members, have its lifetime extended to assure task achievement, most will have a planned ending point that was established well before the group convened for the first time. Although the rationale for an ISG's having a limited life has been discussed in Chapter One, it is appropriate to reconsider it in regard to planning the group's termination.

Some researchers (Schiff, 1962; Phillips, 1968) indicate that any therapeutic growth process is incomplete without a successful termination. London (1982) notes that individuals who pass the boundary from one experience to another without recognizing that passage in a significant manner detract from the fullness of the event. "We diminish the experience we come from and the experience we go toward. Equally important, we completely ignore the possibility of having an experience of the transition itself" (p. 414). Just as there is a need to provide members with an orientation and an opportunity to join up with fellow members at the group's beginning, there is a need to help members disengage from the group and bring the ISG to an appropriate and timely end. Termination of the ISG, from this perspective, is not only desirable but essential. Planners and leaders need to consider termination an integral part of the ISG.

The most difficult feat in this regard is accurately predicting the amount of time it will take to accomplish the desired outcomes without either shortchanging the participants by underestimating the time needed or providing overkill by seeking to maintain the group's life beyond the time required. Most professional practitioners have experienced both these situations and know how irritating, frustrating, and humbling they can be. Accurate timing, therefore, is of the essence when designing ISGs.

Carefully planned adjournment processes are as important as any other aspect of the group experience. Depending on the type and length of the ISG, informal, formal, or even symbolic approaches to termination can be used effectively. In some groups, participants simply desire to touch or hug fellow members as a farewell gesture. A closed circle in which participants can hold hands or place their arms on one anothers' shoulders and sing a familiar song such as "Auld Lang Syne" may be sufficient. Often a formal activity prior to an informal "good-bye" can be helpful in bringing closure to the group. An opportunity for each group member to share one last time with the group is particularly valuable. For instance, a process circle in which participants share "I learned. . ." or "I will always remember. . ." statements has utility. Likewise, a group evaluation, in which members are invited to give feedback to the group leader and other participants, can be of value. In some circumstances, especially for ISGs of longer duration and where clearly defined knowledge and skill development was involved, a symbolic rite-of-passage activity is most desirable. For instance, the

ISG could include a graduation ceremony, at which certificates of completion or achievement are distributed, or a group meal, at which members "break bread" and "drink a toast" to symbolize the ending of the group and the passing of members from the group to new enterprises. It is appropriate to involve the group members in deciding how termination should come about. The key point is that the group's termination and adjournment are an important part of the ISG, and, as such, should be systematically integrated into the overall plan. It is here that the leader's skill often comes most clearly into play, for the leader needs to model how to terminate a relationship, how to bring an ISG to a close, and how to deal with termination in positive ways.

Psychological Closure. Numerous authorities (Bennis and Shepard, 1956; Lifton, 1966; Spitz and Sadock, 1973; Braaten, 1974; Dunphy, 1973; La Coursiere, 1974; Gibbard, Hartman, and Mann, 1973; Mann, 1975; Yalom, 1975; Tuckman and Jensen, 1977) who have studied and written about the stages or phases of group development have found that termination causes group members concern, sadness, and, in some unusual instances, anxiety. Although individuals respond differently to the group's ending, some personal response can be expected from each. Group participants often form close attachments to others in the group and have great affection for them (Dunphy, 1973). These feelings tend to intensify the separation phase, when individual members are required to disengage from the group. Although this reaction is most noticeable with long-term groups, it can be assumed that many of the same feelings of loss and its resulting tension will be present among ISG members, especially if they have become to some degree dependent on the group for support. As Luft (1984) reports, the ending may also promote defensive responses such as intellectualization, denial, and displacement depending on the group members' personalities. As noted in the discussion of premature termination, some participants anticipate the group's termination with such dread that they begin to deal with it by becoming increasingly less involved as the group moves toward its end.

ISG planners must help participants deal with the sadness

or anxiety that they may experience during the termination by providing opportunities for group members to experience some form of psychological closure. Such provisions need not be exotic, but participants need to express their feelings of affection and concern for the fact that "we shall never meet again." Leaders should also be especially sensitive to those group members who appear to be experiencing termination anxiety, for they may need special attention following the group to help them process their feelings. In some instances referral to other support services, such as a counseling center, may be desirable.

Follow-Through Strategies. If the ISG learnings are of special value for enhancing the group members' lives and if the group met on a relatively long-term basis (more than five or six sessions), a plan for a three- or six-month reunion may be worth considering for both easing termination anxieties and providing impetus for members to use the new learnings after the ISG has ended. A skill-development ISG focusing on weight loss, assertiveness, leadership skills, peer-helper skills, or similar topics might well be enhanced by planning a reunion where post-ISG experiences can be shared. If the group members fail to follow through with their contracts or personal commitments, then the reunion will likely be aborted. This kind of follow-up, however, can be of immense value to ISG leaders and evaluators because concrete evidence on how well the group's original goals and objectives were achieved can be obtained.

The plan-of-action technique, designed to provide individual group members with specific plans to follow after the ISG is completed, has much utility. Individuals can develop practice schedules or other ways to systematically use the new learnings in specified ways. Such a plan of action gives participants the opportunity to make personal commitments to goals they helped create and that they can "own." Although not all group members will respond positively to a self-devised plan-of-action proposal, many will appreciate the opportunity to develop and ultimately implement such a plan as an outgrowth of the ISG experience. The personal-commitment contract previously mentioned can be combined with the plan-of-action proposal to encourage group members to apply their new learnings on a regular basis after the ISG is ended. Such contracts typically include an accountability process, usually in the form of a feedback from the ISG leader or another individual. This approach also provides group members with the opportunity to be reunited with the ISG leader or other members following the group's termination should they so desire. These reunions can be especially helpful for those who find disengagement particularly difficult or who desire to establish or maintain a continuing support system.

Postgroup Considerations

Detecting and Meeting Needs for Further Work. Is there a need on the part of some participants to continue study of the content or development of the skills beyond the ISG? Do some members need to deal with other issues or concerns that came about as a result of the ISG? If such needs exist, what alternatives are available for further instruction or advanced practice? And what other resources can group members use to aid their development in this particular area?

Because individual learning styles differ and students enter ISGs at different developmental levels, some group members will need longer periods of time or different types of group activities than were planned originally to assimilate the new learnings or to accommodate their thinking processes to them. In other words, although most participants may have achieved the desired outcomes by the time the ISG formally ends, a few may not. To extend the time allotted for a given ISG because a few members have not achieved their goals is generally not an appropriate solution. Other alternatives, therefore, need to be identified and considered.

The best group leaders are sensitive to and have the ability to identify the cues that group members who need such additional help give them. Some of the most important cues are (1) references to a lack of understanding about the relevance of what was learned in the ISG; (2) recurring questions about how to apply the knowledge or skills in daily situations; (3) apparent inability to relate relevant concepts, principles, or procedures to ISG discussions; (4) lack of involvement in ISG processing discussions; (5) hostility toward the leader or other group members; (6) loss of interest in ISG activities; and (7) direct requests for help. It is perfectly acceptable for a leader to broach the possibility that a group member needs special attention.

Experienced ISG leaders who are sensitive to the needs of group members will readily note these cues and will be responsive to them. Beginning leaders should be especially aware of the individual differences present in any group and should not overlook the unique approaches some people use to call attention to their special needs. Another good reason for having coleaders in fact is so that cues for additional help can be observed. While one leader is totally immersed in the group's immediate activities, the other can objectively observe subtle calls for help or dysfunctional behaviors within the group. If the leadership team is not aware of these cues, it may not be able to bring the ISG to an effective close for some members. In a sense, nonclosure may be the reverse of premature termination. Even though the ISG has formally ended as planned, for some members the group's termination may be premature.

It is incumbent on ISG leaders to assist the individuals involved to find appropriate help. One option may be for the ISG leader to provide a series of additional skill-building sessions or to hold individual sessions for those who wish to continue the learning process. Another option may be to encourage these individuals to enroll in another comparable ISG for the purpose of continuing the learning process. Yet another alternative may be to refer the individual to another campus or community resource where the learnings may be individualized or the blockages dealt with directly by a counselor or therapist. All these options call for skill on the part of ISG leaders for diagnosing special needs and making appropriate and effective referrals.

Continuing Relationships. ISG leaders may also be called on by the group to provide strategies for members' future relationships. In most instances it is wise to place such responsibility directly in the hands of the group. For the leader to make decisions about or plan strategies for continuing group members' relationships is tantamount to saying that the group is not terminating at this time and to encouraging group members to exhibit leader dependency beyond an appropriate point (see Chapter Six). If the group members feel strongly that they wish to continue to have contact with one another, then it should be left to them to make that decision and to formulate plans for doing so. In most instances, the ISG group members will not wish to pursue a continuing close relationship over time, but if they do, it should be their responsibility to make all necessary arrangements.

Ethical Considerations. Confidentiality of personal information should continue to be maintained after the group has disbanded. Although group ethics must always be incorporated into the ISG and group members made cognizant of their importance, ethics are easy to forget once the group has terminated. It behooves group leaders to inform members that even though the group no longer exists, they are held accountable for the way they deal with information of a confidential nature obtained through group interaction. The fact that the group has terminated does not mean that either the individual members' or the leader's responsibility for holding confidences has lapsed.

Referrals. As we have mentioned, ISG leaders must be prepared to refer individual members to other campus and community resources from time to time. To do so, the leader must be knowledgeable about (1) the nature and location of support resources that can help students deal with developmental issues and/or personal, educational, career, and physical problems; (2) the established procedures for accessing the resources; (3) when to make a referral; and (4) how to make a referral. The first two areas necessitate the ISG leader's having a wealth of information about resources, both on the campus and in the larger community.

For the third area — knowing when to make a referral to a

campus or community agency—perhaps the best rule is: When in serious doubt, refer the individual to a resource more qualified than yourself. This strategy relies on the leaders' knowledge of personal resources and competence and on their ability not to get in over their heads. Often it is a good idea to consult a colleague, supervisor, or staff member from the potential referral agency. In most instances, it is wise for the ISG leader not to attempt to develop a continuing counseling relationship with an individual who is currently participating in an ISG. Such a relationship presents a potential conflict of interest with which both the leader and the group member must deal. If one is qualified to establish a continuing counseling relationship with a student following the ISG, this option is usually acceptable because it will not directly interfere with the completed ISG.

How to make a referral requires special skill. One does not want to alienate the group member by implying rejection, or frighten the person by implying that something serious is wrong. When the leader identifies cues that suggest that a member may be experiencing problems that the ISG cannot help the person resolve, it is a good policy to discuss such observations directly with the individual privately. In most instances, the better the relationship previously established, the easier it will be for the individual to accept the referral recommendation. The leader should explain in a clear and concise manner why the referral is being recommended and what services can be provided by the referral agency. Likewise, the leader should reassure the group member about the qualifications of those to whom the referral is being made. When possible, it is useful to personalize the referral by sharing the name of the referral-agency representative with the group member. It is also helpful to aid the group member in formulating specific questions to ask or statements to make during the initial session to assure that appropriate help will be forthcoming. In addition, encouraging the group member to let the leader know when an initial contact has been made and stating that the leader will be available for further discussion if it is necessary should be helpful. Probably the most important single factor is that the leader communicate a caring and supportive attitude toward the group member so that the member does not feel alienated or rejected during the referral process.

ΙΟΙ EIGHT ΙΟΙ

Applying Intentionally Structured Groups in Student and Staff Development

The principal focus of this book has been on using ISGs to directly address college students' personal development concerns. In this chapter we suggest other applications of ISGs on campus and also indicate other uses for ISGs, such as in staff development activities and organization development interventions. Finally, we proffer considerations on the wider social implications of the use of ISGs.

Student Subpopulations Appropriate for ISGs

There are a multitude of possible applications of the ISG approach to developmental work with college students. The following examples of selected student subpopulations are presented for consideration. They are not intended to cover either all ISG applications on campus or all college-student constituencies.

Student Paraprofessionals. Resident assistants and graduate residents often express confusion and anxiety about the extent and limits of their responsibilities. ISGs that focus on a definition of responsibilities, mastery of basic helping skills, stress management, identification of support resources, and the processes of referral and personal assistance have considerable utility for students in these peer-helper positions.

Students in Residence Halls. Basing programs where students live makes it somewhat easier to advertise and promote them than does aiming programs at a whole campus. Students residing in campus housing who could readily profit from ISG experiences include those who feel homesick, alienated from peers, or threatened by loss of privacy. ISGs can also be effective interventions for dealing with perennial problems encountered in residence halls, such as roommate conflicts and development of community responsibility as well as many typical developmental tasks—for example, selecting a major, learning study skills, coping with male/female relationships, or managing time.

Foreign Students. Students who come to the United States from abroad often experience psychological disturbances resulting from conflicts between their native cultural values and American mores, perceived rejection by American students, loneliness, and, as graduation nears, anxiety about reentry into their native cultures. ISG experiences can be most helpful in aiding these students to cope with their concerns. The group may include a mix of international and native students, a mix of international students from different countries, or students of a single nationality. Leaders should have a reasonable understanding of the cultures involved, which may be accomplished by providing a foreign student with leadership training so that he or she can function as a leader or coleader.

Married Students. A variety of adjustment problems are often experienced by married undergraduate and graduate students. The nonstudent spouse may feel excluded from much of the partner's life and threatened by the partner's educational advancement. If both are students, the anticipation of a dual-career marriage may be a concern, particularly in relation to childrearing or whose career will take precedence. An ISG may serve as a preventive intervention for many other potential conflicts—for example, the assignment of responsibility for housekeeping and cleaning chores or the development of true intimacy.

Members of Student Organizations. Many student organizations (such as fraternities and sororities, academic clubs, and special-interest groups) occasionally develop internal problems that may respond well to an ISG focused on conflict resolution, goal setting, or development of effective organizational patterns. Organizations that desire to improve communication or the planning and executive functions often respond positively to well-conceptualized ISGs.

ISGs can also be helpful to students who have been rejected by or have withdrawn from social groups—for example, following Greek rush. The focus would not be on rejection but rather on finding ways to become involved in the college environment, as well as on repairing any damage done their self-esteem. This type ISG could likewise allow any student seeking affiliation with a campus group to clarify needs and alternatives prior to applying for membership.

Students Living with Parents. Commuting students may need special help in entering the social mainstream of campus life. An ISG properly advertised and presented could meet those needs through a special kind of campus orientation. Often the only reason students do not become successfully integrated into the campus community is because they do not have the requisite social skills or know-how. An ISG designed to help students develop these skills could therefore be of great benefit.

Returning Adult Students. Nontraditional students often feel out of place and somewhat conspicuous when socializing with students much younger than themselves but still feel a strong need for affiliation with recreational, social, and study groups. These needs could be addressed by an ISG that provides mutual support and the opportunity to identify appropriate leisure activities in the college environment. An ISG composed of older students could also be designed to help them deal with the anxiety related to their ability to perform academically, which they often experience when returning to college (or entering for the first time). Groups that include a mix of students, faculty, and members of the larger community are sometimes effective for this purpose but are often overlooked.

Versatility of ISGs

One of the most important characteristics of ISGs is that they are so versatile. Although throughout this book we have emphasized use of the ISG primarily as an intervention strategy for student development, it has many other uses as well. ISGs, for instance, can be used with professional, allied professional, paraprofessional, and support staff members to help them strengthen practical skills and enhance personal development. Likewise, much that has been presented about ISGs has direct relevance to classroom instruction for preprofessional and paraprofessional training. In addition, the ISG has utility as a tool for organization development. Because of the great versatility of ISGs, it behooves student affairs practitioners to know about the alternative uses for such groups. Some of the strengths and weaknesses of these options are discussed here.

In-Service Education. Bringing staff members together periodically to increase their ability to achieve an organization's designated mission is an excellent approach. These programs, however, are seldom well organized and implemented in systematic ways. One effective staff-development strategy incorporates the ISG to strengthen previously learned skills or to introduce new concepts, competencies, or procedures. Because ISGs can be designed to attend to both cognitive and affective domains (see Chapters One and Three), their use for staff-development purposes is particularly valuable. Not only can the knowledge to be transmitted, the skills to be learned, and the procedures to be followed be included in the ISG framework, but the use of this approach can also enhance the capacity of staff members to work together as a team.

However, several cautions deserve attention when considering ISGs for training intact staff. First, any staff that has been intact for more than a few weeks will have established its unique group norms and characteristics. These group dynamics, although not unalterable, have been established over time in the work arena and will tend to be present in the ISG activity initially as well, along with any conflicts, pieces of unfinished business, or other unique dynamics. The planning of an ISG for an intact staff should include recognition of these norms and acute sensitivity to areas of conflict and possible hidden agendas. An ISG designed for an intact staff needs to be constructed to either work around trouble spots or confront them directly. These factors create the greatest damage when they arise unexpectedly during the ISG. When such difficulties are anticipated, administrative awareness and approval of the ISG format become especially important.

Second, just as an intact staff will bring its previously established dynamics to the ISG, the results of an ISG will carry over into the continuing work situations and relationships of the staff. If problematical situations or events that occur during the ISG are not adequately resolved by those involved, their residue will likely spill over into the on-going work situation. Such unresolved fallout may result in conflicts that continue long after the positive aspects of the ISG have dissipated. A method for coping with this possibility should become a part of the overall ISG plan.

Third, as noted in Chapter Six, the group leader's style is an important consideration in any ISG. Because every program administrator has a personal management style that has been developed over time and that has become part of the intact staff's dynamics, it should not be overlooked when planning ISGs. Supervisors who lead ISGs may be faced with a conflict between their management role and the role they play as an ISG leader. If this appears to be the case, someone other than the staff supervisor should lead the ISG. A well-qualified staff member may be assigned the task or an outside consultant may be brought in to lead the training (either a member of the faculty on campus or a person from another campus). Even if these strategies are used, however, certain group dynamics may yet need attention if the ISG is to be efficacious. No matter who leads the group, its value will be related to the influence it has on the behavior of staff members as they carry out their day-to-day responsibilities. Therefore, if the ISG training is incongruent with the continuing nature and characteristics of the administrative unit involved and if the staff members are distrustful of the leader's intentions for the ISG, its impact will be lessened considerably. If such issues are carried to the extreme, it may be the better part of valor to not even attempt to impose the ISG framework on an already volatile situation. In other words, any administrative unit with an intact staff is part of a larger system, and that overall system will influence all that goes on within it, including attempts to implement in-service education. ISGs have great utility for staff development, but they are no panacea for overcoming intrastaff conflicts.

Fourth, when using ISGs for staff-development purposes, it is always important to consider the psychosocial and intellectual maturity levels as well as the knowledge base of those involved. With student paraprofessionals, such as residence hall assistants or peer counselors, it may be especially obvious that maturity levels are relatively low and that basic knowledge about the unit's programs, practices, and procedures is limited. Professional staff members will often exhibit great variation in their sophistication about the unit's role and function, knowledge about the content and skills involved, and interpretation of the processes and procedures by which the mission is to be carried forward. Because of these factors it is usually wise to limit the scope of a staff-development ISG so that the group can focus on a relatively limited area. To do otherwise provides increased opportunity for irrelevant variables to come into play. For example, unless there is a commitment to openly examine and consider change in lines of authority or extent of control exercised by supervisors, activities focusing on open communication can lead to a worsening, rather than an improvement, in relationships. (For detailed discussions of matching levels of personal maturity to staff-development activities, see Hodgkinson, 1974; DeCoster and Brown, 1983; Thomas, 1985; Werring, 1985; Winston, Hebert, and McGonigle, 1985.)

Many of these same considerations require attention when using ISGs with allied professionals such as faculty members who are being trained to function as student-organization advisors. Not only will these individuals exhibit a wide range of knowledge about programs, procedures, and expectations, but there may be credibility issues to resolve as well. The greater the differences among the participants, the greater the difficulty in structuring an effective ISG. Because of wide differences in the allied professionals' formal educations, work responsibilities, academic disciplines, ideas about the purposes of higher education, and experiences in working with students, it can be expected that an ISG involving such individuals will be difficult. Part of that difficulty will result from the likelihood that the allied professionals will be somewhat skeptical about the nature and intent of the ISG in general and have some concerns about the ISG leader's qualifications in particular. Because of factors such as these, those planning ISGs for training allied professionals need to structure the group's content and process carefully so that these issues may be dealt with and resolved during the establishment stage.

The use of ISGs with clerical and other support staff has great potential for enhancing the quality of their work experiences. There may be some difficulties in formulating appropriate ISGs because of wide ranges in age, education, and experience. Nevertheless, they can benefit greatly from the ISG approach, and, in some instances, the opportunity to participate in ISGs may be viewed as a perquisite or as a reward for a job well done. ISG experiences designed to enhance staff members' employment skills and quality of life are especially valuable and appreciated. ISGs that focus on human relations, communication, time management, career renewal, stress management, and anxiety reduction can be of special value. Because their daily work is often monotonous and mundane, many clerical staff members will value being provided with relevant ISG experiences.

Although the caveats noted here are important to consider, they are not meant to imply that the use of ISGs with an intact staff is not desirable or should not be attempted. They do suggest, however, that the leader not go blithely forward without considering the already-established dynamics that influence the behavior of all involved and the possible consequences that may result.

ISGs in the Classroom. Everyone associated with the higher education enterprise recognizes that transmission of knowledge is the function that integrates academic instruction and is the core of formal education. For many, higher education *is* the academic curriculum—the various disciplines and their groupings of the academic courses that make up the formal programs of study of a college or university.

As the field of student affairs has matured it has increasingly incorporated instructional modalities. Two types of formal instruction, often involving academic credit, have come increasingly to be viewed as appropriate for student affairs practitioners to organize, initiate, and take responsibility for implementing. These are (1) life-skills classes and (2) training courses for student paraprofessionals. Examples of life-skills classes are orientation courses for entering students such as University 101, career-development classes, and training classes for student leaders. Training courses for student paraprofessionals are exemplified by peer-helper training courses to instruct students to work as resident assistants, academic tutors, orientation leaders, peer counselors, peer academic advisors, and information providers. The ISG has utility for both these instructional activities.

There are several important caveats for using ISGs in conjunction with formal classroom activities. These concern appropriateness, relevance, grading procedures, the voluntary nature of ISGs, and role conflicts. One of the primary advantages of using the ISG in conjunction with a formal academic course is that it can add new dimensions to the classroom experience for both students and instructor. In some instances the classroom ISG approach may take only part of the instructional time, whereas in others it may be a complete instructional unit. Whatever the case, it is important that the ISG activity be appropriate for and relevant to the particular course, its content, its processes, and its procedures. It must be appropriate because ISGs usually stimulate participants to establish expectations about process, procedures, and relationships that, if not met, result in negative responses. It must be relevant because if students do not understand the relationships between the class and the ISG or are not given sufficient opportunity to make connections between the goals of the sponsoring class and those of the ISG, they will likely view the ISG as irrelevant to their education and possibly as an invasion of their privacy.

Incorporating ISGs in academic classes can be problematical because it is ethically and philosophically important that individuals participate in ISGs on a voluntary basis. Unless the instructor is willing to let students voluntarily opt not to participate in the ISG without penalty (either formal or informal), its inclusion raises serious concerns. Real and viable alternatives must be available for those students who do not wish to participate fully in the ISG. Such alternatives might include participation in another ISG elsewhere on campus or in the community, involvement in a comparable activity, or some more academic way of being exposed to the ISG's content. Even though most students will opt to participate in the ISG, they must be given the right to choose an alternative without recrimination from the professor for doing so.

Because many ISGs are concerned primarily with the developmental progress a student makes and not with completed products or amounts of knowledge gained, the typical grading system is often inappropriate for ISGs. The ISG leader, if also the class instructor, may thus be faced with a problem when grading the ISG activity as part of the academic course. Probably the best resolution is to separate the formal class from the ISG activities when making decisions about grades. If, however, the ISG imparts information or teaches specific skills, the typical classroom grading and evaluation system (such as written examinations) may well be appropriate. In this case, however, the instructor/evaluator must be careful to evaluate only the acquisition of knowledge and skills or the products developed and not to make judgments on the basis of personality, personal characteristics, or level of participation.

In many instances the issue of control comes into play when the classroom instructor leads an ISG. As noted in Chapter Six, the leader's style shifts during the course of the ISG on the dimensions of structure, facilitation, task behavior, and relationship behavior.

The classroom instructor who also functions as an ISG leader may have a role conflict, and students likewise will have to deal with the different roles played by the instructor as the shifts between the two disparate activities occur. Students will first come to perceive the instructor as an academic authority in the classroom and then experience this same individual in a different, more equal relationship in the ISG. The role conflict will be further complicated when the ISG is complete and the class reverts to its traditional approach. Helping students deal with the conflicting instructor/leader roles may provide valuable life experience for them, but this should be an intentional goal and not something that happens inadvertently. In addition, the instructor/leader will have to deal with the role shifts, which may interfere with effective functioning in either role. A reasonable resolution of this problem in many instances is for the classroom instructor to assign the ISG leadership role to a colleague and to participate in it as a coleader or regular participant or not at all.

Organization Development. The ISG approach may also be used in organization development (OD) within institutions and their subunits. Organization development, according to Conyne (1983), "consists of a broad net of applied behavioral science techniques. Following careful diagnosis, any of these techniques might be used in a planned process for change to benefit both the organization and its members" (p. 54). The ISG can be one of the intervention techniques designed to facilitate the change process. Typically, OD interventions focus on administrators or small work groups and hold to the humanist assumption that a climate of trust within an organization will bring out the best in people, thereby strengthening the quality of life of the organization and of those involved with it (Gallessich, 1982). The content of OD activities often includes interpersonal communications, decision making, leadership-group relations, and conflict management, all of which lend themselves to the ISG approach.

As with ISGs for intact staff, it is important to remember that the ISG may well produce results that will influence the organization in various unanticipated ways and that these results must be properly dealt with within the organization. In other words, the organization must be prepared to deal with the consequences of individuals' participation in ISG experiences.

Because ISGs are deliberately designed to facilitate change in those who participate, and because participants will seek to use their new learnings, insights, and skills within the organizational context, it is extremely important for the ISG process to be relevant and directly applicable to the organization's functioning. For instance, those responsible for designing and presenting ISGs must avoid creating a process for change that is not anticipated by the organization's leadership. To promote changes that the leadership does not understand or accept may frustrate all involved and lead to unnecessary conflict. For the same reason, ISGs used for OD purposes will naturally reflect the organization's prevailing dynamics. Issues of status, power, responsibility, leadership style, interpersonal conflict, and general unfinished business that are present within the organization will be present and influential within the ISG as well. As a result, it is important that ISG planners and facilitators build in plans and processes to deal with these issues as a recognized part of the ISG experience.

Change is always somewhat threatening so it is wise to provide as much security as possible when change interventions are being contemplated. A rule of thumb is that the more specific and limited the focus, the less threatening it will be to both participants and authorities. Establishment of clearly defined parameters provides increased levels of security and comfort for all involved.

It is not uncommon for organizations to employ experts who are external to the organization for consultation and staff-development purposes. Although such individuals can make positive contributions, it is extremely important that they be knowledgeable and well informed about the unique nature, purposes, and characteristics of the organization, for their interactions and activities can be influential in many ways. Use of an outside consultant to present an ISG will be productive and effective only to the extent that the ISG fits the nature of the institution. Hiring an external consultant or ISG facilitator to present the ISG without assuring that the facilitator is knowledgeable about the total organization is tantamount to malpractice in the medical profession.

Social Implications

A broad view of the value of ISGs, as articulated in this book, may carry a societal significance well beyond the college campus. The potential impact of the concepts, principles, and dynamics on which the ISG is founded have become increasingly recognized by authorities in the field of group work (see Chapter Two). Many of these concepts have come to be accepted by segments of the larger society, even if not to the extent one might desire. An impressive amount of knowledge has been gained about the behavior of people in groups of all sorts through research in laboratories, in the field, and with contrived groups such as training groups and psychotherapy groups. An understanding of the conditions and dynamics that produce variable effects in the functioning of groups gives rise to the possibility, even the demand, to use that understanding to produce desired effects. These effects may or may not benefit the people involved; and many unplanned or undesired effects may occur, often because of ignorance or misinterpretation.

The rapidly increasing complexity of American society has led to the dominance of the small group as the organizing and planning element. Most of the important decisions made in corporations, government, and other social institutions are made by small groups of people such as boards of directors, committees, and task forces. Individual control and readily identifiable responsibility are clearly restricted to small businesses, shops, and minor institutions. The trend toward group decisions rather than individual decisions has both positive and negative effects. The danger lies in the possible dictatorial nature of the group norm, or what is perceived to be the prevailing attitude or opinion within the group. This condition has been referred to by Janis (1982) as "group think." Fortunately, this negative dynamic is clearly recognized by most people familiar with group processes, and measures can be taken to counteract it. On the positive side, democratic processes seem more likely to occur when decisions are made by groups of people than when decisions are made by individuals. At least the opportunity is available for a free interchange of opinions.

Membership in small groups appears to be unavoidable if one wishes to play an effective role in the mainstream of American society. "To rebel against or stand aloof from the trend toward social and individual control through group decisions may be individually noble but socially unproductive, if not destructive. The inescapable but difficult solution is the fostering of a sense of individuality, initiative, and creativity within the group setting" (Bonney, 1969, p. 229). Groups that meet these goals can be, and have been, established; they are the major underlying aim of ISGs. The more overt goal of ISGs is the achievement of specific tasks. Each enhances the other.

A group that is too closely controlled by authoritative leadership or restrictive social norms inhibits creativity and encourages dependency. But uncontrolled group processes (as in some forms of group psychotherapy) have little relevance for day-to-day social interaction in the workplace or in leisure activities. The ISG model attempts to strike a balance between these two extremes. It maintains clear direction and purpose but also stimulates in each member the potential for creative living and independence within the group context. The creative impulse and the need to feel in control of our own destinies exist in all of us; they are the most potent force in opposition to pressures toward conformity. Once released and encouraged, they tend to propel themselves. ISGs can be employed in many college settings to prepare graduates to function effectively and purposefully within a group-oriented society.

ƗƠƗ APPENDIX ƗƠƗ

Sample Manual for Setting Up an Intentionally Structured Group

We have fabricated a sample ISG manual to illustrate many of the points introduced in this book. Readers may take ideas presented here and incorporate them into their ISGs. We, however, would discourage practitioners from attempting to use this manual to implement an ISG on their campus. As stated repeatedly throughout this book, ISGs must be specially tailored to the needs of the students in the unique environment of each college or university. The reason for including this manual is to lend a sense of reality to the conception of ISGs as presented in this book, including all the troublesome details that must be attended to in order to lead successful ISGs. We recommend that this manual be used only as a reference to identify what should be included in readers' manuals created for their own ISGs.

MANUAL FOR TAKING CHARGE
OF YOUR COLLEGE EXPERIENCE:
GETTING INVOLVED

Dean of Student Affairs Office
Southern State University

Leadership Teams

Bonnie Jones (assistant director of student activities) and Wayne
Leamer (residence life coordinator)
Janet Schmidt (dean of students) and David Hoff (student orga-
nizations advisor)
Jacob Smith (director of financial aid) and Juanita Gardner
(international student advisor)
Herman Wellman (assistant director of housing) and Ethel John-
son (Wellness Center coordinator)
Linda Mulschio (director of new student programs) and John
Davis (director of the Career Planning and Placement Center)

Schedule

Mondays, 3:30–5:30 P.M. (September 21–October 26) *Location:*
626 Main Library Building
Tuesdays, 7:00–9:00 P.M. (September 22–October 27) *Location:*
402 Ryosan Hall
Wednesdays, 6:00–8:00 P.M. (September 23–October 28) *Loca-
tion:* Polo Hall, 2nd-floor study
Thursdays, 4:00–6:00 P.M. (September 24–October 29) *Location:*
Counseling Center Group Room
Thursdays, 12:30–2:30 P.M. (September 24–October 29) *Loca-
tion:* 202 Jones Student Center

General Overview

Evidence of the Need for the Group

Several incidents indicate that students are not taking full
advantage of opportunities to become actively involved in col-

lege. Evidence also suggests that students want assistance in becoming involved.

1. Participation in the spring 1987 student government elections was at an all-time low; only 12 percent of the undergraduates voted.
2. Within the past year, three once-strong and prestigious student organizations that had been on the campus for over five years have folded for lack of participation.
3. A winter quarter 1986 survey in the residence halls conducted by a graduate student in the Student Personnel Program found that over 40 percent of the students were not involved in any organized student activities. By class, 41 percent of the freshmen were uninvolved, 25 percent of the sophomores, 26 percent of the juniors, and 42 percent of the seniors. When those who were uninvolved were asked whether they would like to be more actively involved, 47 percent indicated that they would.
4. A recent report by the University Retention Committee indicated that the gains made over the past five years are not continuing. This past year, after five consecutive years of improvement, there was a 3 percent decline in the number of freshmen who returned for the sophomore year.
5. In a telephone survey of freshmen conducted by the Student Affairs Research Office during spring quarter 1987, 22 percent of those contacted indicated that they had experienced difficulty in becoming involved with student groups and organizations on the campus. Of those who reported difficulty, 41 percent indicated interest in participating in a program designed to help them become involved.
6. Compared with the previous year, participation in fall 1986 sorority rush was down 4 percent, and in fraternity rush participation was down 6 percent.
7. A survey conducted by the Institutional Research Office in winter quarter 1985 found that only 57 percent of undergraduates were members of a group or organization directly or indirectly (for example, religious centers) affiliated with the university.

These data suggest that overall participation in student activities is declining at Southern State University. These data also suggest that many students are experiencing difficulty in becoming involved and have expressed interest in receiving help. Based on the current trends, it appears that about 20 percent of the entering freshman class (of about 2,000) need and have an interest in participating in a program for promoting involvement. In other words about 400 freshmen and probably an equal or larger number of upperclassmen appear to be likely candidates for participation in an ISG to promote involvement.

Professional Literature Support

A number of studies and reports have documented the benefits of involvement in extracurricular groups and organizations.

1. The Study Group on the Conditions of Excellence in American Higher Education issued a report entitled *Involvement in Learning: Realizing the Potential of American Higher Education* (1984). [References for the Sample ISG Manual are listed separately at the end of the Manual.] In that report the argument was made that "the quality of undergraduate education could be significantly improved if America's colleges and universities would apply existing knowledge about three critical conditions of excellence — (1) student involvement, (2) high expectations, and (3) assessment and feedback" (p. 17). The group further stated that "the first of these three conditions — and perhaps the most important for purposes of improving undergraduate education — is *student involvement*. By involvement we mean how much time, energy, and effort students devote to the learning process. There is now a good deal of evidence to suggest that the more time and effort students invest in the learning process and the more intensely they engage in their own education, the greater will be their growth and achievement, their satisfaction with their educational experiences, and their persistence in college, and [the] more likely they are to continue their learning. Highly involved students demonstrate their commitment in a variety of ways: by devoting considerable energy to studying, by

working on-campus rather than off-campus jobs, *by participating actively in student organizations*, and by interacting frequently with faculty members and student peers" (p. 17; italics added).

2. Astin (1985, p. 136) argues that "the amount of student learning and personal development associated with any educational program is directly proportional to the quality and quantity of student involvement in the program," and that "the effectiveness of any educational policy or practice is directly related to the capacity of that policy or practice to increase student involvement."

3. Williams and Winston (1985) report that students who participate in one or more student organizations have greater interdependence, more appropriate educational plans, more mature career plans, and more mature life-style plans than nonparticipants.

4. Hood (1984) and Hood, Riahinejad, and White (1986) found in four-year longitudinal studies that students who participated in organized recreational activities developed greater self-confidence than did nonparticipating students and the quality of the participating students' interpersonal interactions were more satisfying.

5. Astin (1977, 1985) concludes that students who participate in extracurricular activities of almost any type are less likely to drop out and more likely to be satisfied with the college experience that are nonparticipants. He (1977) found that members of social fraternities and sororities (compared with nonmembers) were far more likely to graduate and to express high levels of satisfaction with the college environment.

6. In studies of liberal arts colleges, Winter, McClelland, and Stewart (1981) found that participation in formal, organized extracurricular activities enhanced students' maturity and development of management and career decision-making skills.

7. In studies conducted with industry managers (American Telephone and Telegraph Human Resources Study Group, 1984), the number of college extracurricular activities in which managers had participated was found to be related positively to development of administrative skills (especially decision making and creativity), interpersonal skills (particularly lead-

ership, behavioral flexibility, and personal influence), and promotion to middle-management positions.

Statement of Goals

As a result of this group, participants will reach these
goals:

1. Participants will learn about the benefits (both while attend-
    ing college and afterward) associated with involvement in
    extracurricular activities.
2. Participants will explore their personalities and interests
    and the college environment as a means of identifying
    enjoyable avenues for involvement outside the classroom.
3. Participants will identify specific activities, groups, or orga-
    nizations in which they desire to become involved.
4. Participants will develop a realistic plan for achieving their
    involvement goals.

Group Composition

Five groups of twelve students each are planned (group
needs at least eight members). Members will be freshmen in
their first quarter of enrollment. If there is greater demand for
the groups than there are spaces, a *waiting list* will be established.
All persons on the waiting list will be given an opportunity to
participate in similar groups at the beginning of winter quarter.
As an interim measure, all persons on the waiting list will be
invited to a mass meeting one week after the ISGs begin. At that
meeting, literature about student organizations will be distributed, a short lecture will be given about the importance of
involvement, and the general content of the ISG (in which they
are invited to participate in the winter quarter) will be described. A selected group of student-organization leaders will be
invited to attend the mass meeting and will be available to
answer questions informally about their specific organizations
and about their personal experiences in student organizations.
If there are upperclassmen or nontraditional students

who seek to participate, they will be placed on the waiting list and will be invited to take part in a special ISG composed of upperclassmen during winter quarter. If there is undersubscription of freshman students for the planned ISGs for fall, then these upperclass students will be placed together in one of the planned fall ISGs.

All members will participate in *screening interviews* held during the week preceding the first meetings of the ISGs. Interviews will be conducted by appointment. Wayne Leamer (101 Polo Hall), David Hoff (A-3 Jones Student Center), Ethel Johnson (505 Harpe Hall), and Linda Mulschio (320 Jones Student Center) will conduct the interviews. Ms. Jackson in the Dean of Students Office will maintain the master list. Students will be given their choice of group (by location and time). Once a student is selected, the interviewer will (in the presence of the the student) call Ms. Jackson and enter the student's name. If a group is filled, the student will have an opportunity to select another day or time or to be placed on waiting list for a particular group should a vacancy occur. To the extent possible, the goal is to have members with different academic majors, places of residence, and ethnicities, and to have approximately the same number of men and women in each group.

The purpose of the screening interview is to ascertain (1) whether the student has adequate interest and motivation to commit the time and energy required for a six-week experience, (2) the individual's likely impact on other group members, and (3) whether the student is currently experiencing any psychological problems that either would be exacerbated by participation or would create an adverse climate in the group. Interviewers should be especially alert for individuals who display negative or hostile attitudes, extreme passivity, bizarre behavior patterns, or pronounced ambivalence about key aspects of the ISG.

The interview can best be structured by giving the student a printed handout describing the purposes of the ISG and the basic ground rules. The interviewer should elicit the student's reaction to each of the major points listed. Particular attention should be given to responses related to the time schedule, degree of commitment expected, willingness to interact with other group members, and possibility that personal attitudes and perceptions may be altered as a consequence of the experience. Students should also be informed that they will be requested to complete the Myers-Briggs Type Indicator (to obtain a personality profile), the Student Developmental Task and Lifestyle Inventory, and the Extracurricular Involvement Inventory and to share their personality profiles with others in the group. Students should be informed that sessions will be audiotaped or videotaped for purposes of evaluating the leaders' performance and studying the group's dynamics. Ask student to sign the Informed-Consent Form before leaving the interview. [See Manual appendix for form.]

If the exclusion of a student is based on suspected personality disorders or a peculiar behavioral style, individual counseling should be suggested in place of the group experience. Dr. Joan Wild in the Counseling and Testing Center has agreed to accept direct referrals of these students. If the student expresses a willingness to enter individual counseling, call the Counseling Center (555-6677) and tell the receptionist that "[student name] is being referred to Dr. Wild from the Involvement Group." (The receptionist has been instructed to make as early an appointment as possible for the student to see Dr. Wild.)

Note: *Many interviewers find it extremely difficult to turn away people who have volunteered for a group experience on the basis of their personal characteristics. They may very well need the experience more than anyone. The welfare and success of the group, however, must come first in selection. Remember, not all students can benefit equally from any given ISG, and one "bad apple" really can "spoil the barrel" (for other participants and for themselves as well).*

There will be a $10 refundable *deposit* for participation. (Students who request a scholarship because of financial hardship do not need to make the deposit.) Students who attend sessions and complete assignments will be refunded the deposit at the last session of the ISG. Students who cancel their reservations before the first meeting will also be refunded their deposits. Give students a receipt for their deposits. Encourage students to pay by check. Ms. Jackson in the Dean of Students Office will handle the paperwork associated with the deposits. Deposits and receipt books should be turned in to Ms. Jackson before the first session.

Staffing and Support

Dr. Joan Wild, counselor, Counseling and Testing Center (555-6677), will accept referrals of students identified as "unsuitable" for the ISG (if the students want individual counseling) or students who identify concerns during the course of the ISG that indicate that they could benefit from individual counseling.

Dr. Howell Goldberg, clinical psychologist, Campus Mental Health Center (office: 555-1234; home: 444-1110), will handle emergencies, such as potential suicides and highly emotional episodes during sessions.

Dr. Helen Wilson, president of the Campus Ministers' Association (office: 444-0098; home: 444-6651), will take referrals related to religious concerns. She will contact religious personnel of the appropriate sect according to the student's preference.

Students with general personal concerns should be referred to the Counseling and Testing Center (555-6677).

Students with career-planning concerns should be referred to the Career Planning and Placement Center (555-3399).

Students with academic questions or concerns (including classroom-related problems) should be refered to the Academic Advising and Assistance Center (555-0011).

Advertising and Promotion Plan

The group will be promoted in these ways:

Available Media
Campus newspaper, *The Southern State Star*
Campus radio station, WSSU

Other Campus Communication Possibilities
Residence-hall mailboxes
Student Center bulletin boards

Bulletin boards in residence halls and classroom buildings
New-student orientation
Announcement in admission letter
Word of mouth

Advertising Strategies
Prepare short *Southern Star* newspaper announcement
(two paragraphs)
Prepare newspaper advertisement (two column inches)
for first week of classes
Prepare thirty-second spot announcement for campus
radio station
Prepare Getting Involved flyer for bulletin boards (150
copies)
Contact orientation director to include an announcement in new-student orientation program (possibly develop slide and tape presentation on involvement for
inclusion in orientation program)
Prepare draft of information letter and contact director
of admissions for possible inclusion in regular mail-
ings to new students
Inform campus leaders about Getting Involved and encourage them to spread the word about its importance
to beginning students

Advertising Flyer and Announcement Ideas

Have you ever wondered. . .
- How to go about getting involved in the academic and
student-activities programs at Southern State University?
- What opportunities for involvement are available at SSU?
- How to decide in what to become involved?
- How to become a student leader?
- Who are the best people on campus from whom to obtain
information about becoming involved?
- What your true interests are?
- How to make the most out of your college experience and
obtain the best education possible?

If you have ever asked yourself two or more of these questions, Getting Involved is a great opportunity for new students at SSU that is RIGHT FOR YOU.

Getting Involved is designed to provide you with a unique opportunity to examine, along with a small group of your fellow students, how you can make the most of your college experience through becoming involved in one or more of the programs or organizations at SSU.

Getting Involved has these goals:
- To help students explore the purposes of a college education
- To teach students about the values and rewards of becoming involved in college
- To provide students with an opportunity to meet other students
- To assist students in developing their own approaches to choosing involvement opportunities
- To assist students in meeting those on campus who can be of help in the future
- To help students learn to set achievable goals
- To assist students in making self-assessments
- To assist students in planning strategies for getting involved in SSU programs

Expectations if you wish to join Getting Involved:
- Complete the short application form
- Have a short interview (about fifteen minutes) with one of the Getting Involved leaders
- Complete several questionnaires and personality inventories (takes about ninety minutes)
- Make a personal commitment to meet with ten to twelve other students in a group for six two-hour sessions beginning the week of September 21 and ending the week of October 26
- Pay a $10 Getting Involved deposit (deposits will be returned to students who complete all six sessions; students who drop out before completion will forfeit deposit)

Summative Evaluation Plan

Summative evaluation will be accomplished by a pretest/posttest design. The ISG will be judged successful if the participants become more intensely involved in extracurricular activities than students who expressed an interest but who did not participate in the ISG. The following data will be collected on the ISG participants:

1. Participants will identify all student groups or organizations of which they are members during the screening interview.
2. Participants will complete the Student Developmental Task and Lifestyle Inventory (SDTLI) (Winston, Miller, and Prince, 1987) following the screening interview.
3. During the last ISG session participants will complete the Extracurricular Involvement Inventory (EII) (Winston and Massaro, 1987).
4. Within the first two weeks of winter quarter, all participants will be contacted by telephone and requested to identify all student groups or organizations of which they are currently members. They will also be requested to complete the EII and to return it by mail.
5. ISG participants will be contacted by telephone shortly after mid-term spring quarter. They will be asked (1) to identify all student groups and organizations of which they are currently members and (2) to complete the EII, SDTLI, and a short questionnaire designed to ascertain overall satisfaction with the first year at Southern State University, and to return them by mail. Grade point averages will be obtained from the registrar (the students' informed consent will be obtained during the fall).

The following data will be collected on the comparison group:

1. Students who expressed an interest in participating in the ISG but were unable to be accommodated because of space limitations will constitute the comparison group and will be

contacted by telephone prior to the large group meeting during fall quarter. They will be requested to complete the EII and SDTLI and to return them by mail. (*Students who were deemed unsuitable for participation in the ISG will not be used as part of the comparison group.*)

2. At the beginning of winter quarter, the students who expressed an interest in the ISG but who could not be accommodated will be contacted to participate in the ISG and will be asked (1) whether they attended the large group meeting held in the fall, (2) to identify any student groups or organizations of which they have become members, and (3) to complete the EII and SDTLI and to return them by mail.

3. Shortly after mid-term of spring quarter, students who participated in the winter quarter ISG and those who expressed an interest in the fall ISG but participated in neither of the ISG sessions will be contacted by telephone. They will be asked (1) to identify all student groups and organizations of which they are currently members and (2) to complete the EII, SDTLI, and a short questionnaire designed to ascertain overall satisfaction with the first year at Southern State University, and to return them by mail. Grade point averages will be obtained from the registrar (the students' informed consent will be obtained during the fall).

Contents

Session One

Goals

1. To introduce the workshop
2. To acquaint group members with each other and to begin to build a community atmosphere
3. To establish a group norm of openness and acceptance
4. To build commitment to accomplishment of workshop goals
5. To develop an appreciation of the value of purposive involvement in the college experience
6. To begin exploration of the purposes of a college education
7. To begin the process of group formation and development of group identity

Welcoming Comments

   Goals. The goals at the beginning of the group are:

1. To introduce the workshop
2. To begin the process of group formation

   Time Limits. Five to ten minutes.

   Physical Arrangements. Facilities required include a circular or U-shaped seating arrangement where everyone can see each other's faces.

   Equipment Requirements. The name of the group and the names of the leaders (with their phone numbers) should be posted somewhere in the room, perhaps on a chalkboard or a flip chart. The same equipment is required to enable the leaders to post a set of ground rules. *Throughout the group it will be important to have chalk, masking tape, markers, and sheets of newsprint for group activities.*

Instructions: Details. These announcements need to be made:

- Mention name of ISG.
- Briefly introduce coleaders (mention names, usual work responsibilities, experience and credentials in group work or in student development or counseling).
- Provide overview of time, frequency, duration, and location of meetings.
- Give brief explanation of why the meeting's physical facility has been arranged as it has.
- Share excitement about getting to know new students on a personal level and helping students learn how to take charge of their college experience.
- Acknowledge possible feelings of awkwardness and uneasiness. Deflect any possible concerns that the ISG will deal with deep psychological analysis.

Instructions: Ground Rules. Group rules need to be covered:

- Provide members with a copy of the ground rules for the ISG. [See appendix of Manual.]
- Convince group members of the importance of promptness and attendance by describing the interactive nature of group work.
- Introduce parameters of group focus, giving examples of acceptable behaviors (self-disclosure and feedback) and unacceptable behaviors (violence, punitiveness).
- Notify members of potential risks of group involvement — that is, that their lives may be changed somewhat by their participation and that the changes may be unsettling in the short term, particularly if they're trying out a new behavior like assertiveness or meeting new people.
- Emphasize the voluntary nature of participation in ISG activities and the freedom to pass on any activity.
- Explain why there must be a prohibition of substance use and describe any unique or extra rules associated with the

facility or institution (such as no smoking or rearranging furniture after the session).

Instructions: Goals and Expectations. Group goals and expectations of members need to be discussed:

- Identify and explain the group goals [see Manual appendix], commenting briefly on the assessment data from which the group evolved.
- Mention that later on in this first session members will have an opportunity to discuss the ISG's goals and possibly fine-tune them.
- Describe general expectations for active participation and the particular value of "learning by doing" in this type of activity.

Suggestions, Cautions, and Hints. Leaders need to begin winning the group over by encouraging involvement and establishing a sense of "I'm glad I'm doing this." Much of the early interaction of the group will depend on members' responses to the leaders' personalities. The challenge for the leaders, therefore, is to favorably impress the members and simultaneously set the stage for group goal achievement. Leaders ought to deflect "heavy" involvement (for example, premature self-disclosure) at this introductory point. Defer any substantive questions until later. The purposes of this activity are to disseminate basic information and to set the stage for group formation by encouragement and by initiating the development of a comfortable, sharing atmosphere. Be ready to respond positively and yet strategically to group members who have decided to play a "blocking/dominating" role in the group, for they likely will start early in a quest for attention.

Processing Guidelines. The group should be allowed the opportunity to have input at this point and to react to the proposed ground rules. No additional processing will be required if the information is presented quickly, concisely, and comfortably. Questions and comments about the ISG's goals and procedures will be encouraged later in the session.

Variations. The content to be covered will not change a great deal regardless of approach used, but several variations in approach can be employed. For example, one leader could do the entire presentation, or the coleaders could share responsibilities equally. Much of the information could be given orally or it could be put on posters and charts or it could be given orally and written down.

Suggested Readings. None.

Handouts. Distribute handout on the ground rules and goals of the ISG. (See Manual appendix.)

Progressive-Signatures Exercise

Goal. To initiate group formation and to facilitate getting acquainted.

Time Limits. Twenty to thirty minutes.

Physical Arrangements. Place seats in a circle.

Equipment Requirements. None.

Instructions. This introductory exercise is designed to enable group members to learn each others' names in a spirited and light exchange. Members state their given names and add a brief adjective depicting something they enjoy doing. In a progressive fashion, the next person has to first repeat all others' names and adjectives in order before sharing his or her own. Leaders go last.

Suggestions, Cautions, and Hints. Leaders should watch for signs of excessive anxiety and respond to a member exhibiting such anxiety with a comforting and accepting assurance that it's

OK to make mistakes. Laughter and excitement will help most members relieve their anxiety. If a student begins experiencing difficulty, the leader should step in and help out. No student should be placed under undue stress in this exercise.

Processing Guidelines. In processing this opening group activity, leaders should begin to facilitate group formation. One way is to give special attention to members who seem to be a bit quiet or nervous. Such attention can come in the form of encouraging feedback and solid eye contact. Another technique is to link group members through such comments as "Jackie, you and Ruth sure seemed to pull that off smoothly. I guess you both have pretty good memories. Do you find that kind of exercise easy?" If someone criticizes the activity, it is important for the leaders to accept that criticism without becoming defensive. One of the leaders might say, "That is a difficult exercise, and my guess is that you're not alone in your reaction to it. But I really appreciate how you hung in there with it even though it wasn't a particularly enjoyable activity. You know, I'm always looking for some new ideas to help groups get acquainted. Do you recall any icebreaker activities you have enjoyed? So I don't put Jackie on the spot, how about the rest of you? Any great, fun activities of this type?" A caution, however, is that time can get away from leaders on this activity, so they need to be vigilant.

Variations. Leaders might decide to use a different base for the adjectives instead of the "thing you enjoy doing." The replacement should have a direct and obvious connection to involvement, such as hobbies or favorite places to visit.

Suggested Readings. None.

Handouts. None.

Involvement-Experience Exercise

Goals. The goals of this exercise are:

1. To enhance self-understanding through reflecting on past involvement experiences or lack of such experiences
2. To enhance the level of interaction among group members
3. To further promote group formation

Time Limits. Fifteen to twenty minutes.

Physical Arrangements. This dyadic exercise will require movable chairs so that pairs of group members can face each other. In the absence of movable chairs, the exercise will need to be conducted standing.

Equipment Requirements. A chalkboard or an easel with a pad is needed to display the stimulus questions.

Instructions. Members become acquainted through a brief exchange of introductory information with the person sitting directly across from them (unless they already know that person well) and then share with that person responses to the following stimulus questions regarding past experiences in organizations, activities, groups, teams, or clubs (formal or informal):

1. Experiences in which they were glad to have been involved
2. Experiences in which they wish they had become involved but failed to take advantage of opportunities to do so
3. Experiences in which they would have preferred not to participate

Suggestions, Cautions, and Hints. Leaders should include themselves in this activity, joining with group members in recalling and discussing involvement experiences. Before the group forms dyads, ask the members to recall past involvement experiences. To prevent premature and excessive self-disclosure, indicate that members should share only those recollections with which they feel comfortable. The intention of the activity is to promote recollection more than self-disclosure. Leaders should establish the time limit in introductory comments and keep the group on task with a mid-point reminder of time remaining.

Processing Guidelines. The processing of this activity takes place in the next activity.

Variations. The content of the stimulus questions may be changed as long as they are still directed toward discussing involvement experiences.

Suggested Readings. None.

Handouts. None.

Introduction-of-Partner-to-Group Exercise

Goals. This exercise has three goals:

1. To stimulate the recollection of personal thoughts and feelings related to involvement experiences
2. To provide members with an opportunity to speak aloud to the group as a whole for the first time
3. To facilitate the continuing formation of the group

Time Limits. Thirty minutes.

Physical Arrangements. Arrange chairs in a circle.

Equipment Requirements. None.

Instructions. Members of the dyads formed in the previous activity briefly introduce their partners to the group as a whole by sharing something about the partners' involvement experiences as well as appropriate personal background and other introductory information.

Suggestions, Cautions, and Hints. Leaders should keep this process moving or it will take more time than allotted.

Processing Guidelines. Leaders may want to address follow-up questions to the member being described to help expand the information provided. However, in line with the main purpose of this exercise, the leaders should finish the go-round with an invitation for a few students to complete the stem "I learned..." in reference to the group experience thus far.

Variations. A leader may prefer to concentrate on processing reactions and "I learned..." statements rather than on introductions of partners and the content of the dyadic interactions.

Suggested Reading. Simon, Howe, and Kirschenbaum (1972) give a good description of strategies for using "I learned..." statements as wrap-up activities.

Handouts. Leaders may wish to compose and hand out a completion form for the "I learned..." activity to provide members with a tangible product at the end of the session.

Purposes-of-a-College-Education Exercise

Goals. The goals of this exercise are:

1. To stimulate members to examine their reasons for pursuing a college education
2. To increase members' awareness of the many learning possibilities available in an academic environment

Time Limits. Thirty minutes.

Physical Arrangements. Arrange chairs in a circle for this full-group, open-discussion activity.

Equipment Requirements. Because this activity involves recording brainstorming lists, either chalkboard or newsprint (which can be temporarily taped to a wall) or a number of easels with pads are required, along with markers or chalk.

Instructions. Each member shares perceptions of the characteristics normally associated with an "educated person" (or describes characteristics of the "best educated" person each has known). Descriptions should be short — "knowledgeable," "critical thinker," "involved."

As the students share their descriptors in a brainstorming fashion, the coleader writes the terms on the chalkboard or easel paper. Each proposed term is written in one of three columns or on separate sheets. The coleader considers each term proposed and purposefully lists it in one of three designated learning categories that are not written or shown to the participants when the exercise begins. Based on Bowen (1977), the headings used are cognitive learning, emotional and moral development, and practical competence (for citizenship, work, family relations, consumption, leisure, and health).

Following the brainstorming session, the coleader writes the category titles at the top of the page, and the leader processes the descriptors reported by the students on the basis of the three categories. (In most instances every descriptor presented by the students will fit reasonably well under one of the three headings.) Through this process, the students will come to understand how their perceptions fit logically into a conceptual model of college-student development. (The emphasis should be on using the Bowen model to confirm the students' work, not to correct it.)

Suggestions, Cautions, and Hints. Brainstorming sessions require leaders to serve as both stimulators and controllers. Members will have to be actively encouraged to risk sharing some of their ideas, at least at first. Then leaders will likely need to slow down the tempo a bit without destroying the creativity and participation of the members. Another caution is to be wary of allowing members to make evaluations; encourage evaluators to reframe their critiques into positive statements. Leaders need to be prepared to briefly describe the Bowen model, relating it to the purposes of a college education.

Processing Guidelines. Ask group members to give their reactions to the lists of identified purposes for attending college.

What implications do these characteristics have for involvement? Which kinds of involvement?

Variations. The brainstorming could take place in two small groups (of four to six members each) instead of keeping the group together as a whole. This variation is especially useful when time is limited.

Suggested Readings. Bowen's (1977) first chapter and other materials related to purposes of a college education should be read by leaders as background information.

Handouts. None.

Purposive-Plans Exercise

Goals. This exercise has two goals:

1. To discuss a variety of ways in which the identified goals of a college education could be achieved
2. To encourage members to consider the relationship between the purposes of a college education and the development of personal plans for involvement in the college environment

Time Limits. Ten minutes.

Physical Arrangements. Arrange seats in a circle.

Equipment Requirements. Newsprint, masking tape, and markers.

Instructions. Leaders facilitate discussion of possible ways to achieve selected goals of a college education. The task is to help members understand the relationship between purposes and involvement. One of the leaders summarizes comments on newsprint while the other leader facilitates the discussion.

Suggestions, Cautions, and Hints. Time limits are likely to be significant at this point in the session; therefore, leaders will need to remain especially cognizant of the amount of time remaining.

Processing Guidelines. Encourage members to join in the general discussion, particularly those who have previously been least active. Review the list recorded on the newsprint. Look for common themes.

Variations. If time is limited, this exercise could be postponed until next session.

Suggested Readings. None.

Handouts. None.

Closure Activity

Goals. The goals for this final activity are:

1. To provide closure for the session
2. To explain homework assignment

Time Limits. Ten minutes.

Physical Arrangements. Arrange seats in a circle.

Equipment Requirements. None.

Instructions. In an open-ended discussion participants share what they learned from the session. Stimulus questions may include: What did you think this group would be like? What would you like this group experience to be like?

Describe and explain the homework assignment, which is to interview two upperclassmen, residence-hall staff, or faculty members regarding their undergraduate experiences. (1) Inquire about the kinds of involvement they found most meaningful during college. (2) How did they become involved in those particular activities or organizations? (3) What did they learn as a result of their involvement? (4) What activities do they wish they would have pursued or participated in?

Suggestions, Cautions, and Hints. Closure activities should serve as both a synthesizer and a stimulator. Members should be gently persuaded to reflect on their involvement in the group session, not so much in a critical as in a holistic manner. The leader might also want to spark the interest of members in returning for the next session by identifying some of the areas to be covered. The leaders will need to relieve some of the anxiety resulting from receiving an assignment. Members will need to be convinced of the potential value of the interviews.

Processing Guidelines. Closure can sometimes be achieved through silence as effectively as through verbal participation. Because time is likely to be of the essence at the end of the first session, this activity can be lengthened or shortened accordingly. Most of the attention will need to be devoted to lessening the anxiety about and making plans for the interview. It will be important to listen to this anxiety, accept it nondefensively, and respond by gently but firmly persuading the members of the potential value of the activity.

Variations. Leaders may invite group members to pair up to plan and conduct interviews if they note during the discussion that the task seems too threatening or overwhelming.

Suggested Readings. None.

Handouts. None.

Formative Evaluation Plan

The coleaders should meet together briefly after the session to compare observations and evaluations. Each coleader should describe perceptions of the quality and quantity of participation by the members in each activity. The general tone of the group should move from obvious anxiety in the beginning, marked by nervous giggling, excessive chatter, somewhat superficial interchanges, some role testing, and a good bit of hesitancy, to a calm interchange among members toward the end of the session.

Formative evaluation should focus on the individual and collective behavior of the members and the behavior of the leaders. The leaders should share observations of any unusual resistance on the part of a member or any evidence of passive resistance to group activities. The coleaders should compare perceptions of the relative effectiveness of the dyadic exercises and the group exercises. Likewise, they should share views of leadership effectiveness, such as the degree to which they were able to encourage reluctant or shy members, the degree to which they modeled desirable behaviors, the clarity of instructions given to the members during the activities, the leaders' ability to pair and link group members, and their ability to keep the group comfortably on task.

The relative quality of the session can be determined from such factors as the level of interaction during the dyadic exercise, the extent of involvement in full-group activities, and the degree to which members spoke directly to each other as well as to the group coleaders. In addition, the members should be able to give their reasons for coming to Southern State University and to articulate how becoming involved may help them achieve their goals.

The leaders might use the evaluation ratings to compare on a formal basis their individual perceptions of the session. [See Manual appendix.]

Session Two

Goals

1. To give group members information about the value of involvement in the college experience

2. To encourage group members to identify personal preferences as to involvement experiences
3. To stimulate the development of group cohesiveness

Interview-Dialogues Exercise

Goals. The goals for this first exercise are:

1. To form a link with Session One
2. To enable members to learn about involvement by sharing
interview information with each other

Time Limits. Thirty minutes.

Physical Arrangements. Arrange chairs in a circle.

Equipment Requirements. None.

Instructions. The leader asks members to share what they
learned from the interviews about involvement in the college
experience. The exercise should be voluntary; a person may
choose to listen rather than talk. Also, the leader should allay the
anxieties of anyone who was unable to complete the assignment
and refrain from asking members their reasons for not completing the assignment.

Suggestions, Cautions, and Hints. If pairs did the interviews
together and are doing the reporting in this exercise, then the
leaders might expect some animation and lively interchanges. It
is important to keep comments light but meaningful. Some
members may get sidetracked and give their impressions of the
interviewee, which was not the purpose of the activity.

Processing Guidelines. The leader will need to encourage
reluctant members to participate but at the same time allow
them not to participate. If several members have not done their
homework, the atmosphere might be heavier than is conducive
to good interaction, so the leader will need to remain flexible

and help keep the focus on what was learned by those who did complete the interview assignment. The key is to keep the attention positive and yet at the same time to convey the message that assignments are important.

Variations. If there is sufficient time, leaders may volunteer to be interviewed by a group member about their involvement experiences while undergraduates in college.

Suggested Readings. None.

Handouts. None.

Definition-of-Involvement Exercise

Goals. The goals for this exercise are:

1.   To continue group formation through linking of mutual experiences
2.   To integrate and "publish," or publicly confirm, what was learned individually and collectively from the interviews

Time Limits. Ten minutes.

Physical Arrangements. Arrange seats in a circle.

Equipment Requirements. Three easels with pads of paper and appropriate markers or extra long and wide pieces of butcher paper (or newsprint).

Instructions. Facilitate a group discussion on commonalities and differences in the definition of involvement emerging from the collective interview data. Ask the group to reflect on their own previous involvement experiences. One of the leaders may serve as a recorder to note the characteristics of involvement identified in the discussions of the interviews. Or the leader may ask for volunteers to serve as recorders.

Suggestions, Cautions, and Hints. By selectively responding to the most meaningful content shared by the group members and ignoring the incidental details, the leader can maintain a degree of control over the exercise. The critical focus needs to remain on the nature of involvement and its meaning to the interviewees and, in turn, to the group members.

Processing Guidelines. This summary session should not be extended beyond the brief time allotted to it, for it is to serve principally as a synthesis activity. But the synthesis is important to firm up the members' transfer of learning from the interviews to their own experiences.

Variations. Instead of recording on paper the identified commonalities and differences, leaders may want to simply conduct a group discussion.

Suggested Readings. None.

Handouts. None.

Brief Lecture on the Benefits of Involvement

Goal. To present information about the value of involvement to college students.

Time Limits. Ten minutes.

Physical Arrangements. A U-shaped seating arrangement would be the most appropriate because members will be attending to one speaker.

Equipment Requirements. None.

Instructions. The leader presents a brief lecture (see outline) summarizing the data available on the contributions of involvement to personal growth and development. The leader should present data from the professional literature and from personal experience regarding direct and indirect benefits of taking charge of the college experience. The leader should avoid sermonizing or presenting comments as irrefutable facts. The goal is to stimulate discussion among members, not to replace personal values or perceptions.

Outline. The Study Group on the Conditions of Excellence in American Higher Education (1984) issued a report entitled *Involvement in Learning: Realizing the Potential of American Higher Education.* In that report the argument was made that "the quality of undergraduate education could be significantly improved if America's colleges and universities would apply existing knowledge about three critical conditions of excellence — (1) student involvement, (2) high expectations, and (3) assessment and feedback" (p. 17). The group further stated that "the first of these three conditions — and perhaps the most important for purposes of improving undergraduate education — is *student involvement.* By involvement we mean how much time, energy, and effort students devote to the learning process. There is now a good deal of evidence to suggest that the more time and effort students invest in the learning process and the more intensely they engage in their own education, the greater will be their growth and achievement, their satisfaction with their educational experiences, and their persistence in college, and [the] more likely they are to continue their learning. Highly involved students demonstrate their commitment in a variety of ways: by devoting considerable energy to studying, by working on-campus rather than off-campus jobs, *by participating actively in student organizations,* and by interacting frequently with faculty members and student peers" (p. 17; italics added).

Astin (1985) asserts that students learn by becoming involved. *Involvement* is defined as "the amount of physical and psychological energy the student devotes" to the college experience (p. 133). He identifies a number of verbs that connote involvement: commit oneself to, take part in, show enthusiasm for, immerse oneself in, devote oneself to, plunge into, and join in. His research clearly shows that students who are actively involved in college life (in contrast with those who are not) are more likely to persist to graduation, are generally positive about their education and express satisfaction with the institution, and are more likely to become well-educated individuals.

In a study by the American Telephone and Telegraph Human Resources Studies Group (1984) of managerial employees, the researchers sought to identify variables that predicted promotion in the organization. Involvement in extracurricular activities was positively related to future success as a manager. Specifically, they found that persons who had been active in student groups and organizations (in contrast with those who had not) developed better administrative skills (especially decision making and creativity) and better interpersonal skills (particularly leadership skills, behavioral flexibility, and personal influence). Having held leadership positions in these organizations was found to be positively correlated with resourcefulness.

Other research has shown that students who are involved in student organizations have more mature career plans, more appropriate educational plans, and a greater sense of personal autonomy than uninvolved students (Williams and Winston, 1985). Others (Hood, 1984; Hood, Riahinejad, and White, 1986) have found that students who are involved in extracurricular activities have better developed interpersonal relationships and are more satisfied with their college educational experiences.

It seems safe to conclude that involvement outside the classroom has immediate rewards in personal satisfaction and provides a rich experience for students. Involvement also provides opportunities to develop skills that will be useful after college. Students who elect not to become involved seem to be missing valuable learning opportunities that are unlikely to be found anywhere else.

Suggestions, Cautions, and Hints. Information should be clearly and concisely presented, possibly using transparencies.

Processing Guidelines. Presentation should be informal; group members should be able to contribute or ask questions during the presentation.

Variations. None.

Suggested Readings. Astin (1977, 1985); Study Group on the Conditions of Excellence in American Higher Education (1984); Williams and Winston (1985); Winston and Massaro (1987); Hood (1984); Hood, Riahinejad, and White (1986); Feldman and Newcomb (1969); Winter, McClelland, and Stewart (1981).

Handouts. None necessary.

Preferences-for-Involvement Exercise

Goals. There are two goals for this exercise:

1.   To help members identify preferences for activities or organizations (or both) that they might like to become involved in at Southern State University
2.   To increase the interaction and interdependence of the group members

Time Limits. Fifty minutes.

Physical Arrangements. Movable seats are needed to shift from dyadic interaction to full-group discussion.

Equipment Requirements. None.

Instructions. Hand out the sheet that asks participants to list "a dozen things I'd like to do at SSU." [See Manual appendix.] Introductory comments ought to include a light-hearted reference to the need to restrict the activities to those one would feel comfortable telling others in the group about. Leaders may want to set some further parameters on the exercise by mentioning that members may want to review ways in which they have spent their time in the last several months and to select those activities they most preferred. It is not essential, however, that they have done the activity in the past. Leaders may want to offer examples of their own favorite activities as a stimulus. Encourage members to think of specific activities (not just sports, but swimming), regardless of how big or insignificant the activity may appear to others. After the lists are complete, ask follow-up questions (such as those listed on the sheet) to enable the members to look at their favorite things from different perspectives. Once group members have completed their lists and added responses to the follow-up queries, have the group form into dyads and discuss their favorite things to do. The exercise can be concluded by regrouping and having members talk about what they have learned about themselves and each other.

Suggestions, Cautions, and Hints. Leaders should continue to encourage the development of a group identity and the interactive commitment of the members by pairing and linking similar responses of members. The activity should easily generate interest in what each dyadic partner is saying. Also, it is important at this stage of group development that leaders encourage as much communication as possible to go between group members rather than between the members and the leader.

Processing Guidelines. In processing this activity, leaders should facilitate a discussion that focuses both on content and on group dynamics. In the closing part of the activity, the sharing of "I learned. . ." statements, the leader can enhance the quality of the comments by giving feedback to some of the members that makes them take a look at the unique strengths they may possess or challenges they may face in becoming involved in preferred activities. One of the questions that encourages members to look carefully at their level of involvement is, "When was the last time you participated in your five most favorite things to do?"

Variations. The amount of time devoted to different parts of the exercise can be altered depending on available time. Also, a variation might be to add different questions to those currently on the top of the sheet.

Suggested Readings. None.

Handouts. The sheet should be given to the group members to complete and discuss.

Closure Activity

Goals. The goals for this activity are:

1.   To facilitate development of group identity and satisfaction with progress of group toward goals
2.   To explain purpose of and procedure for homework assignment

Time Limits. Ten minutes.

Physical Arrangements. Arrange seats in a circle.

Equipment Requirements. None.

Instructions. In a relatively quick fashion, the leader should check to see how members are progressing toward their goals in the group. Check to see whether members feel that any major changes in the type of group activity need to be made. Also, the leader should take the opportunity to encourage members by making reinforcing comments to some of the members about their involvement in the group. Finally, give each member a profile based on the Myers-Briggs Type Indicator (MBTI) completed during screening for study before the next session. Ask members not to discuss their profiles with anyone prior to the next session.

Suggestions, Cautions, and Hints. Remind group members that there are no perfect MBTI profiles, that the MBTI describes "normal personalities," and that each set of types has pluses and minuses so to speak. In fact, the profiles simply reflect on paper what we tend to know about ourselves anyway; they simply provide the picture somewhat more clearly. The task is to use the personality constructs as displayed and described on the profile as guides to thinking about past and present involvement experiences.

Processing Guidelines. Because the purpose of the closure activity is to enhance group identity, the processing should provide a quick review of group progress and encourage risk taking and attempts at new behaviors in the group. Members should be encouraged to ask questions regarding their assignment.

Variations. Group members may be given an opportunity to give positive feedback to each other about group interaction.

Suggested Readings. None.

Handouts. Each member should be given the MBTI profile.

Formative Evaluation Plan

The coleaders should meet after the session to share formative assessments. Particularly, they may want to share perceptions of the quality of the members' comments about their assigned interviews, thereby gaining a perspective on the relative success of the assignment as well as the degree of members' participation. It should be expected that not every member will complete the assignment or demonstrate an ability to learn, at least directly, from the assignment. Particular attention ought to be given to the participation in the preferences-for-involvement exercise. The interaction ought to be fairly lively during parts of this activity. If not, then coleaders may need to give extra consideration to determining whether group commitment to goal achievement is developing appropriately. Leadership effectiveness ought to be apparent in the balanced involvement of all members of the group. A noticeable increase in the comfort level of group members ought to be evident by the end of the session. Group members ought to be able to describe personal preferences for becoming involved.

The coleaders may choose to use the assessment ratings

scales for further formative evaluation data. [See Manual appendix.]

Session Three

Goals

1. To provide opportunities for self-exploration within the group through use of the assessment instruments employed
2. To introduce members to the concept of challenge and support in college environments
3. To encourage students to develop an understanding of the natural relationship of person and environment and the relevance of the relationship to decisions about involvement
4. To facilitate continued movement toward the transition stage, to increase sensitivity to the members' commitment to each other, to build identification with group goals, and to enhance commitment to group process

Welcoming Comments

Goals. The welcoming comments have three goals:

1. To facilitate the group's movement into the transition stage
2. To enhance members' abilities to self-disclose appropriately
3. To help add to members' self-understanding, particularly in reference to involvement behaviors and characteristic styles of interaction

Time Limits. Five minutes.

Physical Arrangements. Arrange seats in a circle.

Equipment Requirements. None.

Instructions. Leaders should make opening comments, focusing on recognition of members' effort, reinforcement of members for cooperation in the group, and reference to evidence of commitment to members' goals. Also, leaders need to prepare members for the mild risk taking and self-disclosure required in the discussion of MBTI profiles, as required in this session.

Suggestions, Cautions, and Hints. This activity should be brief; questions and comments more than likely should be deferred.

Processing Guidelines. None.

Variations. None.

Suggested Readings. None.

Handouts. None.

Learning About Self and Others from MBTI Profiles

Goal. To enhance members' understanding of the relationship of personality types and ways of becoming involved in the college experience.

Time Limits. Seventy minutes.

Physical Arrangements. Open room is required where separate small subgroups can convene, either standing or sitting. If they are sitting, then movable chairs are required to allow dyads as well as the full group to interact.

Equipment Requirements. An overhead transparency projector is needed to display a sample MBTI profile and interpretation guide.

Instructions. First, display an MBTI profile and give a short lecture about the meaning of I and E, N and S, T and F, P and J. (See Briggs and McCaulley, 1985.) Ask Introverts (I) and Extroverts (E) to form two groups. Ask each person to briefly answer the questions listed here and then to share responses with others in the group. Each subgroup should select a recorder, who will report the general or most common responses to the following questions in the larger group.

1. What kind of parties or social activities do you most enjoy?
2. What kinds of projects do you most prefer — one big project that takes lots of time and planning or several small projects that are quite different from each other?
3. When given a term-paper assignment, what do you usually do first?
4. "When I meet someone whom I think I would really like to get to know better, I usually. . ."
5. Do you prefer to work alone or in groups?
6. "When I go to a party or other social event where I don't know many people, I usually. . ."
7. What are your hobbies?

Subgroups then re-form into the larger group and report their findings.

Leaders should facilitate a discussion of how the members of the subgroups seem to be similar to and different from each other.

Second, ask Intuitive (N) types and Sensing (S) types to form two groups. Ask each person to briefly answer the questions listed here and then to share responses with others in the group. Each subgroup should select a recorder, who will report the general or most common responses to the following questions in the larger group.

1. Do you like to try to solve puzzles or problems? Why?
2. "My favorite kind of leisure reading is. . ."
3. Which is true of you? "I prefer to play a new game or sport." "I prefer to play a game or sport I already know how to play."
4. When you entered this room today, what did you notice first?
5. Do you like doing work that requires a lot of precision or careful attention?

6. What is most true of you? "Uncompleted projects worry me until I get them done." "I like to have several projects going at the same time; I always have uncompleted projects around."

Subgroups then re-form into the larger group and report their findings.

Leaders should facilitate a discussion of how the subgroups seem to be different and similar.

Third, ask Feeling (F) and Thinking (T) types to form two groups. Ask each person to briefly answer the questions listed here and then to share responses with others in the group. Each subgroup should select a recorder, who will report the general or most common responses to the following questions in the larger group.

1. "When I meet someone new, I am most interested in finding out . . ."
2. "When I have a job to do that involves other people, the first thing I prefer to do is . . ."
3. "When I voice my opinions in class, I make sure that everyone . . ."
4. "When I am in a leadership position and other people are doing their job, I tend to . . ."
5. Which is true of you? "Most of my friends are very much like me." "Most of my friends are all different types."

Subgroups then re-form into the larger group and report their findings.

Leaders should facilitate a discussion of how the subgroups seem to be similar and different.

Fourth, ask Perceiving (P) types and Judging (J) types to form two groups. Ask each person to briefly answer the questions listed here and then to share responses with others in the group. Each subgroup should select a recorder, who will report the general or most common responses to the following questions in the larger group.

1. Which is true of you? "I feel most comfortable when things are changing fast." "I feel most comfortable when things are pretty smooth and predictable."
2. When going to dinner would you rather go to a place where you have made reservations or a place where you do not have reservations and hope that you can get in?
3. Describe your usual style of making important decisions.
4. Which best describes you? "When I interview for a job, I always have lots of questions." "When I interview for a job, I want just the essential information and don't usually have too many questions."
5. Which best describes you? "Once I have made a decision, I am usually satisfied and go on to something else." "Once I have made a decision, I usually continue to think about it and to wonder whether I made the right choice."

Subgroups then re-form into the larger group and report their findings.

Leaders should facilitate a discussion of how the subgroups seem to be similar and different.

Fifth, as a large group, discuss the possible relationship of personal profiles to past experiences (twenty minutes).

Suggestions, Cautions, and Hints. In the comments initiating this set of activities, the leaders need to make clear that the types are merely ideal or pure personality types, and that individuals should try to keep from making value judgments or assigning excessively tight descriptions or definitions of type to themselves. The most appropriate use of MBTI scores is as stimuli to encourage introspection and analysis of personal experience.

A word of caution is necessary regarding possible attempts to disrupt, block, or side-track the group. Not only is the content of the activity conducive to this kind of behavior, but also the group is likely in the stage of development where it is going to challenge the leader as a natural part of the push to the next stage of group commitment and work.

Processing Guidelines. Leaders should walk around throughout this activity, giving help in the form of feedback or interpretations of scores, or by making suggestions for looking at one's involvement experiences in relation to the scores and profile types. Time limits are also relatively important in this exercise. But the most important point in processing this exercise is to keep the focus more on the individual than on the MBTI. If members react negatively to their profiles, disagreeing with the description of the high-score type, then give them support and encourage them to talk about how they see themselves in relation to the type of behavior noted on the profile. Leaders should avoid defending the instrument.

Variations. Instead of breaking into subgroups by each letter in the type code, the large group may be divided according to the four-lettered codes. The resulting groups would have increased time to discover similarities and differences among themselves. In some instances, however, only one person may have a particular four-letter profile.

Suggested Readings. Briggs (1980), Briggs and McCaulley (1985), Lawrence (1982), Keirsey and Bates (1984), Provost and Anchors (1987).

Handouts. May wish to present data of relative distribution of types in the population (Keirsey and Bates, 1984, p. 25).

Brief Lecture on Challenge and Support

Goals. The goals of this brief lecture are:

1. To help members learn about their characteristic ways of interacting with the college environment through a comparison of their knowledge of themselves and their typology scores on the personality instrument
2. To help group members improve their understanding of the nature of the interaction between students and college environments
3. To introduce group members to the twin concepts of chal-

lenge and support and their relationship to taking charge of one's college experience

Time Limits. Fifteen minutes.

Physical Arrangements. Arrange chairs in a U shape.

Equipment Requirements. None.

Instructions. The leaders introduce the concept of matching person and environment, provide descriptions of such concepts as challenge and support, and confirm research data related to involvement in the college experience. See outline for further details.

Outline. Sanford's constructs of differentiation and integration (1962) and challenge and response (1967) are a key to involvement of college students. They can be summarized as follows:

1. Challenges faced by the individual are stimuli for change.
2. Support provided by the institution encourages change to occur.
3. Response by the individual reflects the way the individual brings about the changes that occur.
4. Differentiation is the presentation of new conditions and experiences that require individuals to develop new competencies, attitudes, or approaches.
5. Integration is the process individuals go through to resolve the dissonance created by the environment's demand that they respond in a new or different way than in the past.

Chickering (1969) expanded on Sanford's cycles of differentiation and integration by proposing two laws of human development. The first is that differentiation and integration (challenge and response) are often accompanied by disequilibrium and equilibrium. An awareness that accustomed ways of dealing with people, things, or ideas are no longer satisfactory generally precedes a change in behavior. The feeling of dissatisfaction or the realization that something does not seem quite right acts as a stimulus to reevaluate behaviors or responses and to discover ones that seem more sensible or comfortable. In other words, dissatisfaction or unease is an indication of disequilibrium; to regain equilibrium requires action. The second law of human development is that the impact of an experience depends on the characteristics of the person who encounters it. Students differ in significant ways that affect their responses to the college, its staff and faculty members, and their peers; different subject matter, tasks, and activities; different conditions of stress and release; different levels of satisfaction and frustration. (Provide an example that illustrates each of the points.)

Involvement plays a part in development. Becoming involved in college activities (both academic and nonacademic) promotes challenge and differentiation in one's life. Exposing one's self to new experiences and different people is a challenge that can require one to learn new skills, practice different styles, and apply new strategies. Taking the risk of getting involved means taking responsibility for one's own life and learning. Becoming purposefully involved in the college experience is viewed by some authorities as one of the most significant developmental acts a student can undertake (Astin, 1977, 1985).

Suggestions, Cautions, and Hints. Presentation will need to be sharp and crisp to retain interest of members in lecture content.

Processing Guidelines. Processing is accomplished through the next activity.

Variations. None.

Suggested Readings. None.

Handouts. None.

Group Discussion

Goal. To help group members personalize the principal concepts of challenge and support described in the presentation.

Time Limits. Fifteen minutes.

Physical Arrangements. Arrange chairs in a circle to enable face-to-face group discussion.

Equipment Requirements. None.

Instructions. Facilitate a group discussion of the concepts of challenge and support, focusing on the kind of risk taking that is critically important if one is to take charge of one's college experience. Encourage group members to share feelings of personal challenge at accepting "challenges" in pursuit of desired involvement.

Suggestions, Cautions, and Hints. Encourage the participation of all group members, paying particular attention to the less verbal members, who perhaps have not participated as actively as some others. Consider responding to dominators by giving the problem back to the group. For example, the leader may ask the group, "Why do we as a group encourage Ralph to take all the risks or to always be the first or the strongest and loudest? Are we making him the fall guy for some reason, or are you, Ralph, concerned about making sure you get a good solid chance to influence the thinking of the group?"

Processing Guidelines. To introduce the activity and model the kind of content and style of communication desired, leaders may consider disclosing a situation in which they took a risk in order to get involved in a new activity in college.

Variations. Discussion can be extended if time permits. The focus could be shifted to risk-taking behaviors of friends and acquaintances, including the positive and negative aspects of risk taking and the differences between reckless risk taking and thoughtful risk taking.

Suggested Readings. None.

Handouts. None.

Closure Activity

Goal. To introduce the homework assignment.

Time Limits. Ten minutes.

Physical Arrangements. None.

Equipment Requirements. None.

Instructions. Leaders should describe the homework assignment, which is to identify opportunities for involvement on campus by interviewing one or two people associated with activities, organizations, or groups; these interviews may be conducted with a partner from the group if desired. Leaders should then distribute materials describing campus activities, organizations, and groups; discuss the kinds of information one might need to obtain to ascertain or to pursue interests (or both); and coordinate the resulting set of interviews with campus personnel.

Suggestions, Cautions, and Hints. Leaders need to sell this activity somewhat by stressing the importance of everyone's doing a part of the job of discovering information about many of the campus opportunities for involvement.

Processing Guidelines. Leaders need to be upbeat about the promise of this activity in their discussion of the details of the assignment.

Variations. If desired, members may be paired up to achieve the goal.

Suggested Readings. None.

Handouts. Lists of campus organizations, activities, and clubs; copy of student handbook.

Formative Evaluation Plan

The activity level of the group ought to have been notice-ably livelier during this third session than during the previous ones. If this was not the case, the coleaders should reflect on possible shifts in design. Toward the end of this session, the members' emerging resistance or hostility toward the leaders may have appeared. Evaluation observations should include perceptions of the quality of the interchanges in the small groups when members were sharing MBTI profiles and identify-ing similarities and differences. Also, special note ought to be taken of leaders' behavior toward members who became notice-ably withdrawn or less involved and toward unproductive mem-bers. Evidence of increasing group cohesion ought to be apparent.

The leaders should assess the degree to which the com-ments of the group members reflect a growing awareness of the connections between their own personal characteristics and their involvement experiences. In other words, do the members show an understanding of the relationship of person and en-vironment, and of the related concepts of challenge and sup-port? Do the members seem to grasp the nature of risk taking, particularly as it applies to themselves?

Coleaders may use the assessment scales to obtain other comparisons of observations and perceptions. [See Manual appendix.]

Session Four

Goals

1. To help the group move solidly into and through the transi-
    tion stage, where members may struggle with the nature of
    the group and the nature of their participation in the group
2. To facilitate involvement of all group members in process-
    ing the group experience
3. To assist participants in developing their own process of
    choosing involvement opportunities
4. To help group members learn the kinds of valuable infor-
    mation that can be obtained from persons involved in
    various campus activities, organizations, and groups

Group Process

   Goal. To help group members reflect on their own involvement in the group and to share what they have learned about
themselves and about the group thus far.

   Time Limits. Thirty to sixty minutes.

   Physical Arrangements. Arrange chairs in a circle.

   Equipment Requirements. None.

   Instructions. Facilitate a group discussion about involvement as it relates to each member's experience in this group. The
leader will need to help draw a definite connection between
involvement in the group and elsewhere, and help members see
the group as a kind of laboratory by asking such questions as:
"How are you involved in this group?" "Are you satisfied with your
involvement in this group?" "What are you learning about yourself or about others and about involvement that you can transfer
to out-of-group activities?" "What have you learned about group
process?"

Suggestions, Cautions, and Hints. The discussion may start off slowly, so the leader will need to be patient. Also, some dissatisfaction may be expressed with the slow pace or the vagueness of the stimulus, or even with the leader for not doing something directly to get things moving. This dissatisfaction is a key to the success of the group. Achievement of this task will enable the group to begin to work directly on the group's goal. However, if the discussion stalls or breaks down prior to natural completion or closure, individual interests will continue dominating concern for others and commitment to the group goal. (In other words, the group will have refused to confront and move through the transition stage.) Avoid responding defensively to attacks of any sort, but respond nevertheless. A time to pause and reflect will generally stimulate a natural and genuine interaction about roles and substance.

Processing Guidelines. More than likely, anxious members of the group will query the leader as to what this opening discussion has to do with the group's goals. It is important for a leader to accept this statement or question as reflecting that person's need for security or positive support. Direct questions of some members by the leaders may be helpful in stimulating the group and in modeling the kind of processing desired. For example, it would be appropriate to ask a member who seems to play the role of comedian in the group: "Are you often put into the role of clown? Was that a role in your family of origin? How do you feel about that role? Do you ever experience pressure about it from others? Is that type of involvement something you'd like to continue?"

Variations. None.

Suggested Readings. None.

Handouts. None.

Interview Reports

Goal. To give members opportunities to learn from each other about the many involvement possibilities on the campus.

Time Limits. Thirty to sixty minutes. The length of this discussion can be varied depending on the length of the previous activity.

Physical Arrangements. Circle of seats.

Equipment Required. None.

Instructions. Ask group members to share results of their interview assignment and then briefly process the discussion. If time permits, once group members have had a chance to share the information gleaned from their interviews as well as their reactions to the experience, the focus should shift to a group synthesis effort, in which members identify similarities and differences in campus opportunities for involvement and in the procedures for initiating involvement in different activities.

Suggestions, Cautions, and Hints. More than likely members will enjoy sharing the content and process of their campus interviews. Therefore, the leader may need to serve only as an occasional "traffic officer" during the discussion. However, an active role may be required if the sharing becomes misfocused on noninvolvement matters, such as personal impressions or detailed descriptions of the process used to collect the data.

Processing Guidelines. Critical to the processing of the synthesis effort is consideration of the specific data learned about how the interviewee initially became involved in an activity. A similarly important concern is to focus on similarities and differences in the group members' experiences.

Variations. A chart could be developed listing things learned about involvement by the group.

Suggested Readings. None.

Handouts. None.

Closure Activity

Goals. There are two goals for closure:

1. To stimulate members to reflect on their understanding of involvement and the nature of their involvement in this group
2. To build group cohesiveness

Time Limits. Twenty minutes.

Physical Arrangements. Arrange seats in a circle.

Equipment Requirements. None.

Instructions. Facilitate a brief discussion aimed at a review of what members have learned about involvement in general and about their involvement in this group in particular. Also, ask group members to share any desires or plans for continuing or modifying that involvement.

Suggestions, Cautions, and Hints. A helpful hint is to pick up on the feelings and thoughts expressed about interviewees by group members and to mention those feelings and thoughts when appropriate as links to personal involvement styles or desires of the individual members.

Processing Guidelines. This closure activity will serve as a wrap-up of the session by taking the content full circle back to the session's beginning discussion. The key strategy is to help participants continue to look at the nature of their involvement in this group as a training ground or experiment for future involvement activities. Small groups can be excellent laboratories for real-life experiences outside the group. But often members need to be helped to reflect on the meaning of the experience for them.

Variations. The leaders can ask volunteers to complete the stem "From today's session, I learned. . ."

Suggested Readings. None.

Handouts. None.

Formative Evaluation Plan

Evaluation of this session should focus on (1) the relative effectiveness of the ways in which the coleaders handled the processing of the group interaction during this session, and (2) the depth of members' understanding of the relationship between their involvement in the group and the possibilities for involvement in other campus activities and organizations. How well are the members transferring their learning from this experience to the college environment? Members ought to be able to articulate what they are learning about their involvement preferences from the group experience. Members should demonstrate that they have learned from their interviews and the follow-up discussion specific details about how to become involved and stay productively involved in college. Also, the results of the session will provide clear evidence of the degree to which the group is developing cohesion and increased commitment toward mutual goal achievement.

Session Five

Goals

1. To encourage group members to identify preferred involvement activities

2. To help members consider potential obstacles to involvement in the personally preferred activities as well as strategies for overcoming the identified obstacles
3. To help members learn how to set achievable goals

Involvement Preferences

Goal. To increase the specificity of group members' plans for future involvement on campus.

Time Limits. Thirty minutes.

Physical Arrangements. Arrange seats in a circle.

Equipment Requirements. None.

Instructions. Distribute the decision-making grid [see Manual appendix] and ask members to complete it privately. Once everyone has completed the grid, ask the members to share in dyads the results of the grid exercise and their present thinking about preferred alternatives for taking charge of their college experience through involvement. In other words, members will be asked to specify the activities or organizations that they would most like to join and become involved in.

Suggestions, Cautions, and Hints. Leaders may assist the process of exchanging personal preferences for involvement by walking around the room, spending a few minutes with each of the dyads.

Processing Guidelines. The announcement of personal preferences to a partner can be a bit threatening, particularly if a person is not quite ready to make that decision. Therefore, leaders will need to be aware of anxious responses and lighten up the exercise for members who feel excessively anxious about selecting specific alternatives for involvement. Leaders will want to solicit the help of the group in processing these kinds of reactions to see whether the group as a whole can provide some feedback to such members. It is important that the group attend to individual members' indecisiveness or indecision, not so much to change that indecisiveness as to offer support, feedback, and encouragement.

Variations. None.

Suggested Readings. None.

Handouts. Decision-making grid.

Group Brainstorming Session

Goal. The purpose of the brainstorming session is to obtain quickly a variety of views about each person's stated preference for an initial activity or organization.

Time Limits. Sixty minutes.

Physical Arrangements. Movable seats are essential.

Equipment Requirements. Newsprint and markers, or chalkboards.

Instructions. Group members identify for the group the activity or organization in which they want to become involved and how they plan to do so. The group brainstorms on ideas, thoughts, and suggestions about that plan. In addition, the group may wish to offer, *without judging the choice*, thoughts about (1) the kinds of obstacles (both personal and environmental) the individual may confront in pursuing the preferred choice and (2) possible strategies for overcoming such obstacles. A leader and other volunteers may be recruited to record the comments on wall charts.

Suggestions, Cautions, and Hints. Each group member should remain silent while the full group is brainstorming ideas relative to his or her preferred choice and plan. The pace should be rapid, not allowing for evaluative comments or reactions. It is crucial that leaders maintain control during this exercise without putting themselves in the position of evaluating suggestions. Leaders should remain alert to any comments that may negatively affect a group member and clarify or remedy the situation should it arise.

Processing Guidelines. The feedback given to each member may take the form of added information, constructive suggestions for skill enhancement, ideas for initiating involvement, thoughts about possible dilemmas related to the choice or to the individual's plan for initiating involvement, or simply a sharing of support and encouragement. The leaders need to provide additive and helpful feedback throughout the session. Once the round has been completed, the member should be allowed to respond or to ask general questions to clarify input and feedback.

Variations. The same activity could also be conducted in triads.

Suggested Readings. None.

Handouts. None.

Brief Lecture on Goal Setting

Goal. To help members learn how to set achievable goals.

Time Limits. Fifteen minutes.

Physical Arrangements. Arrange seats in a U shape.

Equipment Requirements. None.

Instructions. Group leader provides information about setting achievable goals. A critical element of setting goals is to make them achievable with reasonable effort. Goals should serve not to punish but to stimulate. The presentation should be brief and focused on the five rules for goal setting (see outline).

Outline. Goal setting is a map to involvement. It is helpful to keep in mind these basic facts about goal setting:

1. Goal setting is not wishful thinking.
2. Realistic goal setting is action oriented.
3. Setting goals provides people with the power to achieve.
4. Goal setting is a first step toward purposeful involvement and change.

There are five rules for goal setting:

1. Goals should be personal and owned. Other people's goals are not very meaningful.
2. Goals should be stated positively, not negatively. You attract what you think.
3. Goals should be written and specific. Writing crystallizes one's thinking.
4. Goals should be compatible and attainable. Inappropriate goals in, poor achievement out.
5. Goals should include some behavior changes.

The types of goals are:

1. Tangible: anything concrete such as membership in a club, an elected office, a committee assignment, contact with an officer of an organization
2. Intangible: nonconcrete things like leadership skills, behavior changes, listening skills
3. Short range: an objective that can be accomplished in a relatively limited period of time (day, week, month)
4. Long range: an objective that may take six months or a year or more to be achieved (like a five-year plan)

The characteristics of a good goal are that it:

1. Is realistic and attainable
2. Covers only one issue or responsibility
3. Is fair to everyone involved (does not require others to change behavior drastically)
4. Is in written form
5. Clearly fixes accountability for completion of the task
6. Expresses results to be attained in terms of: quantity, quality, time, or costs
7. Covers only those factors over which the goal setter has control
8. Involves only those factors related to the situation
9. Guarantees that outcome measurement can be accomplished by the goal setter
10. Can be prioritized in relation to other goals and objectives

Here are some suggested areas in which involvement goals can be set:

1. Academic activities and organizations
2. Career activities and organizations
3. Fine- and performing-arts activities
4. Religious activities and organizations
5. Residence life programs
6. Service and volunteer activities
7. Social clubs and organizations
8. Sports and recreation programs
9. Student government and honorary societies

Goals need to be written down following this format:

1. Identify the goal.
2. Identify specific behaviors (results or outcomes) that will satisfy the goal setter that the goal has been achieved.
3. For each behavior (specific result) clearly describe the quality, quantity, time, or cost required for minimal acceptance.
4. Evaluate the written statements by determining whether all involved agree that the goal will have been achieved when the specified results are accomplished.

Suggestions, Cautions, and Hints. At the end of the brief lecture, group members ought to try setting a goal aloud in order to crystallize what they have learned. Examples do not need to be perfect, but the goals need to include a positive change in observable personal behavior.

Processing Guidelines. The group members ought to be allowed a brief moment for reacting to the content of the lecture, as well as an opportunity to try stating an acceptable goal.

Variations. Instead of a lecture, the content may be shared via a handout with group exercises included.

Suggested Readings. None.

Handouts. None.

Closure Activity

Goals. The goals of closure are:

1. To close the session with encouragement for effort
2. To describe homework assignment

Time Limits. Five to ten minutes.

Physical Arrangements. Arrange chairs in a circle.

Equipment Requirements. None.

Instructions. Leaders should commend members for their involvement in the group. Ask group members to review their original goal for attending the ISG and to share their perceptions of the group's progress toward that goal. Also, the closure activity might contain a look to the next meeting, when members will be asked to share the goal for personal involvement that they prepare. Each goal statement should be accompanied by a plan for achievement.

Suggestions, Cautions, and Hints. Because this session included feedback, leaders will want to systematically check with group members to see whether the session raised any unfinished business that needs attention.

Processing Guidelines. In processing this discussion leaders will need to be especially sensitive to signs of unfinished business on the part of members or the group as a whole. Anytime feedback is a major part of the session, leaders need to remain alert to injured feelings or the emergence of self-doubts.

Variations. More time could be spent on the goal-setting activities rather than on the content of the brief lecture.

Suggested Readings. None.

Handouts. None.

Formative Evaluation Plan

Group members should be able to identify preferred involvement activities, describe associated risks and obstacles, and specify plans for initiating such activities. Therefore, assessment ought to focus on members' abilities to select involvement goals and make plans for pursuing such goals. Evidence of such conceptual ability will be recognizable in group discussion. The quality of the discussion will be especially enhanced by member-to-member interaction. If formative evaluation measures reveal that a major portion of the discussion is a leader/member interchange, goal achievement is lacking. Other, more formal measures are obtainable through the use of the rating scales. [See Manual appendix.]

Session Six

Goals

1. To help members appraise the kinds of personal characteristics or behaviors (or both) they would like to possess to

be successful in the roles they desire to play in the chosen involvement activity

2. To provide opportunities to practice the kinds of behavior required in initiating contact and in following through on initial involvement efforts

3. To achieve successful group closure

Goal-Sharing Exercise

Goal. To provide group members individually with an opportunity to announce personal goals.

Time Limits. Sixty minutes.

Physical Arrangements. Arrange seats in a circle.

Equipment Requirements. None.

Instructions. Ask each group member to share a personal goal for becoming involved in a campus activity, organization, or group, and to describe the kind of role he or she would like to assume. Follow-up questions to the initial statement should include:

- How are you going to use your own personal strengths and characteristics to achieve your involvement goal?
- How will you need to behave differently than you have in the past to achieve your involvement goal? In other words, will you need to change? If so, how?
- Imagining that you have been successful, how will you feel after your involvement experience? What will you have gotten out of the experience? What reward will you receive? How will you build on this successful involvement?

Suggestions, Cautions, and Hints. Leaders should employ good verbal following skills to help each member elaborate and expand on statements. Yet, at the same time, leaders need to remain cognizant of the clock and the involvement of the rest of the group.

Processing Guidelines. The follow-up questions will enable the leader to initiate the processing of the discussion.

Variations. Fewer specific questions might be asked by the leaders, and more emphasis could be given to a free-flowing discussion carried largely by the group.

Suggested Readings. None.

Handouts. None.

Closure Activity

Goal. To stimulate the sharing of immediate plans to implement involvement goals.

Time Limits. Thirty to forty minutes.

Physical Arrangements. Arrange seats in a circle.

Equipment Requirements. None.

Instructions. Initiate a series of activities designed to allow members to achieve psychological closure.

1. Ask each member to finish the statement: "My next step in taking charge of my college experience through increasing my involvement will be to . . ."
2. Ask each group member to share "I learned . . ." statements in regard to the total ISG experience.
3. If the group has been at least marginally successful, allow each member to offer a closing comment, perhaps to complete the statement: "One thing I want to tell the group is . . ."

Suggestions, Cautions, and Hints. The main caution is for the leaders to consult their formative evaluations in order to decide whether the group has been sufficiently successful to encourage members to share positive feelings and personal thoughts. It is important that all groups end on an upbeat note if possible. Groups do need to achieve closure, so leaders ought to deflect attempts to continue the group.

Processing Guidelines. Without exerting undue pressure, leaders ought to encourage each individual to announce a next step. If a member has attempted to come up with a viable plan but cannot, then some time ought to be devoted by the whole group to the task. Each of the three statements may elicit emotions, so the leader needs to be alert to the intensity and act accordingly. This closing activity should help members realize that their participation in *this group* was itself an exercise in involvement and that how they acted or felt in this group was indicative of how they act and feel in other involvement situations.

Variations. The three statements may be provided on paper so that members can respond in writing before they respond orally.

Suggested Readings. None.

Handouts. None.

Summative Evaluation

Goal. To evaluate goal achievement.

Time Limits. Twenty minutes.

Physical Arrangements. Arrange seats so that members have some privacy for writing.

Equipment Requirements. Pencils for all members.

Instructions. Ask group members to complete the Extracurricular Involvement Inventory: Summative Evaluation Form [see Manual appendix]. Ask members to provide an address where they can be reached for a follow-up evaluation to be conducted during winter quarter.

Suggestions, Cautions, and Hints. Encourage participation by acknowledging the quality and quantity of members' efforts throughout the group. Provide an accurate time estimate to complete the forms (fifteen minutes).

Processing Guidelines. Respond to direct questions.

Variations. None.

Suggested Readings. None.

Handouts. Evaluation forms.

MANUAL APPENDIX

Informed-Consent Form

I, the undersigned, voluntarily elect to participate in the group entitled "Taking Charge of Your College Experience: Getting Involved."

I understand that if I am to receive maximum benefit from participation, I have several obligations. Namely, I agree to (1) attend all six sessions, (2) actively participate in the activities, (3) conscientiously complete assignments between sessions, and (4) make efforts to contribute to the learning of other members of the group. I understand that I may elect not to participate (without penalty) in any activity or exercise that causes me discomfort and that I can withdraw from membership in the group at any time.

I agree to make a $10 deposit, which will be refunded if I attend and participate in all sessions. (In case of need, I understand that scholarships are available.) I forfeit the deposit if I fail to attend a session or fail to make a good-faith effort to complete assignments. I understand that the purpose of the deposit is primarily to remind me of the commitment I have made to myself and to the other group members.

As part of participation in this group I agree to provide information that will allow the leaders to evaluate the group's effectiveness. Specifically, I agree to complete the *Extracurricular Involvement Inventory* and the *Student Developmental Task and Lifestyle Inventory* several times during the course of the year and also agree to participate in several telephone interviews after the group has been completed. I also give my permission for the registrar to release my grade point averages and SAT scores to the leaders for the purpose of evaluating the group's effects. I understand that any information I provide or that is otherwise obtained about me by the leaders will be kept confidential and will not be released in any personally identifiable form without my written permission or unless required by law.

Date: _____ Student's signature: _____
Student's name (please print clearly): _____
Social Security number: _____
Campus/local address: _____
Local telephone number: _____
Home/parents' telephone number:_____

Goals and Ground Rules

Goals of the Group

1. Participants will learn the benefits (both while attending college and afterward) associated with involvement in extra-curricular activities.
2. Participants will explore themselves (their personalities and interests) and the college environment as a means of identifying avenues of involvement outside the classroom that will be enjoyable and that will enrich their college experience.
3. Participants will identify specific activities, groups, or organizations in which they desire to become involved.
4. Participants will develop a plan for achieving their involvement goals.

Basic Ground Rules

In order for this experience to be beneficial, a number of basic understandings or ground rules need to be specified. These ground rules are established to help participants get an understanding of how the group will function and to assure that everyone's rights are protected.

Attendance and Involvement. Members are expected to attend all sessions and to be prompt because their absence or tardiness adversely affects all group members. Members who cannot attend a session should call a group leader prior to the session and explain the reason for the absence. Sessions will last for two hours and will meet once per week for six weeks.

Deposit. Members who elect to participate in this group pay $10 deposits which will be refunded at the end of the last session provided they have attended all sessions and have made a good-faith effort to complete all assignments. The purpose of this deposit is to help participants maintain the commitment to complete the group that they have when they sign up.

Voluntary Participation. Members may elect not to participate in any part of the group experience or any exercise or activity by saying simply "I pass"; they will not be required to give an explanation. It should be understood, however, that in order to gain maximum benefit from this experience, members need to stretch themselves or to try some things that they have never done before. If that were not the case, the experience would likely have little to offer participants. (Members may elect to withdraw from the group at any time.)

Substance Use. Members may not use alcohol or other drugs during the course of sessions and should not come to sessions under their influence.

Violence. Use or threat of physical violence will not be permitted at any time.

Confidentiality. Although this group is not designed to elicit highly personal or embarrassing material, trust and respect among members are essential. In order to build that trust and respect it is essential that members feel confident that whatever is said in the group will remain confidential. What is said during sessions, therefore, should not be communicated to others who are not members of the group (while the group is going on as well as after it is over) and should not be discussed privately among members outside the group. Members should be warned, however, that there is no legal means for enforcing this rule and should, therefore, keep this lack of enforcement in mind before revealing highly personal material.

Potential Risk. Physical and psychological risks to participants are judged to be minimal. Members may experience some discomfort as they are encouraged to look at themselves critically and to attempt new behaviors or ways of relating to other people. The focus of this group, however, is developmental; it deals with activities and adjustments most college students face. Minimal risk and discomfort are expected.

Completion of Instruments. Members will be asked to complete the *Myers-Briggs Type Indicator*, which is a questionnaire designed to describe normal personality characteristics, and will be asked to share their profiles with others in the group. Members will also be requested to complete several other questionnaires and surveys, including the *Extracurricular Involvement Inventory* and the *Student Developmental Task and Lifestyle Inventory*. These two instruments evaluate the group's effect on members and are designed to determine how effectively this group accomplished its goals. Results from these instruments will be kept confidential and will not be revealed in any personally identifiable form unless required by law. Personal identities will be removed from instruments as soon as the final data collection is complete.

Recording. Sessions will be recorded (either audiotape or videotape). These recordings will be used to help the leaders evaluate their performance as leaders and help them learn how to lead groups effectively. These recordings will be viewed (heard) by only the leaders and such other professionals as the leaders may need to consult. The content will not be revealed to anyone else. Tapes will be erased within six months from the time the group terminates.

A Dozen Things I'd Like to Do at SSU

List twelve activities, projects, programs, or organizations in which you are involved or in which you think you might like to become involved at Southern State University. Write them under "Things/Activities."

Things/Activities	*Characteristics of preferences*
1.	
2.	
3.	
4.	
5.	
6.	
7.	
8.	
9.	
10.	
11.	
12.	

After listing the twelve activities, programs, or organizations, mark the appropriate symbols under "Characteristics of preferences."

1. Place a $ after each activity that requires more than $5 to do or become involved in.

2. Place an **N** after any activity you've begun within the last two years. Place an **O** after any activity you've been involved in for more than two years.

3. If the activity requires taking risks (that is, doing something that you feel uneasy about), indicate how much risk is involved for you (1 = very little risk to **10** = great deal of risk). Now identify the type of risk involved (**P** = physical, **I** = intellectual, **E** = emotional, or **S** = social).

4. Identify what kind of activity it is (**R** = recreation or leisure, **W** = work or career, **E** = educational or learning, **SE** = social or entertainment).

5. Place a **G** after any activity that involves a group of five or more people; an **A** after all activities performed alone; an **F** after activities involving four or fewer people.

6. Place **PS** after all activities requiring skills you presently possess. Place **NS** after all activities requiring you to develop new skills.

7. Place a **C** after any activity you know is available at SSU. Place a **?** after any activity you are unsure is available at SSU.

8. After each activity, indicate how much time per week it requires (**X** = four hours or less, **Y** = four to eight hours, **Z** = more than eight hours).

9. Rank the activities according to how interested you are in becoming or remaining involved (**L** = little or low interest, **M** = moderate interest, **V** = very interested).*

Decision-Making Grid

This decision-making grid is provided to aid students in identifying preferred alternatives for becoming involved in college activities.

Step 1. List the opportunities for involvement at Southern State University that particularly appeal to you. Be as specific and yet as comprehensive as possible in identifying your involvement options. It is permissible to list a small number of options, as long as the total sufficiently represents a composite of your interests and preferences.

1.
2.
3.
4.
5.
6.
7.
8.
9.
10.

Step 2. Compare each alternative in turn with every other alternative and circle the one that has the most appeal for you

* Reproduced by permission of Dodd, Mead, and Company, Inc. From *Values Clarification: A Handbook of Practical Strategies for Teachers and Students* by Sidney B. Simon, Leland W. Howe, and Howard Kirschenbaum. Copyright © 1972, 1978, by Hart Publishing Company, Inc.

on the chart. Your reason for making the selection is not as important as making the forced choice. Later, after all comparisons have been made, it will be important to think and talk about the reasons for your choices.

1 2									
1 3	2 3								
1 4	2 4	3 4							
1 5	2 5	3 5	4 5						
1 6	2 6	3 6	4 6	5 6					
1 7	2 7	3 7	4 7	5 7	6 7				
1 8	2 8	3 8	4 8	5 8	6 8	7 8			
1 9	2 9	3 9	4 9	5 9	6 9	7 9	8 9		
1 10	2 10	3 10	4 10	5 10	6 10	7 10	8 10	9 10	

Step 3. Enter the total number of times each number was circled.

1: _____ 2: _____ 3: _____ 4: _____ 5: _____

6: _____ 7: _____ 8: _____ 9: _____ 10: _____

Step 4. Make a list of priorities based on the results documented in the chart. In case of ties, use the grid's comparison of the two numbers tied to select one.

1.
2.
3.
4.
5.
6.
7.
8.
9.
10.*

* Based on the Prioritizing Grid from *What Color Is Your Parachute?* Copyright 1988 by Richard N. Bolles. Reprinted with permission by Ten Speed Press, Berkeley, Calif.

Session One
Formative Evaluation Form

Consider each of the activities during the session and then complete this chart. Make notes about activities or events that you want to discuss before the next session.

Session Activities	Leader Effectiveness	Goal Achievement
Welcoming comments	1 2 3 4 5	1 2 3 4 5
Progressive signatures	1 2 3 4 5	1 2 3 4 5
Involvement experience	1 2 3 4 5	1 2 3 4 5
Introduction of partner to group	1 2 3 4 5	1 2 3 4 5
Purposes of education	1 2 3 4 5	1 2 3 4 5
Purposive plans	1 2 3 4 5	1 2 3 4 5
Closure	1 2 3 4 5	1 2 3 4 5

Notes: _____

_____

_____

Key to Leadership Effectiveness
1 = Exceptionally effective
2 = Very effective
3 = Effective
4 = Ineffective
5 = Very ineffective

Key to Degree of Goal Achievement
1 = Completely achieved
2 = Achieved to a great extent
3 = Partially achieved
4 = Minimally achieved
5 = Not achieved

Session Two
Formative Evaluation Form

Consider each of the activities during the session and then complete this chart. Make notes about activities or events that you want to discuss before the next session.

Session Activities	*Leader Effectiveness*	*Goal Achievement*
Interview dialogues	1 2 3 4 5	1 2 3 4 5
Definition of involvement	1 2 3 4 5	1 2 3 4 5
Brief lecture	1 2 3 4 5	1 2 3 4 5
Preferences for involvement	1 2 3 4 5	1 2 3 4 5
Closure	1 2 3 4 5	1 2 3 4 5

Notes: _____

_____

_____

Key to Leadership Effectiveness	*Key to Degree of Goal Achievement*
1 = Exceptionally effective	1 = Completely achieved
2 = Very effective	2 = Achieved to a great extent
3 = Effective	3 = Partially achieved
4 = Ineffective	4 = Minimally achieved
5 = Very ineffective	5 = Not achieved

Session Three
Formative Evaluation Form

Consider each of the activities during the session and then complete this chart. Make notes about activities or events that you want to discuss before the next session.

Session Activities	Leader Effectiveness	Goal Achievement
Welcoming comments	1 2 3 4 5	1 2 3 4 5
MBTI profiles	1 2 3 4 5	1 2 3 4 5
Brief lecture	1 2 3 4 5	1 2 3 4 5
Group discussion	1 2 3 4 5	1 2 3 4 5
Closure	1 2 3 4 5	1 2 3 4 5

Notes: _____

_____

_____

Key to Leadership Effectiveness
1 = Exceptionally effective
2 = Very effective
3 = Effective
4 = Ineffective
5 = Very ineffective

Key to Degree of Goal Achievement
1 = Completely achieved
2 = Achieved to a great extent
3 = Partially achieved
4 = Minimally achieved
5 = Not achieved

Session Four
Formative Evaluation Form

Consider each of the activities during the session and then complete this chart. Make notes about activities or events that you want to discuss before the next session.

Session Activities	Leader Effectiveness	Goal Achievement
Group process	1 2 3 4 5	1 2 3 4 5
Interview reports	1 2 3 4 5	1 2 3 4 5
Closure	1 2 3 4 5	1 2 3 4 5

Notes: _____

_____

_____

Key to Leadership Effectiveness
1 = Exceptionally effective
2 = Very effective
3 = Effective
4 = Ineffective
5 = Very ineffective

Key to Degree of Goal Achievement
1 = Completely achieved
2 = Achieved to a great extent
3 = Partially achieved
4 = Minimally achieved
5 = Not achieved

Session Five
Formative Evaluation Form

Consider each of the activities during the session and then complete this chart. Make notes about activities or events that you want to discuss before the next session.

Session Activities	Leader Effectiveness	Goal Achievement
Involvement preferences	1 2 3 4 5	1 2 3 4 5
Group brainstorming	1 2 3 4 5	1 2 3 4 5
Brief lecture	1 2 3 4 5	1 2 3 4 5
Closure	1 2 3 4 5	1 2 3 4 5

Notes: _____

_____

_____

Key to Leadership Effectiveness
1 = Exceptionally effective
2 = Very effective
3 = Effective
4 = Ineffective
5 = Very ineffective

Key to Degree of Goal Achievement
1 = Completely achieved
2 = Achieved to a great extent
3 = Partially achieved
4 = Minimally achieved
5 = Not achieved

Session Six
Formative Evaluation Form

Consider each of the activities during the session and then complete this chart. Make notes about activities or events that you want to discuss before the next session.

Session Activities	Leader Effectiveness	Goal Achievement
Goal sharing	1 2 3 4 5	1 2 3 4 5
Closure	1 2 3 4 5	1 2 3 4 5
Summative evaluation	1 2 3 4 5	1 2 3 4 5

Notes: _____

_____

_____

Key to Leadership Effectiveness	*Key to Degree of Goal Achievement*
1 = Exceptionally effective	1 = Completely achieved
2 = Very effective	2 = Achieved to a great extent
3 = Effective	3 = Partially achieved
4 = Ineffective	4 = Minimally achieved
5 = Very ineffective	5 = Not achieved

Summative Evaluation Forms

Taking Charge of Your College Experience: Getting Involved

1. How effectively did this group accomplish its goals to help participants (*Circle one number*):
   A. Learn the benefits associated with involvement in college activities

      Not addressed or   Completed,
      accomplished at all   **1   2   3   4   5**   accomplished
   B. Explore their personalities and interests as a means of identifying avenues of involvement

      Not addressed or   Completed,
      accomplished at all   **1   2   3   4   5**   accomplished
   C. Identify activities that are enjoyable and will enrich their college experience

      Not addressed or   Completed,
      accomplished at all   **1   2   3   4   5**   accomplished
   D. Decide which activities they wish to become involved in

      Not addressed or   Completed,
      accomplished at all   **1   2   3   4   5**   accomplished
   E. Develop a plan for achieving their involvement goals

      Not addressed or   Completed,
      accomplished at all   **1   2   3   4   5**   accomplished
2. How effective were the leaders in addressing the goals of the workshop?

      Not effective at all   **1   2   3   4   5**   Very effective
3. What aspect(s) of this workshop were most beneficial or helpful to you?

   _____

   _____

4. What aspects or parts of the workshop would you recommend be changed or omitted if it were to be offered in the future?

   _____

   _____

5. What suggestions do you have for the leaders for improving their performance in this workshop?

Leader's name: _____. I suggest that you: _____

Leader's name: _____. I suggest that you: _____

6. What was the most important thing you learned from this workshop?

7. Please make other comments about the workshop that you think it important for the leaders to know.

Extracurricular Involvement Inventory
(by Anne V. Massaro and Roger B. Winston, Jr.)

This inventory is concerned with your involvement in extracurricular activities. Membership in any organized student group for which you *are not paid and do not receive academic credit* is considered involvement in extracurricular activities.

Examples of Extracurricular Groups and Organizations

- Residence-hall council
- Wesley Foundation, Hillel Foundation, Newman Center, etc.
- Intramural football/basketball/softball team
- Student government council/senate, committee, or task force
- Bible (or other religious) study group
- Young Democrats/Republicans/Liberals, etc.
- Intercollegiate athletic team
- Biology Club, Advertising Club, Historical Society
- Student center/union committee or concert/lecture program committee
- Social fraternity/sorority
- Service organization
- College newspaper, yearbook, magazine, or radio station
- Drama club/production or debate team

- Choir/band or other performing group
- Mortar Board, Blue Key, Phi Eta Sigma, and other honor or leadership societies

1. What is your name? _____
2. What is your local address? _____
    _____ Telephone:_____
    (We will need to contact you during Winter Quarter. If you plan to move, please provide your new address and telephone number. _____
    _____ Telephone: _____)
3. What is your gender? ☐ Male ☐ Female
4. What was your age at your last birthday? _____
5. What is your class standing? ☐ Freshman
    ☐ Sophomore ☐ Junior ☐ Senior
6. What is your academic major? _____
    (If undecided, write undecided.)
7. In how many extracurricular organizations or groups are you currently involved? (*Check one.*)
    ☐ None. . . *You need complete no more of the Inventory. Thank you!*
    ☐ One
    ☐ Two
    ☐ Three
    ☐ Four
    ☐ Five or more

If you answered that you are involved in one or more organizations or groups, please fill out an Involvement Index *for each extracurricular activity in which you are involved.*

Remember, complete an Involvement Index *for each organization of which you are a member.*

[There are 5 Involvement Indexes attached. If more are needed, please ask the leader for additional copies.]

Involvement Index

Please indicate: (1) the type of organization it is, (2) the approximate number of hours you have been involved (for example, attending meetings or practices, working on projects, or playing in games) with this group or organization in the last four weeks, and (3) leadership positions held, if any. Then, answer questions 1 through 5 below.

What type of student organization is it? (*Check the one best description.*)
☐ Social Fraternity/Sorority
☐ Religious
☐ Leadership or Academic Honorary
☐ Intramural Sports Team
☐ Service
☐ Governance (e.g., residence-hall council, student government, student judiciary)
☐ Intercollegiate Athletic Team
☐ Academic (academic-department or major-related) Club or Society
☐ Programming (e.g., Student Center/Union, lecture or concert committee)
☐ Student Publication (e.g., newspaper, magazine, or yearbook)
☐ Performing Group (e.g., choir, drama production, debate team)
☐ Other (Please Specify): _____

In the last four weeks, for approximately how many hours (total) have you been involved with this group or organization and its activities, projects, or programs? (*Check one.*)
☐ None   ☐ 33–40 hours
☐ 1–8 hours   ☐ 41–48 hours
☐ 9–16 hours   ☐ 49–56 hours
☐ 17–24 hours   ☐ 57–64 hours
☐ 25–32 hours   ☐ 65 or more hours

In the last four weeks have you held one of the offices in this organization or a position equivalent to one of the following offices? If you have held more than one, check the one in which you put the most effort. (*Check only one.*)
☐ President/Chairperson/Team Captain

☐ Vice President
☐ Secretary
☐ Treasurer
☐ Committee/Task Force/Project Chairperson
☐ I held no office.
☐ Other Office, Please specify:_____

Please respond to the following statements about your involvement in the above student organization or group. Check the *one best* response for each statement.

During the past four weeks...
1. When I attended meetings or other functions, I took an active part in the discussion or other activities.
   ☐ Very Often   ☐ Often   ☐ Occasionally   ☐ Never
   ☐ I attended no meetings or other functions in the past four weeks.
   ☐ The group/organization held no meetings or functions in the past four weeks.
2. When I was away from members of the group/organization, I talked with others about the organization and its activities, wore a pin, jersey, etc., or did something to let others know about my membership.
   ☐ Very Often   ☐ Often   ☐ Occasionally   ☐ Never
3. When the group/organization sponsored a program or activity, I made an effort to encourage other students and/or members to attend.
   ☐ Very Often   ☐ Often   ☐ Occasionally   ☐ Never
   ☐ The organization had no program or activity during the past four weeks.
4. I volunteered or was assigned responsibility to work on something that the group/organization needed to have done.
   ☐ Very Often   ☐ Often   ☐ Occasionally   ☐ Never
5. I fulfilled my assigned duties or responsibilities to the group/organization on time.
   ☐ Very Often   ☐ Often   ☐ Occasionally   ☐ Never

☐ I had no duties or responsibilities except to attend meetings or other functions.

Please continue until you have completed an Involvement Index *for every student group or organization in which you are currently involved.**

References to Appendix

American Telephone and Telegraph Human Resources Studies Group. "College Experiences and Managerial Performance: Report to Management." Unpublished paper, 1984. (Available from Division Manager, Human Resources Studies, AT & T, Room 29-1231, New York, N.Y. 10022.)

Astin, A. W. *Four Critical Years: Effects of College on Beliefs, Attitudes, and Knowledge.* San Francisco: Jossey-Bass, 1977.

Astin, A. W. *Achieving Educational Excellence: A Critical Assessment of Priorities and Practices in Higher Education.* San Francisco: Jossey-Bass, 1985.

Bolles, R. N. *What Color Is Your Parachute?* Berkeley, Calif.: Ten Speed Press, 1988.

Bowen, H. R. *Investment in Learning: The Individual and Social Values of American Higher Education.* San Francisco: Jossey-Bass, 1977.

Briggs, I. B. *Gifts Differing.* Palo Alto, Calif.: Consulting Psychologists Press, 1980.

Briggs, I. B., and McCaulley, M. H. *Manual: A Guide to the Development and Use of the Myers-Briggs Type Indicator.* Palo Alto, Calif.: Consulting Psychologists Press, 1985.

Chickering, A. W. *Education and Identity.* San Francisco: Jossey-Bass, 1969.

Feldman, K. A., and Newcomb, T. M. *The Impact of College on Students.* (2 vols.) San Francisco: Jossey-Bass, 1969.

Hood, A. B. "Student Development: Does Participation Affect Growth?" *ACU-I Bulletin,* 1984, *52,* 16–19.

* From Winston and Massaro (1987). Reprinted by permission of the American Association for Counseling and Development.

Hood, A. B., Riahinejad, A. R., and White, D. B. "Changes in Ego Identity During the College Years." *Journal of College Student Personnel*, 1986, 27, 107–113.

Keirsey, D., and Bates, M. *Please Understand Me: Character and Temperament Types*. Del Mar, Calif.: Prometheus Nemesis Books, 1984.

Lawrence, G. *People Types and Tiger Stripes*. Gainesville, Fla.: Center for the Applications of Psychological Type, 1982.

Provost, J. A., and Anchors, S. "Student Involvement and Activities." In J. A. Provost and S. Anchors (Eds.), *Applications of the Myers-Briggs Type Indicator in Higher Education*. Palo Alto, Calif.: Consulting Psychologists Press, 1987.

Sanford, N. "The Developmental Status of the Entering Freshman." In N. Sanford (Ed.), *The American College*. New York: Wiley, 1962.

Sanford, N. *Where Colleges Fail*. San Francisco: Jossey-Bass, 1967.

Simon, S. B., Howe, L. W., and Kirschenbaum, H. *Values Clarification: A Handbook of Practical Strategies for Teachers and Students*. New York: Hart, 1972.

Study Group on the Conditions of Excellence in American Higher Education. *Involvement in Learning: Realizing the Potential of American Higher Education*. Washington, D.C.: National Institute of Education, 1984.

Williams, M. E., and Winston, R. B., Jr. "Participation in Organized Student Activities and Work: Differences in Developmental Task Achievement of Traditional Aged College Students." *National Association of Student Personnel Administrators Journal*, 1985, 22(3), 52–59.

Winston, R. B., Jr., and Massaro, A. V. "Extracurricular Involvement Inventory: An Instrument for Assessing Intensity of Student Involvement." *Journal of College Student Personnel*, 1987, 28, 169–175.

Winston, R. B., Jr., Miller, T. K., and Prince, J. S. *Student Developmental Task and Lifestyle Inventory*. Athens, Ga.: Student Development Associates, 1987.

Winter, D. G., McClelland, D. C., and Stewart, A. J. *A New Case for the Liberal Arts: Assessing Institutional Goals and Student Development*. San Francisco: Jossey-Bass, 1981.

ΙΟΙΟΙΟΙΟΙΟΙΟΙΟΙΟΙΟΙΟΙ

References

Alley, P. M. "The Graduate Student Coleader in the Student Counseling Group: A General Theme and a Specific Case." *School Counselor*, 1981, *29*(1), 51–53.

American Association for Counseling and Development. "Ethical Standards." In R. Callis, S. K. Pope, and M. E. DePauw (Eds.), *APGA Ethical Standards Casebook*. (3rd ed.) Alexandria, Va.: American Association for Counseling and Development, 1982.

American College Personnel Association. "Statement of Ethical and Professional Standards." *Journal of College Student Personnel*, 1981, *22*, 184–189.

Anderson, S. B., Ball, S., Murphy, R. T., and Associates. *Encyclopedia of Educational Evaluation: Concepts and Techniques for Evaluating Education and Training Programs*. San Francisco: Jossey-Bass, 1975.

Arbes, B. H. "Intervention Style Survey." In J. W. Pfeiffer and J. E. Jones (Eds.), *Annual Handbook for Group Facilitators*. La Jolla, Calif.: University Associates, 1972.

Aronson, E. *The Social Animal*. (3rd ed.) Chicago: W. H. Freeman, 1980.

Aslanian, C. B., and Brickell, H. M. *Americans in Transition: Life Changes as Reasons for Adult Learning*. New York: College Entrance Examination Board, 1980.

Association for Specialists in Group Work. "Ethical Guidelines for Group Leaders." In R. Callis, S. K. Pope, and M. E. DePauw (Eds.), *APGA Ethical Standards Casebook*. (3rd ed.) Alexandria, Va.: American Association for Counseling and Development, 1982.

Astin, A. W. *Four Critical Years: Effects of College on Beliefs, Attitudes, and Knowledge.* San Francisco: Jossey-Bass, 1977.

Astin, A. W. *Achieving Educational Excellence: A Critical Assessment of Priorities and Practices in Higher Education.* San Francisco: Jossey-Bass, 1985.

Aulepp, L. A., and Delworth, U. *Training Manual for an Ecosystem Model.* Boulder, Colo.: Western Interstate Commission for Higher Education, 1976.

Bach, G. R. *Intensive Group Psychotherapy.* New York: Ronald Press, 1954.

Baldridge, J. V. *Power and Conflict in the University.* New York: Wiley, 1971.

Banning, J. H. (Ed.). *Campus Ecology: A Perspective for Student Affairs.* Washington, D.C.: National Association of Student Personnel Administrators, 1978.

Banning, J. H. "The Campus Ecology Manager Role." In U. Delworth, G. R. Hanson, and Associates, *Student Services: A Handbook for the Profession.* San Francisco: Jossey-Bass, 1980.

Banning, J. H., and McKinley, D. L. "Conceptions of the Campus Environment." In W. H. Morrill, J. C. Hurst, and Associates, *Dimensions of Intervention for Student Development.* New York: Wiley, 1980.

Barr, M. J. "Internal and External Forces Influencing Programming." In M. J. Barr, L. A. Keating, and Associates, *Developing Effective Student Services Programs: Systematic Approaches for Practitioners.* San Francisco: Jossey-Bass, 1985.

Barrow, J. C. *Fostering Cognitive Development of Students: A New Approach to Counseling and Program Planning.* San Francisco: Jossey-Bass, 1986.

Baxter Magolda, M. B. "Comparing Open-Ended Interviews and Standardized Measures of Intellectual Development." *Journal of College Student Personnel*, 1987, *28*, 443–448.

Baxter Magolda, M. B., and Porterfield, W. D. "A New Approach to Assessing Intellectual Development on Perry Scheme." *Journal of College Student Personnel*, 1985, *26*, 343–351.

Beane, J. A., Toepfer, C. F., Jr., and Alessi, S. J., Jr. *Curriculum Planning and Development.* Boston: Allyn & Bacon, 1986.

Benne, K. D., and Sheats, P. "Functional Roles of Group Members." *Journal of Social Issues*, 1948, *6*(2), 42–47.

Bennis, W. G., and Shepard, H. A. "A Theory of Group Development." *Human Relations*, 1956, *9*, 415–437.

Bennis, W. G., and Shepard, H.A. "A Theory of Group Development." In G. S. Gibbard, J. J. Hartman, and R. D. Mann (Eds.), *Analysis of Groups: Contributions to Theory, Research, and Practice.* San Francisco: Jossey-Bass, 1973.

Biddle, B. J., and Thomas, E. J. *Role Theory: Concepts and Research.* New York: Wiley, 1966.

Bion, W. R. *Experiences in Groups.* New York: Basic Books, 1961.

Blake, R. R., and Mouton, J. S. *The Managerial Grid.* Houston: Gulf, 1964.

Blake, R. R., and Mouton, J. S. "An Overview of the Grid." *Training and Development Journal*, 1975, *29*, 29–37.

Blake, R. R., Mouton, J. S., and Williams, M. S. *The Academic Administrator Grid: A Guide to Developing Effective Management Teams.* San Francisco: Jossey-Bass, 1981.

Blocher, D. H. "Toward an Ecology of Student Development." *Personnel and Guidance Journal*, 1974, *52*, 360–365.

Blocher, D. H. "Campus Learning Environments and the Ecology of Student Development." In J. H. Banning (Ed.), *Campus Ecology: A Perspective for Student Affairs.* Washington, D.C.: National Association of Student Personnel Administrators, 1978.

Blocher, D. H. *The Professional Counselor.* New York: Macmillan, 1987.

Bloom, A. *The Closing of the American Mind: How Higher Education Has Failed Democracy and Impoverished the Souls of Today's Students.* New York: Simon & Schuster, 1987.

Blos, P. *The Adolescent Personality: A Study of Individual Behavior.* New York: Appleton-Century-Crofts, 1941.

Bolles, R. N. *What Color Is Your Parachute?* Berkeley, Calif.: Ten Speed Press, 1985.

Bonney, W. C. "Group Counseling and Developmental Processes." In G. M. Gazda (Ed.), *Theories and Methods of Group Counseling in the Schools.* Springfield, Ill.: Thomas, 1969.

Bonney, W. C. "The Maturation of Groups." *Small Group Behavior*, 1974, *5*, 445–461.

Bonney, W. C., and Foley, W. J. "The Transition Stage in Group Counseling in Terms of Congruity Theory." *Journal of Counseling Psychology*, 1963, *10*, 136–138.

Bowers, D. G., and Seashore, S. E. "Predicting Organizational Effectiveness with a Four-Factor Theory of Leadership." *Administrative Science Quarterly*, 1966, *11*, 238–263.

Braaten, L. J. "Developmental Phases of Encounter Groups: A Critical Review of Models and a New Proposal." *Interpersonal Development*, 1974, *75*, 112–129.

Brown, R. D. *Student Development in Tomorrow's Higher Education: A Return to the Academy.* Alexandria, Va.: American College Personnel Association, 1972.

Brown, R. D. "How Evaluation Can Make a Difference." In G. R. Hanson (Ed.), *New Directions for Student Services: Evaluating Program Effectiveness*, no. 1. San Francisco: Jossey-Bass, 1978.

Brown, R. D. "Key Issues in Evaluating Student Affairs Programs." In G. D. Kuh (Ed.), *Evaluation in Student Affairs.* Alexandria, Va.: American College Personnel Association, 1979.

Brown, R. D., and DeCoster, D. A. (Eds.). *New Directions for Student Services: Mentoring-Transcript Systems for Promoting Student Growth*, no. 19. San Francisco: Jossey-Bass, 1982.

Brown, R. D., and Sanstead, M. J. "Using Evaluation to Make Decisions About Academic Advising Programs." In R. B. Winston, Jr., S. C. Ender, and T. K. Miller (Eds.), *New Directions for Student Services: Developmental Approaches to Academic Advising*, no. 17. San Francisco: Jossey-Bass, 1982.

Brown, R. D., and others. "Aesthetic Development in College Students." *College Student Journal*, 1982, *16*, 358–365.

Brubacher, J. S., and Rudy, W. *Higher Education in Transition: A History of American Colleges and Universities, 1936–1976.* (3rd ed.) New York: Harper & Row, 1976.

Byrum-Gaw, B., and Carlock, C. J. "Modeling: Teaching by Living the Theory." In J. W. Pfeiffer and J. E. Jones (Eds.), *Annual Handbook for Group Facilitators.* La Jolla, Calif.: University Associates, 1983.

Campbell, D. T., and Stanley, J. C. *Experimental and Quasi-*

Experimental Designs for Research. Chicago: Rand McNally, 1966.

Capelle, R. G. *Changing Human Systems.* Toronto: International Human Systems Institute, 1979.

Caple, R. B. "The Sequential Stages of Group Development." *Small Group Behavior,* 1978, *9,* 470–476.

Carkhuff, R. R. "Rejoinder: What's It All About Anyway? Some Reflections on Helping and Human Resource Development Models." *Counseling Psychologist,* 1972, *3,* 79–87.

Cartwright, D. "Achieving Change in People: Some Applications of Group Dynamics Theory." *Human Relations,* 1951, *4,* 381–392.

Cartwright, E., and Zander, A. *Group Dynamics: Research and Theory.* (3rd ed.) New York: Harper & Row, 1968.

Chickering, A. W. *Education and Identity.* San Francisco: Jossey-Bass, 1969.

Chickering, A. W. *Commuting Versus Resident Students: Overcoming the Educational Inequities of Living Off Campus.* San Francisco: Jossey-Bass, 1974.

Chickering, A. W., and Havighurst, R. J. "The Life Cycle." In A. W. Chickering and Associates, *The Modern American College: Responding to the New Realities of Diverse Students and a Changing Society.* San Francisco: Jossey-Bass, 1981.

Cissna, K. N. "Phases in Group Development, the Negative Evidence." *Small Group Behavior,* 1984, *15,* 3–32.

Clack, R. J. "Skill Development: Human Relations Skills Training Groups." In R. K. Conyne (Ed.), *The Group Workers' Handbook: Varieties of Group Experience.* Springfield, Ill.: Thomas, 1985.

Clark, B. R., and Trow, M. "The Organizational Context." In T. M. Newcomb and E. K. Wilson (Eds.), *College Peer Groups: Problems and Prospects for Research.* Hawthorne, N.Y.: Aldine, 1966.

Commission on Professional Development of the Council of Student Personnel Associations in Higher Education. "Student Development Services in Post-Secondary Education." In G. L. Saddlemire and A. L. Rentz (Eds.), *Student Affairs—A Profession's Heritage: Significant Articles, Authors, Issues, and Documents.* Alexandria, Va.: American College Personnel Association, 1972/1983.

Conyne, R. K. "Group Leadership Functions Scale." In J. W. Pfeiffer and J. E. Jones (Eds.), *Annual Handbook for Group Facilitators*. La Jolla, Calif.: University Associates, 1975.

Conyne, R. K. "Organization Development: A Broad Net Intervention for Student Affairs." In T. K. Miller, R. B. Winston, Jr., and W. R. Mendenhall (Eds.), *Administration and Leadership in Student Affairs: Actualizing Student Development in Higher Education.* Muncie, Ind.: Accelerated Development, 1983.

Conyne, R. K. "Organization Change: The Social Climate Group." In R. K. Conyne (Ed.), *The Group Workers' Handbook: Varieties of Group Experience.* Springfield, Ill.: Thomas, 1985a.

Conyne, R. K. "Preface." In R. K. Conyne (Ed.), *The Group Workers' Handbook: Varieties of Group Experience.* Springfield, Ill.: Thomas, 1985b.

Coons, F. W. "The Developmental Tasks of College Students." In S. C. Feinstein, P. L. Glovacchini, and A. A. Miller (Eds.), *Adolescent Psychiatry: Developmental and Clinical Studies.* Vol. 1. New York: Basic Books, 1971.

Cooper, C. L. "Adverse and Growthful Effects of Experiential Learning Groups: The Role of the Trainer, Participant, and Group Characteristics." *Human Relations,* 1977, *30,* 1103–1129.

Cooper, C. L., and Harrison, K. "Designing and Facilitating Experiential Group Activities: Variables and Issues." In J. W. Pfeiffer and J. E. Jones (Eds.), *Annual Handbook for Group Facilitators.* La Jolla, Calif.: University Associates, 1976.

Corey, G., and Corey, M. S. *Groups: Process and Practice.* Monterey, Calif.: Brooks/Cole, 1977.

Corey, G., and others. *Group Techniques.* Monterey, Calif.: Brooks/Cole, 1982.

Corey, M. S., and Corey, G. *Groups: Process and Practice.* (3rd ed.) Monterey, Calif.: Brooks/Cole, 1987.

Council for the Advancement of Standards for Student Services/Development Programs. *General Standards.* Washington, D.C.: Council for the Advancement of Standards, 1986.

Crockett, D. S. (Ed.). Academic Advising: A Resource Document. Iowa City, Iowa: American College Testing Program, 1978.

Cronbach, L. J. "Course Improvement Through Evaluation." *Teachers College Record,* 1963, *64,* 672–683.

Cronbach, L. J. *Designing Evaluations of Educational and Social Programs.* San Francisco: Jossey-Bass, 1982.

Cross, K. P. *Accent on Learning: Improving Instruction and Reshaping the Curriculum.* San Francisco: Jossey-Bass, 1976.

Daane, C. J. *Vocational Exploration Groups.* (4th ed.) Tempe, Ariz.: Studies for Urban Man, 1972.

Dagley, J. C., and Hartley, D. H. *Career Guidance in Georgia.* Atlanta: Georgia Department of Education, 1976.

Dalton, J. C. (Ed.). *Promoting Values Development in College Students.* Washington, D.C.: National Association of Student Personnel Administrators, 1985.

DeCoster, D. A., and Brown, S. S. "Staff Development: Personal and Professional Education." In T. K. Miller, R. B. Winston, Jr., and W. R. Mendenhall (Eds.), *Administration and Leadership in Student Affairs: Actualizing Student Development in Higher Education.* Muncie, Ind.: Accelerated Development, 1983.

Deffenbacher, J. L., and McKinley, D. L. "Stress Management: Issues in Intervention Design." In E. M. Altmaier (Ed.), *New Directions for Student Services: Helping Students Manage Stress,* no. 21. San Francisco: Jossey-Bass, 1983.

Dewey, J. *Democracy and Education.* New York: Macmillan, 1916.

Drum, D. J. "Understanding Student Development." In W. H. Morrill, J. C. Hurst, and Associates, *Dimensions of Intervention for Student Development.* New York: Wiley, 1980.

Drum, D. J., and Knott, J. E. *Structured Groups for Facilitating Development: Acquiring Life Skills, Resolving Life Themes, and Making Life Transitions.* New York: Human Sciences Press, 1977.

Dunphy, D. C. "The Function of Fantasy in Groups." In G. S. Gibbard, J. J. Hartman, and R. D. Mann (Eds.), *Analysis of Groups: Contributions to Theory, Research, and Practice.* San Francisco: Jossey-Bass, 1973.

Durkheim, E. *Moral Education.* New York: Free Press, 1961.

Elman, D., and Rupple, D. "Group Discussion Members' Reactions to a Structured Opening Exercise." *Small Group Behavior*, 1978, *9*, 363–371.

Erikson, E. H. *Childhood and Society*. New York: Norton, 1950.

Erikson, E. H. "Identity and the Life Cycle." *Psychological Issues Monograph 1* (1). New York: International Universities Press, 1959.

Erikson, E. H. *Childhood and Society*. (2nd ed.) New York: Norton, 1963.

Erikson, E. H. *Insight and Responsibility*. New York: Norton, 1964.

Erikson, E. H. *Identity, Youth and Crisis*. New York: Norton, 1968.

Evans, N. J., and Jarvis, P. A. "Group Cohesion: A Review and Re-evaluation." *Small Group Behavior*, 1980, *11*, 359–370.

Feldman, K. A., and Newcomb, T. M. *The Impact of College on Students: An Analysis of Four Decades of Research*, Vol. 1. San Francisco: Jossey-Bass, 1969a.

Feldman, K. A., and Newcomb, T. M. *The Impact of College on Students: Summary Tables*. Vol. 2. San Francisco: Jossey-Bass, 1969b.

Festinger, L., Schachter, S., and Bock, K. *Social Pressures in Informal Groups: A Study of Human Factors in Housing*. Stanford, Calif.: Stanford University Press, 1950.

Fiedler, F. E. *A Theory of Leadership Effectiveness*. New York: McGraw-Hill, 1967.

Fiedler, F. E., Chemers, M. M., and Mahar, L. *Improving Leadership Effectiveness*. New York: Wiley, 1976.

Fiedler, F. E., and Mahar, L. "The Effectiveness of Contingency Model Training: A Review of the Validity of Leader Match." *Personnel Psychology*, 1979, *32*, 45–62.

Fink, A., and Kosecoff, J. *An Evaluation Primer*. Beverly Hills, Calif.: Sage, 1978.

Foley, W. J., and Bonney, W. C. "A Developmental Model for Counseling Groups." *Personnel and Guidance Journal*, 1966, *44*, 576–580.

Francis, K. C., McDaniel, M., and Doyle, R. E. "Training in Role Communication Skills: Effect on Interpersonal and Academic Skills of High-Risk Freshmen." *Journal of College Student Personnel*, 1987, *28*, 151–156.

Fried, J. (Ed.). *New Directions for Student Services: Education for Student Development*, no. 15. San Francisco: Jossey-Bass, 1981.

Fromm, E. *Escape from Freedom*. New York: Holt, Rinehart and Winston, 1941.

Galinsky, M. J., and Schopler, J. H. "Structuring Co-leadership in Social Work Training." *Social Work with Groups*, 1981, *3*, 51–63.

Gallessich, J. *The Profession and Practice of Consultation: A Handbook for Consultants, Trainers of Consultants, and Consumers of Consultation Services*. San Francisco: Jossey-Bass, 1982.

Gardner, H. *The Arts and Human Development: A Psychological Study of the Artistic Process*. New York: Wiley, 1973.

Gaw, B. A. "Processing Questions: An Aid to Completing the Learning Cycle." In J. W. Pfeiffer and J. E. Jones (Eds.), *Annual Handbook for Group Facilitators*. La Jolla, Calif.: University Associates, 1979.

Gazda, G. M. *Group Counseling: A Developmental Approach*. (2nd ed.) Boston: Allyn & Bacon, 1978.

Gazda, G. M. "Life Skills Training." In E. K. Marshall, P. D. Kurtz, and Associates, *Interpersonal Helping Skills: A Guide to Training Methods, Programs, and Resources*. San Francisco: Jossey-Bass, 1982.

Gazda, G. M., Childers, W. C., and Brooks, D. K., Jr. *Foundations of Counseling and Human Services*. New York: McGraw-Hill, 1987.

Gazda, G. M., and others. *Human Relations Development: A Manual for Educators*. (3rd ed.) Boston: Allyn & Bacon, 1984.

Gelwick, B. P. "Cognitive Development of Women." In N. J. Evans (Ed.), *New Directions for Student Services: Facilitating the Development of Women*, no. 29. San Francisco: Jossey-Bass, 1985.

Gibbard, G. S., Hartman, J. J., and Mann, R. D. (Eds.). *Analysis of Groups: Contributions to Theory, Research, and Practice*. San Francisco: Jossey-Bass, 1973.

Gill, S. J., and Barry, R. A. "Group-Focused Counseling: Classifying the Essential Skills." *Personnel and Guidance Journal*, 1982, *60*, 302–305.

Gilligan, C. "Moral Development." In A. W. Chickering and Associates, *The Modern American College: Responding to the New*

Realities of Diverse Students and a Changing Society. San Francisco: Jossey-Bass, 1981.

Gilligan, C. *In a Different Voice: Psychological Theory and Women's Development.* Cambridge, Mass.: Harvard University Press, 1982.

Gleason, J. M., Seaman, F. J., and Hollander, E. P. "Emergent Leadership Processes as a Function of Task Structure and Machiavellianism." *Social Behavior and Personality,* 1978, *6,* 33–36.

Goodson, W. D. "Do Career Development Needs Exist for All Students Entering Colleges or Just the Undecided Major Students?" *Journal of College Student Personnel,* 1981, *22,* 413–417.

Gordon, V. N. *The Undecided College Student: An Academic and Career Advising Challenge.* Springfield, Ill.: Thomas, 1984.

Green, K. C., and others. *The American College Student, 1982: National Norms for 1978 and 1980 College Freshmen.* Los Angeles: American Council on Education and the Higher Education Research Institute, University of California, 1983.

Guba, E. G., and Lincoln, Y. S. *Effective Evaluation: Improving the Usefulness of Evaluation Results Through Responsive and Naturalistic Approaches.* San Francisco: Jossey-Bass, 1981.

Hansen, J. C., Warner, R. W., and Smith, E. J. *Group Counseling: Theory and Process.* (2nd ed.) Chicago: Rand McNally, 1980.

Hanson, G. R., and Lenning, O. T. "Evaluating Student Development Programs." In G. D. Kuh (Ed.), *Evaluation in Student Affairs.* Alexandria, Va.: American College Personnel Association, 1979.

Hanson, G. R., and Yancey, B. D. "Gathering Information to Determine Program Needs." In M. J. Barr, L. A. Keating, and Associates, *Developing Effective Student Services Programs: Systematic Approaches for Practitioners.* San Francisco: Jossey-Bass, 1985.

Havighurst, R. J. *Developmental Tasks and Education.* New York: Longman, 1952.

Havighurst, R. J. *Human Development and Education.* (Rev. ed.) New York: Longman, 1972.

Heath, D. *Growing Up in College: Liberal Education and Maturity.* San Francisco: Jossey-Bass, 1968.

Heath, R. *The Reasonable Adventurer*. Pittsburgh: University of Pittsburgh Press, 1964.

Heath, R. "Form, Flow, and Full-being." *Counseling Psychologist*, 1973, *4*, 56–63.

Hersey, P., and Blanchard, K. H. *Management of Organizational Behavior: Utilizing Human Resources*. (3rd ed.) Englewood Cliffs, N.J.: Prentice-Hall, 1977.

Hersey, P., and Blanchard, K. H. *Management of Organizational Behavior: Utilizing Human Resources*. (4th ed.) Englewood Cliffs, N.J.: Prentice-Hall, 1982.

Hettler, B. "Wellness Promotion on a University Campus." *Family and Community Health*, 1980, *3*, 77–95.

Hill, W. F. "Learning: Systematic Group Discussion Method (SGD)." In R. K. Conyne (Ed.), *The Group Workers' Handbook: Varieties of Group Experience*. Springfield, Ill.: Thomas, 1985.

Hodgkinson, H. L. "Adult Development: Implications for Faculty and Administrators." *Educational Record*, 1974, *55*, 263–274.

Holland, J. L. *Making Vocational Choices: A Theory of Careers*. Englewood Cliffs, N.J.: Prentice-Hall, 1973.

Hollander, E. P. *Leaders, Groups and Influences*. New York: Oxford University Press, 1964.

Hood, A. B. "Student Development: Does Participation Affect Growth?" *ACU-I Bulletin*, 1984, *52*, 16–19.

Huebner, L. A. "Interaction of Student and Campus." In U. Delworth, G. R. Hanson, and Associates, *Student Services: A Handbook for the Profession*. San Francisco: Jossey-Bass, 1980.

Hurst, J. C., and Jacobson, J. K. "Theories Underlying Students' Needs for Programs." In M. J. Barr, L. A. Keating, and Associates, *Developing Effective Student Services Programs: Systematic Approaches for Practitioners*. San Francisco: Jossey-Bass, 1985.

Hutchins, R. M. *The Higher Learning in America*. New Haven, Conn.: Yale University Press, 1936.

Isaac, S., and Michael, W. B. *Handbook in Research and Evaluation: A Collection of Principles, Methods, and Strategies Useful in the Planning, Design, and Evaluation of Studies in Education and the Behavioral Sciences*. San Diego, Calif.: Edits, 1971.

Ivey, A. E. *Developmental Therapy: Theory into Practice.* San Francisco: Jossey-Bass, 1986.

Ivey, A. E., and Authier, J. (Eds.). *Microcounseling: Innovations in Interviewing, Counseling, Psychotherapy, and Psychoeducation.* (2nd ed.) Springfield, Ill.: Thomas, 1978.

Ivey, A. E., and Galvin, M. "Skills Training: A Model for Treatment." In E. K. Marshall, P. D. Kurtz, and Associates, *Interpersonal Helping Skills: A Guide to Training Methods, Programs, and Resources.* San Francisco: Jossey-Bass, 1982.

Jackson, L. M., and Hood, A. B. "The Iowa Developing Autonomy Inventory." In A. B. Hood (Ed.), *The Iowa Student Development Inventories.* Iowa City, Iowa: Hitech Press, 1986.

Janis, I. L. *Group Think.* (2nd ed.) Boston: Houghton Mifflin, 1982.

Johnson, C. S., and Figler, H. E. "Career Development and Placement Services in Postsecondary Institutions." In N. C. Gysbers and Associates, *Designing Careers: Counseling to Enhance Education, Work, and Leisure.* San Francisco: Jossey-Bass, 1984.

Johnson, D. W., and Johnson, F. P. *Joining Together: Group Theory and Group Skills.* Englewood Cliffs, N.J.: Prentice-Hall, 1975.

Jones, J. E. "Major Growth Processes in Groups." In J. W. Pfeiffer and J. E. Jones (Eds.), *Annual Handbook for Facilitators, Trainers, and Consultants.* La Jolla, Calif.: University Associates, 1982.

Kasdorf, J., and Gustafson, K. "Outcome Research in Microcounseling." In A. E. Ivey and J. Authier (Eds.), *Microcounseling: Innovations in Interviewing, Counseling, Psychotherapy, and Psychoeducation.* (2nd ed.) Springfield, Ill.: Thomas, 1978.

Katchadourian, H. A., and Boli, J. *Careerism and Intellectualism Among College Students: Patterns of Academic and Career Choice in the Undergraduate Years.* San Francisco: Jossey-Bass, 1985.

Katz, D., Maccoby, N., and Morse, N. C. *Productivity, Supervision, and Morale in an Office Situation.* Ann Arbor, Mich.: Institute for Social Research, University of Michigan, 1950.

Katz, G. M. "Previous Conformity, Status, and the Rejection of the Deviant." *Small Group Behavior,* 1982, *13,* 403–413.

Kegan, R. *The Evolving Self: Problem and Process in Human Development.* Cambridge, Mass.: Harvard University Press, 1982.

Kelly, G. A. *The Psychology of Personal Constructs.* New York: Norton, 1955.

Kimball, R. K., and Hollander, E. P. "Independence in the Presence of an Experienced but Deviate Group Member." *Journal of Social Psychology,* 1974, *93,* 281–292.

King, P. M. "William Perry's Theory of Intellectual and Ethical Development." In L. L. Knefelkamp, C. Widick, and C. A. Parker (Eds.), *New Directions for Student Services: Applying New Developmental Findings,* no. 4. San Francisco: Jossey-Bass, 1978.

Kitchener, K. S. "Ethical Principles and Ethical Decisions in Student Affairs." In H. J. Canon and R. D. Brown (Eds.), *New Directions for Student Services: Applied Ethics in Student Services,* no. 30. San Francisco: Jossey-Bass, 1985.

Kitchener, K. S., and King, P. M. "Reflective Judgment: Concepts of Justification and Their Relationship to Age and Education." *Journal of Applied Developmental Psychology,* 1981, *2,* 89–116.

Knefelkamp, L. L. "Developmental Instruction: Fostering Intellectual and Personal Growth in College Students." Unpublished doctoral dissertation, University of Minnesota, 1974.

Knefelkamp, L. L., Widick, C., and Parker, C. A. (Eds.). *New Directions for Student Services: Applying New Developmental Findings,* no. 4. San Francisco: Jossey-Bass, 1978.

Knowles, M. S., and Knowles, H. F. *Introduction to Group Dynamics.* New York: Association Press, 1965.

Kohlberg, L. "Stages of Moral Development." In C. M. Beck, B. S. Crittenden, and E. V. Sullivan (Eds.), *Moral Education.* Toronto: University of Toronto Press, 1971.

Kohlberg, L. "A Cognitive Developmental Approach to Moral Education." *Humanist,* 1972, *6,* 13–16.

Kohlberg, L. "The Cognitive-Developmental Approaches to Moral Education." *Phi Delta Kappan,* 1975, *56,* 670–677.

Kohlberg, L., and others. *Assessing Moral Stages: A Manual.* Cambridge, Mass.: Center for Moral Education, Harvard University, 1978.

Kolb, D. *Learning Styles Inventory: Technical Manual.* Boston: McBer, 1976.

Kuh, G. D. "Evaluation: The State of the Art in Student Affairs." In G. D. Kuh (Ed.), *Evaluation in Student Affairs.* Alexandria, Va.: American College Personnel Association, 1979.

La Coursiere, R. "A Group Method to Facilitate Learning During the Stages of a Psychiatric Affiliation." *International Journal of Group Psychotherapy,* 1974, *24,* 342–351.

Lambert, M. J. "Relation of Helping Skills to Treatment Outcome." In E. K. Marshall, P. D. Kurtz, and Associates, *Interpersonal Helping Skills: A Guide to Training Methods, Programs, and Resources.* San Francisco: Jossey-Bass, 1982.

Lassey, W. R., and Sashkin, M. "Dimensions of Leadership." In W. R. Lassey and M. Sashkin (Eds.), *Leadership and Social Change.* (3rd ed.) La Jolla, Calif.: University Associates, 1983.

Law, A. I., and Fowle, C. M. *Program Evaluator's Guide.* Princeton, N.J.: Educational Testing Service, 1979.

Leafgren, F., and Elsenrath, D. E. "The Role of Campus Recreation Programs in Institutions of Higher Education." In F. Leafgren (Ed.), *New Directions for Student Services: Developing Campus Recreation and Wellness Programs,* no. 34. San Francisco: Jossey-Bass, 1986.

Levinson, D. J., and others. *The Seasons of a Man's Life.* New York: Knopf, 1978.

Lewin, K. *Principles of Topological Psychology.* New York: McGraw-Hill, 1936.

Lewin, K. "Frontiers in Group Dynamics." *Human Relations,* 1951, *1,* 2–38.

Lewin, K., Lippitt, R., and White, R. K. "Patterns of Aggressive Behavior in Experimentally Created 'Social Climates.'" *Journal of Social Psychology,* 1939, *10,* 271–299.

Lewis, M. D., and Lewis, J. A. "The Counselor's Impact on Community Environments." *Personnel and Guidance Journal,* 1977a, *55,* 356–358.

Lewis, M. D., and Lewis, J. A. "A Schematic for Change." *Personnel and Guidance Journal,* 1977b, *55,* 320–323.

Lieberman, M. A., Yalom, I. D., and Miles, M. D. *Encounter Groups: First Facts.* New York: Basic Books, 1973.

Lifton, W. M. *Working with Groups: Group Process and Individual Growth.* New York: Wiley, 1966.

Lippitt, R. "Community Change: Community Futuring and Planning Groups." In R. K. Conyne (Ed.), *The Group Workers' Handbook: Varieties of Group Experience.* Springfield, Ill.: Thomas, 1985.

Loevinger, J. *Ego Development: Conceptions and Theories.* San Francisco: Jossey-Bass, 1976.

London, M. "How Do You Say Goodbye After You've Said Hello?" *Personnel and Guidance Journal,* 1982, *60,* 412–414.

Luft, J. *Group Processes: An Introduction to Group Dynamics.* (3rd ed.) Mountain View, Calif.: Mayfield, 1984.

Lundgren, D. C., and Knight, D. J. "Sequential Stages of Development in Sensitivity Training Groups." *Journal of Applied Behavioral Science,* 1978, *14,* 204–222.

McCanne, L. P. F. "Dimensions of Participant Goals, Expectations, and Perceptions in Small Group Experiences." *Journal of Applied Behavioral Science,* 1977, *12,* 533–541.

McCoy, V. R. *Lifelong Learning: The Adult Years.* Washington, D.C.: Adult Education Association, 1977.

Mann, R. D. "Winners, Losers and the Search for Equality in Groups." In C. L. Cooper (Ed.), *Theories of Group Processes.* New York: Wiley, 1975.

Mead, G. H. *Self, Mind and Society.* Chicago: University of Chicago Press, 1934.

Middleman, R. R., and Goldberg, G. "The Concept of Structure in Experiential Learning." In J. W. Pfeiffer and J. E. Jones (Eds.), *Annual Handbook for Group Facilitators.* La Jolla, Calif.: University Associates, 1972.

Miller, J. B. *Toward a New Psychology of Women.* Boston: Beacon Press, 1976.

Miller, T. K., and McCaffrey, S. S. "Student Development Theory: Foundations for Academic Advising." In R. B. Winston, Jr., S. C. Ender, and T. K. Miller (Eds.), *New Directions for Student Services: Developmental Approaches to Academic Advising,* no. 17. San Francisco: Jossey-Bass, 1982.

Miller, T. K., and Prince, J. S. *The Future of Student Affairs: A Guide to Student Development for Tomorrow's Higher Education.* San Francisco: Jossey-Bass, 1976.

Miller, T. K., Winston, R. B., Jr., and Mendenhall, W. R. (Eds.). *Administration and Leadership in Student Affairs: Actualizing Student Development in Higher Education.* Muncie, Ind.: Accelerated Development, 1983.

Mines, R. A. "Measurement Issues in Evaluating Student Development Programs." *Journal of College Student Personnel,* 1985, *26,* 101–106.

Montagu, A. *Growing Young.* New York: McGraw-Hill, 1981.

Moos, R. H. *The Human Context: Environmental Determinants of Behavior.* New York: Wiley, 1976.

Moos, R. H. *Evaluating Educational Environments: Procedures, Measures, Findings, and Policy Implications.* San Francisco: Jossey-Bass, 1979.

Moreland, J. R., and Krimsky, E. "Competency-Based Training." In E. K. Marshall, P. D. Kurtz, and Associates, *Interpersonal Helping Skills: A Guide to Training Methods, Programs, and Resources.* San Francisco: Jossey-Bass, 1982.

Morrill, W. H., Hurst, J. C., and Associates. *Dimensions of Intervention for Student Development.* New York: Wiley, 1980.

Morrill, W. H., Oetting, E. R., and Hurst, J. C. "Dimensions of Counselor Functioning." *Personnel and Guidance Journal,* 1974, *52,* 354–359.

Morris, L. L., and Fitz-Gibbon, C. T. *How to Present an Evaluation Report.* Beverly Hills, Calif.: Sage, 1978.

Myers, I. B., and Briggs, K. C. *Manual for the Myers-Briggs Type Indicator.* Princeton, N.J.: Educational Testing Service, 1962.

Napier, R. W., and Gershenfeld, M. K. *Making Groups Work: A Guide for Group Leaders.* Boston: Houghton Mifflin, 1983.

Napier, R. W., and Gershenfeld, M. K. *Groups: Theory and Experience.* Boston: Houghton Mifflin, 1985.

National Institute of Education. *Involvement in Learning.* Washington, D.C.: National Institute of Education, 1984.

Neimeyer, G. J., and Merluzzi, T. V. "Group Structure and Group Process, Personal Construct Theory and Group Development." *Small Group Behavior,* 1982, *13,* 150–164.

Newcomb, T. M., and Wilson, E. K. (Eds.). *College Peer Groups:*

Problems and Prospects for Research. Hawthorne, N.Y.: Aldine, 1966.

Norton, R. W. "Measurement of Ambiguity Tolerance." *Journal of Personality Assessment,* 1975, *39,* 607–619.

Oetting, E. R. "Evaluation Research and Orthodox Science." *Personnel and Guidance Journal,* 1976, *55,* 11–15.

Oetting, E. R., and Cole, C. W. "Method, Design, and Implementation in Evaluation." In G. R. Hanson (Ed.), *New Directions for Student Services: Evaluating Program Effectiveness,* no. 1. San Francisco: Jossey-Bass, 1978.

Oetting, E. R., Morrill, W. H., and Hurst, J. C. "The Purpose of Intervention." In W. H. Morrill, J. C. Hurst, and Associates, *Dimensions of Intervention for Student Development.* New York: Wiley, 1980.

Osipow, S. *Theories of Career Development.* (2nd ed.) Englewood Cliffs, N.J.: Prentice-Hall, 1973.

Pace, C. R. *Measuring Outcomes of College: Fifty Years of Findings and Recommendations for the Future.* San Francisco: Jossey-Bass, 1979.

Pearson, R. E. "Basic Skills for Leadership of Counseling Groups." *Counselor Education and Supervision,* 1981, *2,* 30–37.

Pekarik, G. "The Effects of Employing Different Termination Classification Criteria in Dropout Research." *Psychotherapy,* 1985, *22,* 86–91.

Perry, W. G., Jr. *Forms of Intellectual and Ethical Development in the College Years: A Scheme.* New York: Holt, Rinehart and Winston, 1970.

Perry, W. G., Jr. "Cognitive and Ethical Growth: The Making of Meaning." In A. W. Chickering and Associates, *The Modern American College: Responding to the New Realities of Diverse Students and a Changing Society.* San Francisco: Jossey-Bass, 1981.

Pfeiffer, J. W., and Jones, J. E. "Design Considerations in Laboratory Education." In J. W. Pfeiffer and J. E. Jones (Eds.), *Annual Handbook for Group Facilitators.* La Jolla, Calif.: University Associates, 1973.

Pfeiffer, J. W., and Jones, J. E. "Co-facilitating." In J. W. Pfeiffer and J. E. Jones (Eds.), *Annual Handbook for Group Facilitators.* La Jolla, Calif.: University Associates, 1975a.

Pfeiffer, J. W., and Jones, J. E. "Introduction to the Structured Experiences Section." In J. W. Pfeiffer and J. E. Jones (Eds.), *Annual Handbook for Group Facilitators.* La Jolla, Calif.: University Associates, 1975b.

Pfeiffer, J. W., and Jones, J. E. "Introduction to the Structured Experiences Section." In J. W. Pfeiffer and J. E. Jones (Eds.), *Annual Handbook for Group Facilitators.* La Jolla, Calif.: University Associates, 1976.

Pfeiffer, J. W., and Jones, J. E. "Introduction to the Structured Experiences Section." In J. W. Pfeiffer and J. E. Jones (Eds.), *Annual Handbook for Group Facilitators.* La Jolla, Calif.: University Associates, 1979.

Phillips, B. "Terminating a Nurse-Patient Relationship." *American Journal of Nursing,* 1968, *68,* 1941–1942.

Piaget, J. *The Moral Judgment of the Child.* San Diego, Calif.: Harcourt Brace Jovanovich, 1932.

Piaget, J. *The Origins of Intelligence in Children.* New York: International Universities Press, 1952.

Piaget, J. *The Moral Judgment of the Child.* (Gabain, Trans.) New York: Free Press, 1965.

Piaget, J. *The Psychology of the Child.* New York: Harper Torchbooks, 1969.

Polkosnik, M. C., and Winston, R. B., Jr. "Relationships Between Cognitive and Psychosocial Development in College Students: An Exploratory Investigation." *Journal of College Student Development,* in press.

Provus, M. M. "Evaluation of Ongoing Programs in the Public School System." In R. W. Tyler (Ed.), *Educational Evaluation: New Roles, New Means.* Chicago: National Society for the Study of Education, 1969.

Ragan, T. D., and Higgins, E. B. "The Perceived Needs of Underclass College Students from Diverse Educational Institutions." *Journal of College Student Personnel,* 1985, *26,* 444–449.

Rest, J. R. *Manual for the Defining Issues Test.* Minneapolis: Moral Research Projects, University of Minnesota, 1974.

Rest, J. R. *Development in Judging Moral Issues.* Minneapolis: University of Minnesota, 1979.

Rest, J. R. "Evaluating Moral Development." In J. C. Dalton (Ed.),

Promoting Values Development in College Students. Washington, D.C.: National Association of Student Personnel Administrators, 1985.

Rodgers, R. F. "Theories Underlying Student Development." In D. G. Creamer (Ed.), *Student Development in Higher Education: Theories, Practices, and Future Directions.* Alexandria, Va.: American College Personnel Association, 1980.

Rodgers, R. F. "Theories of Adult Development: Research Status and Counseling Implications." In S. D. Brown and R. W. Lent (Eds.), *Handbook of Counseling Psychology.* New York: Wiley, 1984.

Rogers, C. R. *On Becoming a Person.* Boston: Houghton Mifflin, 1961.

Rogers, C. R. "The Interpersonal Relationship: The Core of Guidance." *Harvard Educational Review,* 1962, *32,* 416–429.

Rubin, D. *Estimating Causal Effects of Treatments in Experimental and Observational Studies.* Princeton, N.J.: Educational Testing Service, 1972.

Rudolph, F. *The American College and University: A History.* New York: Random House, 1962.

Sanford, N. *Self and Society.* New York: Atherton, 1966.

Sanford, N. *Where Colleges Fail.* San Francisco: Jossey-Bass, 1967.

Sashkin, M., and Lassey, W. R. "Theories of Leadership: A Review of Useful Research." In W. R. Lassey and M. Sashkin (Eds.), *Leadership and Social Change.* (3rd ed.) La Jolla, Calif.: University Associates, 1983.

Schiff, S. "Termination of Therapy: Problems in a Community Psychiatric Outpatient Clinic." *Archives of General Psychiatry,* 1962, *6,* 77–82.

Schutz, W. C. *FIRO: A Three Dimensional Theory of Interpersonal Behavior.* New York: Holt, Rinehart and Winston, 1958.

Scriven, M. "The Methodology of Evaluation." In R. E. Stake (Ed.), *Curriculum Evaluation.* American Educational Research Association Monograph Series on Evaluation, No. 1. Chicago: Rand McNally, 1967.

Shaw, M. E. *Group Dynamics.* (3rd ed.) New York: McGraw-Hill, 1981.

Sherif, M. *The Psychology of Social Norms.* New York: Harper & Row, 1936.

Simon, S. B., Howe, L. W., and Kirschenbaum, H. *Values Clarification: A Handbook of Practical Strategies for Teachers and Students.* New York: Hart, 1972.

Sisson, C. J., Sisson, P. J., and Gazda, G. M. "Extended Group Counseling with Psychiatry Residents." *Small Group Behavior,* 1977, *8,* 351–360.

Smith, A. F. "Lawrence Kohlberg's Cognitive Stage Theory of the Development of Moral Judgment." In L. L. Knefelkamp, C. Widick, and C. A. Parker (Eds.), *New Directions for Student Services: Applying New Developmental Findings,* no. 4. San Francisco: Jossey-Bass, 1978.

Smith, M. *A Practical Guide to Value Clarification.* La Jolla, Calif.: University Associates, 1977.

Spitz, H., and Sadock, B. J. "Small Interactional Groups in the Psychiatric Training of Graduate Nursing Students." *Journal of Nursing Education,* 1973, *12,* 6–13.

Stake, R. E. (Ed.). *Evaluating the Arts in Education: A Responsive Approach.* Columbus, Ohio: Merrill, 1975.

Stake, R. E. *Evaluating Educational Programmers: The Need and Response.* Paris: Organization for Economic Cooperation and Development, 1976.

Staub, E. *Positive Social Behavior and Morality: Social and Personal Influences.* Vol. 1. New York: Academic Press, 1978.

Staub, E. *Positive Social Behavior and Morality: Socialization and Development.* Vol. 2. New York: Academic Press, 1979.

Stern, G. G. *People in Context.* New York: Wiley, 1970.

Stockton, B. W., and Hulse, D. "Developmental Sequence in Small Groups." *Psychological Bulletin,* 1981, *63,* 188–194.

Stogdill, R. M. "Personal Factors Associated with Leadership: A Survey of the Literature." *Journal of Psychology,* 1948, *25,* 37–71.

Straub, C. A. "Women's Development of Autonomy and Chickering's Theory." *Journal of College Student Personnel,* 1987, *28,* 198–205.

Strong, E. K., Jr., Hansen, J. C., and Campbell, D. P. *Strong Vocational Interest Blank.* Stanford, Calif.: Stanford University Press, 1985.

Strupp, H. H., and Hadley, S. W. "Specific Versus Nonspecific

Factors in Psychotherapy: A Controlled Study of Outcome." *Archives of General Psychiatry*, 1979, *36*, 1125–1136.

Stufflebeam, D. L., and others. *Educational Evaluation and Decision Making*. Itasca, Ill.: Peacock, 1971.

Super, D. E. "Assessment in Career Guidance: Toward Truly Developmental Counseling." *Personnel and Guidance Journal*, 1983, *61*, 555–562.

Super, D. E., and Kidd, J. M. "Vocational Maturity in Adulthood: Toward Turning a Model into a Measure." *Journal of Vocational Behavior*, 1979, *14*, 225–270.

Super, D. E., and others. *Career Development Inventory*. Palo Alto, Calif.: Consulting Psychologists Press, 1981.

Taylor, M. B. "The Development of the Measure of Epistemological Reflection." Unpublished doctoral dissertation, Ohio State University, 1983.

Thomas, R. E. "Applying Adult Development Theory to Staff Development Programming." *College Student Affairs Journal*, 1985, *6*(2), 39–47.

Titley, R. W., and Titley, B. S. "Initial Choice of College Major: Are Only the 'Undecided' Undecided?" *Journal of College Student Personnel*, 1980, *21*, 293–298.

Titley, R. W., and Titley, B. S. "Initial Choice of College Major and Attrition: The 'Decided' and 'Undecided' After Six Years." *Journal of College Student Personnel*, 1985, *26*, 465–466.

Tryon, C., and Lilienthal, J. W. "Developmental Tasks: The Concept and Its Importance." In *Fostering Mental Health in Our Schools*. Washington, D.C.: National Education Association, 1950.

Tuckman, B. W. "Developmental Sequence in Small Groups." *Psychological Bulletin*, 1965, *63*, 384–399.

Tuckman, B. W., and Jensen, M. A. C. "Stages in Small Group Development Revisited." *Group and Organizational Studies*, 1977, *2*, 419–427.

Tyler, R. W. "General Statement on Evaluation." *Journal of Educational Research*, 1949, *30*, 492–501.

Van Hoose, W. H., and Kottler, J. A. *Ethical and Legal Issues in Counseling and Psychotherapy*. San Francisco: Jossey-Bass, 1977.

Wahrman, R. "Status, Deviance, Sanctions, and Group Discussions." *Small Group Behavior*, 1977, *8*, 147–168.

Walsh, W. B. *Theories of Person-Environment Interaction: Implications for the College Student.* Iowa City: American College Testing Program, 1973.

Weissberg, M., and others. "An Assessment of the Personal, Career, and Academic Needs of Undergraduate Students." *Journal of College Student Personnel*, 1982, *23*, 115–122.

Wellman, F. E. "A Conceptual Framework for the Derivation of Guidance Objectives and Outcome Criteria: Preliminary Statement." In J. M. Whiteley (Ed.), *Research in Counseling.* Columbus, Ohio: Merrill, 1967.

Wellman, F. E. "A Conceptual Framework for the Derivation of Guidance Objectives and Outcome Criteria: Preliminary Statement." In J. M. Whiteley (Ed.), *Research in Counseling.* Columbus, Ohio: Merrill, 1971.

Werring, C. J. "A Continuing Education Model for Student Affairs Professionals: An Adult Learner Perspective." *College Student Affairs Journal*, 1985, *6*(1), 55–62.

Whiteley, J. M., and Associates. *Character Development in College Students: The Freshman Year.* Vol. 1. Schenectady, N.Y.: Character Research Press, 1982.

Whiteley, J. M., and others. "Influences on Character Development During the College Years: The Retrospective View of Recent Undergraduates." In J. C. Dalton (Ed.), *Promoting Values Development in College Students.* Washington, D.C.: National Association of Student Personnel Administrators, 1985.

Widick, C. "An Evaluation of Developmental Instruction in a University Setting." Unpublished doctoral dissertation, University of Minnesota, 1975.

Widick, C., Parker, C. A., and Knefelkamp, L. L. "Arthur Chickering's Developmental Vectors." In L. L. Knefelkamp, C. Widick, and C. A. Parker (Eds.), *New Directions for Student Services: Applying New Developmental Findings*, no. 4. San Francisco: Jossey-Bass, 1978.

Wile, D. B. "Group Leadership Questionnaire." In J. W. Pfeiffer and J. E. Jones (Eds.), *Annual Handbook for Group Facilitators.* La Jolla, Calif.: University Associates, 1972.

Winston, R. B., Jr. "Counseling and Advising." In U. Delworth, G. R. Hanson, and Associates, *Student Services: A Handbook for the Profession.* (2nd ed.) San Francisco: Jossey-Bass, in press.

Winston, R. B., Jr., Hebert, D. A., and McGonigle, R. B. "Professional Staff Development as Management Tool." *College Student Affairs Journal,* 1985, *6*(2), 12–25.

Winston, R. B., Jr., Miller, T. K., and Prince, J. S. *Assessing Student Development: A Preliminary Manual for the Student Developmental Task Inventory.* (2nd ed.) Athens, Ga.: Student Development Associates, 1979.

Winston, R. B., Jr., Miller, T. K., and Prince, J. S. *Student Developmental Task and Lifestyle Inventory.* Athens, Ga.: Student Development Associates, 1987.

Winter, S. K. "Developmental Stages in the Roles and Concerns of Group Co-leaders." *Small Group Behavior,* 1976, 7, 349–362.

Witkin, B. R. *Assessing Needs in Educational and Social Programs.* San Francisco: Jossey-Bass, 1984.

Worthen, B., and Sanders, J. *Educational Evaluation: Theory and Practice.* Worthington, Ohio: Charles A. Jones, 1973.

Wright, D. J. "Minority Students: Developmental Beginnings." In D. J. Wright (Ed.), *New Directions for Student Services: Responding to the Needs of Today's Minority Students,* no. 38. San Francisco: Jossey-Bass, 1987.

Yalom, I. D. *The Theory and Practice of Group Psychotherapy.* (2d ed.) New York: Basic Books, 1975.

Yalom, I. D. *The Theory and Practice of Group Psychotherapy.* (3rd ed.) New York: Basic Books, 1985.

Zander, A. *The Purposes of Groups and Organizations.* San Francisco: Jossey-Bass, 1985.

Zimpfer, D. G. "Planning for Groups Based on Their Developmental Phases." *Journal for Specialists in Group Work,* 1986, *11*, 180–187.

Index

371

Index

K

Kasdorf, J., 358; and leadership skills, 195

Katchadourian, H. A., 358; as typological theorist, 81–82

Katz, D., 358; and theory of leadership, 181–182

Katz, G. M., 358; and leadership dynamics, 66

Kaufman, R.: and needs assessment, 119

Kegan, R., 358; as cognitive-development theorist 77

Keirsey, D., 305, 345

Kelly, G. A., 359; and group roles, 46

Kidd, J. M., 367; as psychosocial-development theorist, 81

Kimball, R. K., 359; and leadership dynamics, 66, 68

King, P. M., 359; and intellectual development, 17; and interview as evaluation, 176

Kirschenbaum, H., 346, 366; activities list designed by, 330–332; and strategies for activities, 285; and value development in college, 102

Kitchener, K. S., 359; and intellectual development, 17; and interview as evaluation, 176; and leadership ethics, 29

Knefelkamp, L. L., 359, 368; and career development, 95; and emotional development, 80, 91; and evaluation instrument, 176; and theories of development in college, 77

Knight, D. J., 361; and stages in group development, 61

Knott, J. E., 353; and purpose of activities in groups, 7; and purpose of groups, 23

Knowles, H. F., 359; and purpose of groups, 53

Knowles, M. S., 359; and purpose of groups, 53

Kohlberg, L., 359; as cognitive-development theorist, 77, 80–81, 84; and moral development, 17–18, 102, 103

Kolb, D., 360; and needs assessments, 124; as typological theorist, 78

Kosecoff, J., 354; and evaluation designs, 171; and steps in summative evaluation, 162, 164

Kottler, J. A., 367; and leadership dynamics, 27

Krimsky, E., 362; and taxonomy of leadership skills, 193–195

Kuh, G. D., 360; and evaluation, 154–155

L

La Coursiere, R., 360; and group termination, 243

Lambert, M. J., 360; and leadership skills, 195

Lassey, W. R., 360, 365; and contingency theory of leadership, 182–183

Law, A. I., 360; and evaluation designs, 171; and randomization, 168–169

Lawrence, G., 305, 346

Leader credibility. *See* Credibility of leaders

Leaders: and ambiguity, 55–56; analyzing competencies of, 133–135; and applications of theories, 187–189; behavior theories of, 181–182; and coleaders, 199–208; and confrontation, 49–50; and contingency theories, 182–187; ethical responsibilities of, 29; facilitating skills of, 195–197; and group dynamics, 34–35, 40–41; and group norms, 49–50; and group roles, 47–48, 49–50; minimum skills of, 30–32; as models, 200; myths in roles of, 137–138; sample session and formative evaluation, 161–162, 163; skills and competencies of, 193–199; structuring skills of, 197–199; styles of, 189–193; successful